CBT Approaches for Children and Young People

CBT Approaches for Children and Young People: A Practical Case Study Guide

Edited by Alison Coad and Nick Wrycraft

McGraw Hill Education
Open University Press

Open University Press
McGraw-Hill Education
McGraw-Hill House
Shoppenhangers Road
Maidenhead
Berkshire
England
SL6 2QL

email: enquiries@openup.co.uk
world wide web: www.openup.co.uk

and Two Penn Plaza, New York, NY 10121-2289, USA

First published 2015

A catalogue record of this book is available from the British Library

ISBN-13: 978-0-33-526294-6
ISBN-10: 0-33-526294-5
eISBN: 978-0-33-526295-3

Library of Congress Cataloging-in-Publication Data
CIP data applied for

Typeset by Aptara, Inc.

Praise for this book

"This timely publication succinctly illustrates the applicability of CBT to enable children and young people to proactively achieve empowerment over a broad range of physical and emotional health problems. The inclusion of real life clinical case vignette provides a welcome human counterpart to a commanding overview of the evidence pertaining this particular population. This book is a valuable addition to the clinical armamentarium of both novice and experienced CBT practitioners alike."

John Davies, Consultant Clinical Psychologist, Accredited Cognitive Behaviour Therapist, Norfolk and Suffolk NHS Foundation Trust, Ipswich, UK

Contents

Contents

Author biographies

May Baker has been a senior lecturer at Liverpool John Moores University since 2004. Her mental health nursing career spans three decades, and she teaches both postgraduate and undergraduate students. She is a former specialist practitioner/manager in drug services in Liverpool and continues to maintain links with frontline services. She completed her MSc in addiction in 2003 and continues to specialise in drug and alcohol awareness, dual diagnosis and motivational interviewing. She has authored several chapters on alcohol and drug use and collaborates with others in the field of addiction and mental health to promote awareness and recovery.

Rob Bode, RSCN, RMN, BA(Hons), PGCert works as a ward manager for Cambridge and Peterborough NHS Foundation Trust. After qualifying as a children's nurse in 1996, Rob worked for 11 years with adolescents in both inpatient and community settings before moving to work with young people experiencing their first episode of psychosis in an early intervention team. He has recently returned to work with children in an inpatient mental health setting.

Alison Coad is an occupational therapist and cognitive behavioural psychotherapist specialising in the treatment of children and young people. She qualified in 2001, having switched careers in her mid-thirties. After a ten-year career in the NHS, she took the decision to work freelance and now works as a member of a team of independent associates based in Norfolk. She has a particular interest in acceptance and commitment therapy, mindfulness and compassion-focused approaches.

Jeannie Gordon trained as a psychiatric nurse with both residential and community experience of working with young children, adolescents and their families. Over the last 18 years she has led the Incredible Years development in Essex. Jeannie is now a director of the Ministry of Parenting CIC, the main aim of which involves the delivery of both parent group programmes and training. Jeannie holds an MA in teaching, is a Queen's nurse and author of the SPOT (Supporting Parents of Teens) parenting programme and the FLASH (Families Learning About Self Harm) parenting programme. Jeannie is the mother of two daughters.

J C Harrison, BA(Hons) RMN MSc PhD is senior lecturer in mental health nursing, Liverpool John Moores University. He trained as a registered mental nurse in Liverpool and worked at the Royal Liverpool Children's Hospital with young people suffering mental health problems. He has also worked in the Army as a community psychiatric nurse and later as a nursing officer. Following a master's degree in nursing from the

University of Liverpool, he undertook doctoral research into the perceptions of clinicians towards child self-harm. His research interests are in the areas of self-harm and eating disorders.

Dr. Vineeta Gupta has, since qualifying as a clinical psychologist in 2004, worked in a variety of children's services and health settings, including children with life-limiting illness, CAMHS, children and adults with cleft palate, and children, teenagers and young adults (0–25) with cancer. She has been working within a paediatric diabetes team since 2012. She passionately believes psychological approaches are a crucial aspect in managing health and illness and believes psychology has much to offer, both directly to the child and family and also to the systems around them.

Tom Marshall is currently studying at the University of Sussex for an MA in literature and philosophy, and will be beginning a PhD at Queen Mary University of London in September 2015. His broad interests include the intersection between literature and philosophy, as well as the history of both.

Dr Sarah Rogers is a clinical psychologist working with children and young people in Norfolk. Sarah began work in the NHS in 1998 and qualified as a clinical psychologist in 2004. Since then she has worked full-time, in CAMHS, for Norfolk and Suffolk NHS Foundation Trust. Sarah is an integrative therapist using skills drawn from a range of therapeutic models, including cognitive behavioural therapy. Anxiety disorders are an area of special clinical interest and Sarah also enjoys working creatively with primary school children.

Sarah Russell RMN, BSc, PGCert is a learning and development consultant with Cambridge and Peterborough Mental Health Trust. Her current role involves optimising learning within clinical placements, supporting student nurses and mentors. She has a long history of working with adults with mental health challenges across inpatient and community settings including early intervention for psychosis. She has also worked as a personal tutor at Anglia Ruskin University.

Dr Jenny Smerdon qualified as a clinical psychologist in 2000. She worked in a busy CAMHS in North London before moving to the West Country. She now works for The Lifetime Service, a community paediatric nursing and psychology service, and for Reading University as a supervisor on the postgraduate diploma in evidence-based psychological treatment for children and young people.

Nick Wrycraft is a senior lecturer with Anglia Ruskin University and teaches on the pre-registration nursing course. He completed his doctorate in 2012, with his thesis on clinical supervision in primary healthcare settings. Nick has a keen interest in promoting mental health nursing, and has previously edited *An Introduction to Mental Health Nursing* and *Case Studies in Mental Health Nursing* and co-wrote *CBT Fundamentals: Theory and Cases* with Vanessa Skinner in 2014, all with Open University Press.

List of figures

Preface

Alison Coad

The aim of this volume is to offer new perspectives on the delivery of cognitive behavioural therapy (CBT) to children and young people. The past decade has been a time of considerable change in the provision of mental health services in the UK. Chapter 1 offers an account of these changes, including the introduction of Improving Access to Psychological Therapies (IAPT) services and the ways in which these ideas were carried through to services for children and young people (CYP-IAPT). These ideas were developed in response to Lord Layard's (2006) pivotal report on the treatment of depression. Evidence-based treatment was a central feature of the new services, and as a consequence a new model of practice – based on outcome measures – evolved. As a clinician working within the National Health Service (NHS) as these changes were introduced, I observed a variety of reactions from my colleagues and from our young clients. This is not the place to provide a detailed critique of the impact of these changes. However, curiosity about that process is part of our motivation for producing this volume.

This is not intended to be a skills manual – there are already several excellent volumes which fulfil this role. Instead, these case studies offer insights into the ways in which CBT approaches can be used as the foundation for highly individual treatment programmes. Therapists and clients bring their experiences into the therapeutic relationship, and various influences will shape the way that therapy progresses. For me, as a late starter in the field of mental health (I qualified as an occupational therapist at the age of 38), those experiences included a master's degree in literature, and training in CBT, systemic therapy and solution-focused therapy. The more I studied, the more I saw links between theories that underpinned a seemingly disparate range of disciplines. I was familiar with the idea of interpreting a novel – a fictional narrative – in certain ways. Could I transfer any of this learning to the understanding of my personal narrative, or of those of my clients? I was intrigued by this, and became curious about ways in which I could combine my interests in therapy, literature and philosophy. The links between philosophical concepts such as Stoicism and modern psychotherapy seemed clear, as the following quotation shows:

> The Stoics realised that a life plagued with negative emotions – including anger, anxiety, fear, grief and envy – will not be a good life. They therefore became acute observers of the workings of the human mind and as a result became some of the most insightful psychologists of the ancient world. They went on to develop techniques for preventing the onset of negative emotions and for extinguishing them when attempts at prevention failed.
>
> (Irvine 2009: 5)

This prompted further reading and discussion with colleagues, the results of which appear in Chapter 2. My aim here is to encourage broad and creative thinking, and to use resources from life outside therapy in order to help clients and therapists to find new answers to questions in therapy. For Eleanor and Robert, two of the clients who generously agreed to participate in this project, the value of reading and literature is clear and has provided new dimensions to our shared understanding. It has also provided common ground between client and therapist, emphasising the collaborative nature of our work.

Central to each case are the experience and the voice of the young person and, as appropriate, those who support and care for them. All client names mentioned within the case studies are pseudonyms. These case studies will be valuable to trainee clinicians, as they offer authentic accounts of successes and pitfalls in the therapeutic relationship. However – and this is a unique feature of this volume – the cases also offer an accessible narrative, represented jointly by the client's and therapist's voice, which it is hoped will be relevant to young people experiencing these kinds of difficulties. The narrative approach in qualitative research has been well documented (Andrews *et al.* 2013) and also highlights links to other disciplines, including philosophy, literature and literary theory. Narrative offers a structure to our efforts to find meaning – stories have long been a metaphor for life experiences, from fairy stories to postmodern theories of the meaning of the text, such as those of Roland Barthes (1915–1980). Therapeutic techniques such as the genogram, the 'lifeline' and life story work all offer ways for clients to gain a clearer understanding of their situation, and what might have led them to their current circumstances. In CBT, formulation performs a similar function. Formulation is central to the case studies presented in this volume, and although the cases are presented according to diagnosis, the therapeutic approach emphasises individual need over protocol.

As a cognitive behavioural therapist I have always strived to work in a collaborative manner with my clients. It was not always easy to translate techniques developed with an adult population in mind to my young clients, and I often struggled to adapt techniques. Good supervision was essential, as was informal case discussion with experienced colleagues of all disciplines. Paul Stallard's work was a key reference for me, and the development of a therapist rating scale was a very welcome addition to the resources available to those training and to those responsible for assessing trainees. Chapter 3 provides a summary of the cognitive behaviour therapy scale for children and young people (CBTS-CYP), together with commentary on its application in practice. The principles which underpin Paul Stallard's work are clear: a collaborative and respectful relationship with the client, whether a child or an adult, is central to the model. Ensuring that conversations in therapy are clear to all involved is the foundation of meaningful interaction. The CBTS-CYP offers a means to structure highly personalised aspects of work with children and young people, including aspects which are not easy to quantify – for example, fun, creativity, and the negotiation of the power relationship. It enables CYP therapists to work in developmentally appropriate ways, without losing sight of key features of CBT such as agenda setting, Socratic dialogue and between-session tasks.

Emphasis on the experience of the young person in therapy has also been evident in initiatives to increase service user participation. The views of children and young people are now actively sought via the use of routine outcome questionnaires and through initiatives such as the Department of Health *You're Welcome* policy document

(Department of Health 2011). Although these initiatives demonstrate commitment to the principle of an open exchange of views, they take place against a backdrop of severe financial constraint within the NHS. Inevitably, this produces tensions which are not always easy to resolve. Increasingly stringent thresholds for access to services, limited resources and a 'value for money' culture have all shaped the delivery of services. A brief review of media coverage of these issues in the 12 months prior to the time of writing illustrates the concerns of the public and politicians alike around these changes. There is no doubt that these are difficult times. Readers will also notice that several of the case studies involve work with clients over extended periods of time, and it is recognised that interventions of this nature are not always feasible. It is hoped that the creativity of the approaches described will provide inspiration and generate new ideas, however long the intervention may be.

In 1952, Aaron Beck wrote a case study based on the outpatient treatment of a patient diagnosed with schizophrenia. Beck's observations on the therapeutic process are as valid today as when they were written:

> The major force in the therapeutic process appears to have been the emotional experience between the patient and therapist. Important components in the therapist's attitude were a strong liking for and interest in the patient. No fixed system of therapeutic techniques was employed other than an attempt to perceive the patient's needs and to deal with them in a flexible way.
>
> (Beck 1952)

Each case study within this volume captures this spirit. The current economic and political climate means that mental health services in the UK have been, and continue to be, under significant pressure. This book cannot change that. What it can do is offer some examples of the ways in which innovative clinicians can respond to the needs of individuals, employing evidence-based practice, while simultaneously negotiating the impact of sustained reductions in resources.

References

Andrews, M., Squire, C. and Tamboukou, M. (eds) (2013) *Doing Narrative Research*. London: Sage.

Beck, A.T. (1952) Successful outpatient psychotherapy of a chronic schizophrenic with a delusion based on borrowed guilt. In A.P. Morrison (ed.) (2014) *A Casebook of Cognitive Therapy for Psychosis*. Abingdon: Routledge

Department of Health (2011) *You're Welcome: Quality Criteria for Young People Friendly Health Services*. Available at https://www.gov.uk/government/publications/quality-criteria-for-young-people-friendly-health-services (accessed 14 January 2015).

Irvine, W.B. (2009) *A Guide to the Good Life: The Ancient Art of Stoic Joy*. Oxford: Oxford University Press.

Layard, R. (2006) *The Depression Report: A New Deal for Depression and Anxiety Disorders*. The Centre for Economic Performance's Mental Health Policy Group. Available at http://eprints.lse.ac.uk/818/1/DEPRESSION_REPORT_LAYARD.pdf (accessed 6 January 2015).

Acknowledgements

Thanks to my wife Alex and children Emily and Hamish for your support, and to Monika Lee and Maria Convey at the Open University for all your help and hard work.

Nick Wrycraft

Thanks to all of the young people who so generously agreed to share their stories for this project. Special thanks to 'Eleanor', 'Hannah' and 'Robert' for their contributions and constructive comments during the process.

Thanks also to my family for their unswerving support: Mike, Tom, Amy, Rob and Alex. And Phoebe of course.

And last but not least, thanks to Noel Sawyer, Nick Wrycraft, Monika Lee and Maria Convey, without whom none of this would have found its way onto paper!

Alison Coad

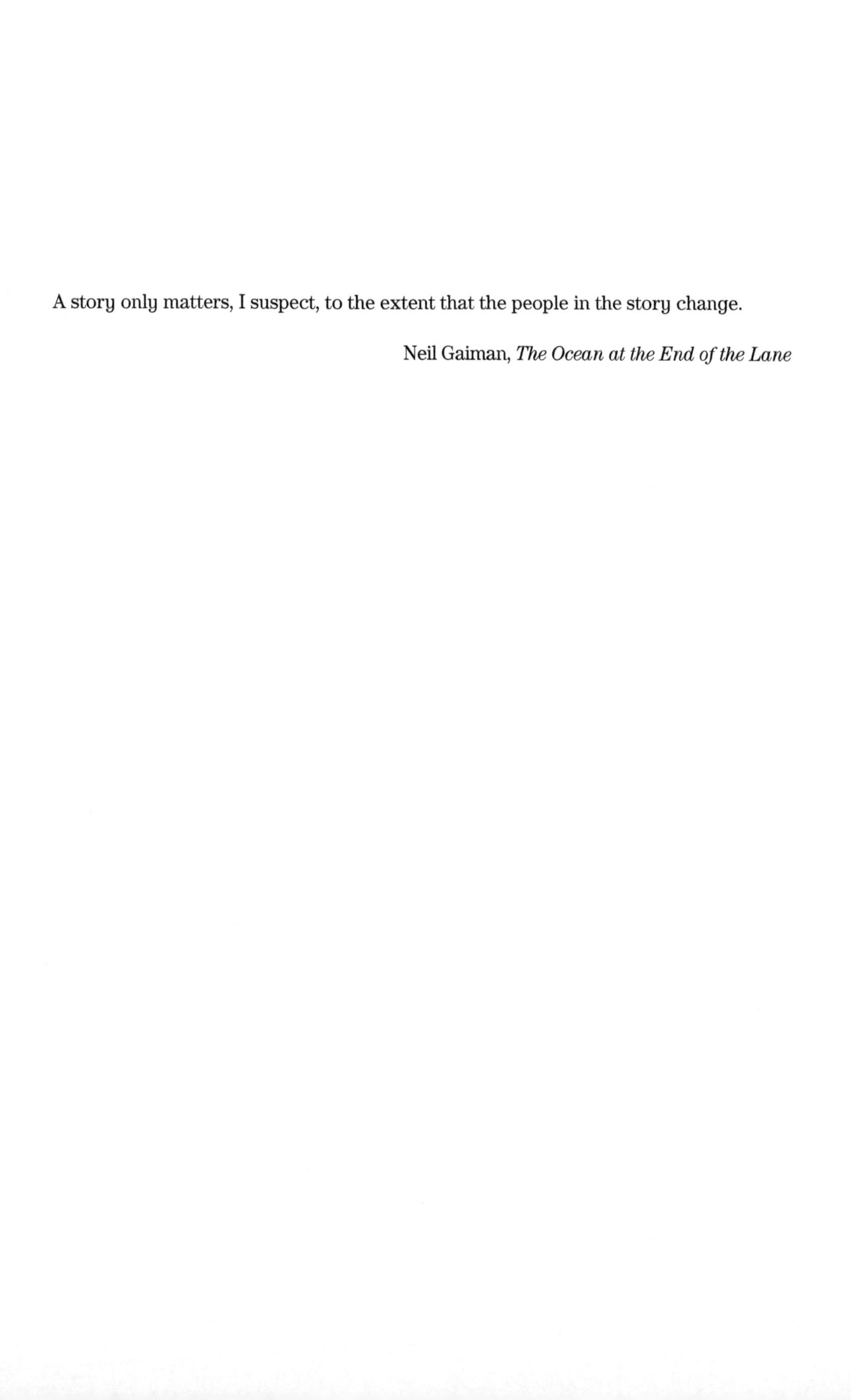

A story only matters, I suspect, to the extent that the people in the story change.

Neil Gaiman, *The Ocean at the End of the Lane*

1 Introduction: changes in mental health services for children and young people

Alison Coad

The aim of this introduction is to provide a context for the case studies presented in this book. Paul Calaminus (2013) offers a succinct summary of recent changes in healthcare policy and provision which provides a useful background to this discussion. The past decade has been one of significant change within the National Health Service. Mental health services have undergone several rounds of restructuring: this is an ongoing process with far-reaching consequences for service users and professionals alike. Calaminus notes changes in public expectations of the health service, highlighting the ways in which service users have been invited to become involved in the design and delivery of services – for example, in service design and the recruitment of staff. The value of experience of chronic conditions has also been acknowledged, in the recognition and training of 'expert patients' (NHS Choices 2014). These changes have led to a shift in the balance of power between those who provide the service and those who are served by it. This is an important point which links to some of the philosophical ideas discussed in Chapter 2 below. The general trend within modern healthcare – what Calaminus (2013: 110) describes as 'the shift away from paternalistic models of care' – does not alter the fact that professionals still tend to have the final say (for example, when a decision is made to section a patient under the Mental Health Act). However, as the case studies in this book show, it is possible for clients and therapists to share decisions, and to learn from this process, even in the context of financial constraint and service redesign discussed below.

There is a growing concern among professionals, charities and individuals that the mental health services provided for young people in the UK cannot meet their needs. This is evidenced not only in academic publications, but also in the national press, where concerns have been voiced on a regular basis in the 12 months prior to the time of writing. Examples of press coverage are provided in the 'soundbites' presented in the illustration on page 6; these give some indication of the extent of public concern about these issues.

The House of Commons Health Committee 2014–15

The concerns noted above have been recognised by the government, and in 2014 the House of Commons Health Committee was asked to review these issues in detail. The Committee heard evidence from a range of expert witnesses, including young people using mental health services, the Minister for Health and the Chief Executive of

NHS England. It is clear from the Committee discussions that concern exists about the impact of changes arising following the restructuring of NHS commissioning, which came into force on 1 April 2013. Since then, local commissioning arrangements have meant that some child and adolescent mental health service (CAMHS) provisions have experienced significant reductions in funding. This has been linked to concerns that thresholds for access to services are growing higher, against a backdrop of increasing numbers of young people seeking help for mental health difficulties. The provision of specialist inpatient services (known as Tier 4 services, and including provision for issues including deliberate self-harm and eating disorders) has also been under scrutiny. CAMHS services have not been exempt from a reduction in the overall number of acute psychiatric beds, and as recent media reports demonstrate, this can cause significant problems for patients and for service providers (Sabin 2014). The fact that the news of this event reached public attention via the Twitter account of an Assistant Chief Constable is also an indicator of the public mood around this issue:

> We have a 16yr old girl suffering from mental health issues held in police custody. There are no beds available in the UK! #unacceptable.
>
> (ACC Paul Netherton, 29 November 2014)

The message was retweeted 2,126 times.

The latest report from the Health Committee, which set up an inquiry into CAMHS in February 2014, was published on 5 November 2014. The opening statement of the report's summary is very clear:

> There are serious and deeply ingrained problems with the commissioning and provision of children's and adolescents' mental health services. These run through the whole system from prevention and early intervention through to inpatient services for the most vulnerable young people.
>
> (House of Commons Health Committee 2014)

Children and Young Persons' Improving Access to Psychological Therapies

The news is not entirely negative, however. Significant recent changes in service provision included, in 2011, the introduction of the Children and Young Persons' Improving Access to Psychological Therapies (CYP-IAPT) initiative. A total of £54 million has been invested in the programme to date. It is aimed to roll out CYP-IAPT to the whole of England by 2017; at the time of writing, approximately two-thirds of the country have access to the service (Norman Lamb, 15 July 2014).[3]

This development was an extension of the original IAPT programme, which came into being in 2007 following the publication of the *Depression Report* (Layard 2006). The Layard

3. http://bit.ly/1A1B00J, *c*.3.34 p.m.

report highlighted the need for greater recognition of treatments that were supported by research evidence. It also placed emphasis on the role of psychological interventions in the treatment of a range of mental health difficulties, concluding that 'most people with mental illness should be offered the choice of psychological therapy' (Layard 2006: 2).

The development of an IAPT service for children and young people was outlined in *Talking Therapies: A Four Year Plan of Action*, published in February 2011 (Department of Health 2011). The introduction to this document, written by Paul Burstow MP, makes reference to the link between the economy and the psychological health of the UK population, speaking of the 'emotional wounds' caused by the economic recession. The figures cited are impressive: £70 million pledged in June 2010, with a further £400 million earmarked over the four years to 2014–15.

There are three key aspects of the delivery of CYP-IAPT which reflect the concept of service transformation: evidence-based practice (EBP), outcome monitoring and participation (see the CYP IAPT Key Facts Document, http://bit.ly/1zzS6SR). Each of these areas is discussed in more detail below.

Evidence-based practice

Sackett *et al.* (2000) define EBP as:

> the integration of clinical expertise, patient values, and the best research evidence into the decision making process for patient care. Clinical expertise refers to the clinician's cumulated experience, education and clinical skills. The patient brings to the encounter his or her own personal preferences and unique concerns, expectations, and values. The best research evidence is usually found in clinically relevant research that has been conducted using sound methodology.

The case studies in this volume aim to demonstrate the practice of integrating these elements in creative ways which reflect the particular needs of younger clients.

There is a distinction between evidence-based practice and evidence-based interventions, and it is important to understand this. Some treatments, such as cognitive behavioural therapy or interpersonal therapy (IPT), have been the subject of a lot of research. Research findings support the use of both of these treatments, and so they have tended to attract investment from major employers such as the NHS. In July 2014, Norman Lamb reported to the Select Committee that 770 individuals had received training in CBT, parent training or IPT to support the CYP-IAPT programme. CAMHS teams are multi-disciplinary and are staffed by a range of professionals – nurses, psychologists, psychiatrists, psychotherapists and social workers, for example. Each professional brings a set of skills, and many will have additional training in specific therapeutic techniques in addition to their core training. Anecdotally, the investment in CBT is seen by some professionals as leading to the neglect of other therapies such as psychodynamic therapy, which does not have such a solid body of empirical research to support its use. Of course, this does not necessarily mean that it is less effective. However, without statistics to demonstrate its effectiveness, it is harder for those who control the budget to justify spending on staff training staff in psychodynamic techniques. A research study, Improving Mood with Psychoanalytic and Cognitive Therapies (IMPACT),[4] has recently been undertaken within a small number of CAMHSs to study the outcomes for young people diagnosed with depression. This study randomises subjects into one of three treatment arms – CBT, psychodynamic therapy or standard clinical care (this includes treatment such as medication reviews). The results of the IMPACT study, which are due to be published in 2015, will provide a useful addition to the evidence base and will offer a new perspective on treatment options for depression in young people.

Outcome monitoring

The Department of Health report *Children and Young People in Mind* (2008) identified a number of areas for improvement within the provision of mental healthcare for children and young people. The report also recognised the need to measure the effectiveness of treatments, so that services can offer interventions that have a proven record of success. Methods of measuring progress are a standard feature of CBT interventions – they can take the form of a brief 'mood check' each session, or a subjective rating of level of anxiety (see Chapter 11, this volume) or more formal questionnaires. Both can also be used to measure progress at regular intervals. A wide variety of standardised measures are available (for more detail, see http://www.corc.uk.net/) and a number of these questionnaires have become a routine part of therapy sessions. Measures such as the revised Child Anxiety and Depression Scale (Chorpita *et al.* 2000) can be useful and even fun, as the results can be represented in graphic form which enhances understanding for young clients, parents and clinicians. Progress can be measured session by session, or at agreed intervals; IAPT services require completion of measures at every session. Some services have invested in tablet technology, such as iPads, as an alternative to paper-based questionnaires. The use of this kind of technology makes capture of data more efficient and less labour-intensive, as computer programs record and calculate results rapidly and with less room for human error. The interest in measuring progress is reflected in other areas of society too. David Cameron has shown an interest in 'happiness' as a measure of success since 2004 (Stratton 2010; but see also Allen 2012). 'Happiness' data is recorded regularly by the Office for National Statistics, most recently in 2014, using categories such as personal wellbeing, relationships, health and finance (see Office for National Statistics 2014). This echoes initiatives in France and Canada to attempt to find a measure other than the strictly economic to reflect quality of life.

Collaboration and participation

Collaboration and participation, like outcome monitoring, are key features of CBT. Within therapy, collaboration and participation take the form of shared activities (agenda setting, goal setting and mutually devised behavioural experiments, for

---

4. http://www.impacttrial.org.uk

example). The client is actively encouraged to shape the course of therapy, and to enter into a relationship of equality with the therapist. Of course, complete equality would be impossible to achieve; a range of issues, including age, professional versus personal status and the relationship between the individual and a huge organisation such as the NHS, mean that a power imbalance is inevitable. The best that can be hoped for is an awareness of these elements, and a relationship which takes them into account.

In terms of service provision, collaboration between all participants in the process of therapy is an essential feature of CYP-IAPT. This includes better coordination between professional agencies, including appropriate information sharing between agencies. It also calls for the routine involvement of young people and their parents in the design of services. This can be achieved by encouraging open and honest feedback about services received, via methods such as end-of-treatment questionnaires, comments and suggestions boxes, and formal discussion groups.

Training of staff is also seen as an opportunity to share knowledge and expertise, with the establishment of learning collaboratives between CAMHS services and higher education institutions such as universities.

Question: What do you see as the main changes in service provision proposed by the CYP-IAPT service?

Answer: There are three key points to think about: evidence-based practice and interventions, the use of routine outcome measures, and collaboration and participation. The paragraphs above give you a summary of what each of these terms mean, and the websites listed in the references provide more detail if you would like to explore these ideas further.

Question: What possible difficulties might there be in implementing these changes within CAMHS services?

Answer: All of the changes described involve an investment of time and resources, and so financial constraint is one of the most obvious potential difficulties. In an organisation as large as the NHS, the implementation of any change requires energy and support from staff at every level. Skilful management of this type of change is needed. Service redesign will inevitably make some staff unsettled and this can lead to the loss of experienced staff, which calls for the recruitment and training of new staff. All of these processes take time, which can have a considerable impact on the level of service provided, at least in the short term. It is also crucial to ensure that the young people who need the service are given the opportunity to have a say about changes which will affect them. The coordination of all of these elements is a complex process.

Conclusion

This introduction has presented two perspectives on recent changes in mental health provision for children and young people. Accounts in the media, and the findings of the House of Commons Select Committee on Health, describe significant concerns about mental health services. There is also indisputable evidence that some service users have suffered as a result of reduction in provision; the young woman who was the subject of the tweet from ACC Paul Netherton, for example. Investment in CYP-IAPT services suggests an alternative picture, and could be said to address many of the concerns raised in the earlier part of the discussion.

The day-to-day reality of service users, clinicians and those who are managing the budgets seems to involve a mixture of concern and optimism. Anecdotally, students training through the CYP-IAPT programme have encountered practical difficulties such as limited access to essential course materials and training manuals. Balancing a busy caseload with the demands of a university-level training programme can also produce challenges. Trainees are likely to be members of a team with responsibility for the provision of crisis care, and these responsibilities cannot be disregarded – this could lead to conflict for the trainee, and possibly to resentment from other team members. On a separate point, the aim of involving service users in the design and delivery of services raises a number of questions. How realistic is it that the views of service

- The Acting Chairman of the Select Committee, David Tredinnick MP, quoted a description of CAMHS as 'a system under siege, reporting significant reductions in resources, and all of that against a background of rising demand' (1 April 2014).[3]
- In 2013, *Young Minds* magazine conducted a survey of staff working in mental healthcare for young people. Of those surveyed, 66% 'reported that quality of care had been affected because of cuts of budget changes' and '77% reported a cut in the 2012/2013 Budget'.[4]
- In May 2014 Maggie Atkinson, the Children's Commissioner for England, raised concerns that 'rising rates of mental health disorders among children are linked to council budget cuts and health restructurings that have denied vulnerable young people early help' (Cassidy 2014).
- Recent UNICEF reports [show] that children in the UK are, relative to children and young people in other European countries, less happy and more affected by poverty than their peers elsewhere (UNICEF 2010, cited by Calaminus 2013).
- On 1 January 2015, the BBC reported the resignation of a consultant child and adolescent psychiatrist:

> A child psychiatrist has said she resigned from her health trust job after becoming disillusioned with the service for young children.
>
> Dr Irene Lampert, who worked for the Norfolk and Suffolk Foundation Trust (NSFT), said she was concerned about a decline in care standards.
>
> She said the trust was putting resources into treating 14 to 26 year olds and neglecting those younger.
>
> (Rigby 2015)

3. http://bit.ly/1A1BK69
4. http://bit.ly/1ICJYTc

users will be taken into account in the appointment of senior members of staff, for example? And in a climate of economic constraint, how likely is it that the suggestions of service users which have resource implications (more staff, for example, or improved clinic facilities) can be taken on board? A recent news item brings another aspect of participation into focus. Lady Elizabeth Butler-Sloss, who in 2014 stepped down as the chair of a high-profile public inquiry into child abuse, commented that 'for [the victims and survivors] to be deciding who should be the person chairing it creates real problems … if you do not have a position of authority, how are you going to be able to run the inquiry?' (Wintour 2014). These remarks have led to debate within the media regarding the nature of 'the establishment' – those who hold power in society, and who has the right to exercise that power. It could be argued that this debate has raised a fundamental question about 'participation' generally: how much difference does it make to the outcome of major public decisions, and how can that difference be measured? There is no straightforward answer to this question, but it is hoped that this volume will encourage readers to reflect on issues like this, and to consider the ways in which they can be addressed within therapeutic relationships.

References

Allen, C. (2012) Why Cameron's happiness agenda can only backfire. *Guardian*, 31 July. Available at: http://www.theguardian.com/society/2012/jul/31/why-camerons-happiness-agenda-backfire (accessed 24 November 2014).

Calaminus, P. (2013) The social policy context of mental health care. In I.J. Norman and I. Ryrie (eds) *The Art and Science of Mental Health Nursing: A Textbook of Principles and Practice*. Maidenhead: Open University Press.

Cassidy, S. (2014) Cuts send rates of mental health disorders among young soaring. *Independent*,18 May. Available at: http://www.independent.co.uk/life-style/health-and-families/health-news/cuts-send-rates-of-mental-health-disorders-among-young-soaring-9392996.html (accessed 25 June 2014).

Chorpita, B.F., Yim, L., Moffitt, C.E., Umemoto, L. A. and Francis, S.E. (2000). Assessment of symptoms of DSMIV anxiety and depression in children: A Revised Child Anxiety and Depression Scale. *Behaviour Research and Therapy*, 38, 835–55.

Department of Health (2008) *Children and Young People in Mind: The Final Report of the CAMHS Review*. London: Department of Health.

Department of Health (2011) *Talking Therapies: A Four Year Plan of Action*. London: Department of Health. Available at: http://www.iapt.nhs.uk/silo/files/talking-therapies-a-four-year-plan-of-action.pdf (accessed 6 January 2015).

House of Commons Health Committee (2014) *Children's and Adolescents' Mental Health and CAMHS. Third Report of Session 2014–2015*, HC342. London: The Stationery Office. Available at: http://www.publications.parliament.uk/pa/cm201415/cmselect/cmhealth/342/34202.htm (accessed 24 November 2014).

Layard, R. (2006). *The Depression Report: A New Deal for Depression and Anxiety Disorders*. The Centre for Economic Performance's Mental Health Policy Group. Available at: http://eprints.lse.ac.uk/818/1/DEPRESSION_REPORT_LAYARD.pdf (accessed 6 January 2015).

NHS Choices (2014) *The Expert Patients Programme (EPP)*. http://www.nhs.uk/NHSEngland/AboutNHSservices/doctors/Pages/expert-patients-programme.aspx (accessed 29 December 2014).

Office for National Statistics (2014) *Measuring National Well-being: Life in the UK, 2014*. http://www.ons.gov.uk/ons/rel/wellbeing/measuring-national-well-being/life-in-the-uk–2014/art-mnwb–life-in-the-uk–2014.html (accessed 30 December 2014)

Rigby, N. (2015) Psychiatrist's concerns over Norfolk and Suffolk children's mental health care. *BBC News*, 1 January. Available at: http://www.bbc.co.uk/news/uk-england-30247002 (accessed 12 January 2015).

Sabin, L. (2014) Girl, 16, with mental health problems held in police cells for nearly 48 hours as 'no NHS beds free'. *Independent*, 29 November. Available at: http://www.independent.co.uk/news/uk/home-news/girl-16-with-mental-health-problems-held-by-police-for-nearly-48-hours-as-no-nhs-beds-free-9892833.html (accessed 6 May 2015).

Sackett, D., Straus, S.E., Richardson, W.S., Rosenberg, W. and Haynes R.B. (2000) *Evidence-Based Medicine: How to Practice and Teach EBM* (2nd edn). London: Churchill Livingstone.

Stratton, A. (2010) Happiness index to gauge Britain's national mood. *Guardian*, 14 November. Available at: http://www.theguardian.com/lifeandstyle/2010/nov/14/happiness-index-britain-national-mood?guni=Article:in%20body%20link (accessed 24 November 2014).

Wintour, P. (2014) Butler-Sloss: victims should not run child abuse inquiry. *Guardian*, 31 December. Available at: http://www.theguardian.com/society/2014/dec/31/butler-sloss-victims-not-run-child-abuse-inquiry (accessed 6 May 2015).

Further reading

IAPT (2012a) *Children and Young People's Improving Access to Psychological Therapies Project* [Online]. Available at: http://www.iapt.nhs.uk/silo/files/children-and-young-peoples-improving-access-to-psychological-therapies-project.pdf (accessed 30 December 2014).

IAPT (2012b) *Children and Young People's Improving Access to Psychological Therapies Project A Practical Guide to Using Service User Feedback & Outcome Tools to Inform Clinical Practice in Child & Adolescent Mental Health* [Online]. Available at: http://www.iapt.nhs.uk/silo/files/a-practical-guide-to-using-service-user-feedback–outcome-tools-.pdf (Accessed: 30 December 2014).

IAPT (2012c) *A Practical Guide to Using Service User Feedback & Outcome Tools to Inform Clinical Practice in Child & Adolescent Mental Health* [Online]. Available at: http://www.iapt.nhs.uk/silo/files/a-practical-guide-to-using-service-user-feedback–outcome-tools-.pdf (accessed 30 December 2014).

Roth, A., Calder, F. and Pilling, S. (2011). A competence framework for Child and Adolescent Mental Health Services [online]. Available at: http://www.ucl.ac.uk/clinical-psychology/CORE/child-adolescent-competences/CAMHS%20Competences%20Framework_V1%20(2).pdf (Accessed 29 April 2012).

Worrall-Davies, A. and Marino-Francis, F. (2008). Eliciting children's and young people's views of child and adolescent mental health services: a systematic review of best practice. *Child and Adolescent Mental Health*, 13, 9–15.

Young Minds (2011) Talking about Talking Therapies: Thinking and planning about how best to make good and accessible talking therapies available to children and young people [online]. Available at: http://www.youngminds.org.uk/assets/0000/2743/iapt-long.pdf (accessed 29 April 2014).

2 CBT: theory, history and wider influences

Nick Wrycraft, Alison Coad and Tom Marshall

Introduction

In this chapter we introduce the concepts and ideas on which the cognitive behavioural therapy (CBT) approach is based. We begin by considering what defines CBT, before exploring the ideas that have fed into its development. Then we look at the various therapeutic approaches that combined to form CBT as we know it today.

CBT has played a prominent role in the in the Improving Access to Psychological Therapies (IAPT) initiative which, as discussed in Chapter 1, has in recent years been extended to services for children and young people (CYP-IAPT).

What is CBT?

Write down what you think are the characteristics of CBT, and then check them against the features that are discussed below.

Cognitive behavioural therapy can be defined as a psychological therapy that:

- Uses a structured approach
- Is evidence-based
- Is focused on collaboration and learning for both client and therapist
- Is usually brief and time-limited
- Looks at problems in the 'here and now'
- Teaches the client to become their own therapist
- Considers relapse prevention.

A structured approach

When working with younger children, sessions would be held jointly with parents or carers; for older children and adolescents, there is a choice of approach, including individual sessions between the young person and the therapist, with involvement of parents or carers as appropriate.

The first stage of therapy takes the form of an **assessment** and **formulation** of the problem. The formulation is collaboratively devised and discussed between the therapist and the client and is revisited and amended or updated as therapy progresses. CBT sessions are conducted using an **agenda** – an agreed list of issues to cover. It can be useful for client and therapist to allocate time for each item at the start of the session.

Sessions generally commence with a brief checking-in to discuss how things have been for the client between sessions, and to highlight any significant changes or developments. In CBT there is also a focus on socialising the client to the model from as early a point in therapy as possible. It is also necessary to focus on pacing the session in accordance with the client's developmental stage and style of learning. Regular **summaries** and **feedback** are provided throughout the session, and the client is encouraged to contribute to this process. Towards the end of the session an overall summary is provided by the therapist, which provides an opportunity to check understanding on the part of both client and therapist. A key aspect of therapy involves testing ideas between sessions and the setting of agreed **homework** tasks is therefore important. Some clients prefer to use a term such as 'home practice' or 'home therapy' – for some, 'homework' has connotations of school and of an authority relationship. Checking out details such as preferred terminology is an important part of the collaborative process. Adopting a shared language is essential to successful engagement.

Children and young people have different needs than adults, and this needs careful consideration when working therapeutically with this client group. This point is discussed in more detail in Chapter 3.

Question: Looking at the above, which aspects of CBT do you think might be the most challenging? In particular, what needs to be considered when adapting techniques so that they are accessible to young people?

Answer: This varies from person to person, as we all have differing strengths and weaknesses. However, many student CBT therapists struggle with time management and keeping to the agenda. Often there is also difficulty in keeping the client on track when they digress – there is a need to be assertive without being perceived as critical, which could impair the therapeutic relationship.

Evidence-based

CBT is evidence-based in two respects. Firstly, in CBT sessions there is an emphasis on gathering and using evidence. This includes carrying out assessment measures as a means of collecting baseline data and later repeating the same assessment to measure therapeutic progress. The client is also encouraged to gather evidence to support or disprove their assumptions or beliefs, using a variety of methods such as thought diaries, surveys and behavioural experiments. Each of these strategies enables client and therapist to understand the client's thoughts and beliefs, and to measure how and when change occurs.

Secondly, there is a significant base of empirical research supporting the effectiveness of CBT as a therapeutic approach, particularly with regard to the treatment of anxiety and depression. It could be argued that, due to being a brief and time-limited approach that is structured, and which emphasises the use of assessment measures, CBT is especially amenable to research.

Focused on learning

CBT encourages curiosity, gathering evidence and reflection on how this evidence might enable therapeutic change. This is true for the therapist as well as the client. The therapist, for example, uses their knowledge of CBT theory to find the right model of treatment for a specific problem. Models are developed as a result of academic research within clinical practice. There are a number of well-known models which have come to represent standard approaches to treatment – for example, Beck's model of depression, or Clark and Wells's model of social anxiety. These models are usually represented in diagrammatic form, and are supported by research which is published in the academic literature. **Psycho-education** is also used, for example, to enable the client to understand the links between uncomfortable emotions and physiological symptoms (see Figure 2.1). Through work within sessions, which is often developed and enhanced by the use of appropriate homework tasks, the client is encouraged to adopt a pragmatic approach and to challenge and test beliefs. Using these strategies, the client is enabled to identify unhelpful assumptions, negative automatic thoughts and thinking styles such as 'black and white' (or inflexible) thinking. Awareness of these factors can help clients to recognise some of the thinking that could be maintaining their problem (see Figure 2.1 for an example).

Brief and time-limited

CBT is time-limited and a course of treatment is usually relatively brief. The models of treatment discussed above include guidance about stages of therapy, and how many sessions should be aimed for (for examples of treatment programmes and suggested numbers of sessions, see Leahy *et al.* 2000). This reduces the risk of dependency developing and ensures that the ending of treatment can be planned for and is part of the process. This means that, from the outset of treatment, the client's ability to manage without continuous support is recognised. Although there is guidance regarding the number of sessions recommended for a particular condition, and this can be very useful for therapists, the number of sessions and duration of treatment is specific to the particular case. As the case studies in this volume demonstrate, models can be used as the basis for a very flexible approach to treatment.

Problems in the 'here and now'

CBT focuses on problems as they are currently experienced. Problems are addressed in a spirit of inquiry and with an open mind. Sometimes it is helpful to reflect on aspects of the client's past experiences, as this helps to understand the function of current patterns of thinking and behaviour. Problems may be linked to events experienced in the past, for example an accident or trauma, or to repeated negative experiences such as abuse. In the case of Sophia, for example (Chapter 14) past events have precipitated the problem. Although in these cases an awareness of the historic origin to the problem is essential, CBT works to resolve the effects of these events on the present situation.

The focus of CBT interventions is often practical in nature. Recognising the connections between the client's thoughts, feelings and behaviours opens up the possibility of new interpretations and of the client's choice to respond in a manner that produces more positive outcomes.

Teaching the client to become their own therapist

As CBT is brief and time-limited, there is an emphasis on the client acquiring effective tools and resources so that they can maintain new-found coping skills and positive change once treatment has ended. The client needs to feel confident in the tools and techniques they use, and such confidence is more likely if they have been effectively socialised to the model and can clearly understand the rationale for the use of particular techniques. Understanding the model not only occurs at a cognitive level but also experientially, so that while understanding CBT intellectually it can also be known to have worked experientially. Homework outside the therapy session is therefore important in reinforcing the understanding that learning which occurs in the therapy session can be translated to the client's everyday life.

Relapse prevention

Although generally focused upon the present, CBT also emphasises the need to plan ahead and maintain positive change. Relapse prevention is therefore a very important aspect of therapy. Measures that are considered in relapse prevention include recognising effective coping strategies and potential 'trigger' situations, which may lead to a recurrence of symptoms. The client is encouraged to develop a sense of self-efficacy and to recognise that contingency plans, which can be called upon in the event of a recurrence of symptoms, are an important aspect of remaining well. When working with children and younger people, the role of parents and carers can be particularly important here, by providing an overview of possible signs of relapse and by encouraging the recall of strategies which have proved helpful in the past. The nature of the client group also means that these issues need to be handled with sensitivity to developmental changes – the young person's needs, and their relationship to their parents, will naturally undergo changes over time and this process may present new challenges.

CBT works on the premise that our thoughts influence how we feel, and that our feelings influence what we feel able to do (or not to do). Our response is determined by not only what happens to us, but also what we make of it. Figure 2.1 presents a diagrammatic representation of this process. The cognitive cycle identifies how thoughts, emotions, behaviours and physical arousal interact in maintaining problems. This information contributes to the formulation – that is, the overall picture of an individual's difficulties which acts as a basis for treatment planning.

An important part of this is for the therapist and client to work together to arrive at a formulation which makes sense to them both. Active collaboration is an essential part of the therapeutic relationship, as it emphasises the client's abilities and skills and encourages problem-solving.

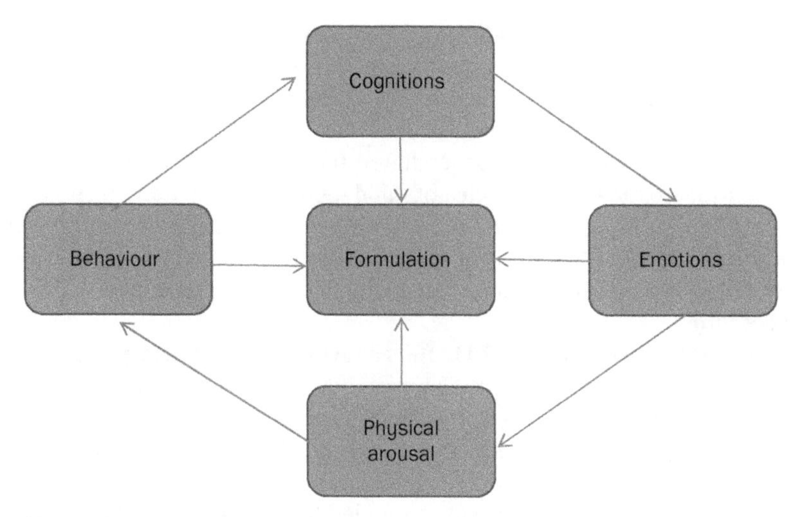

Figure 2.1 The cognitive cycle (Adapted from James *et al.*, 2001)

The philosophy of CBT

Philosophy is the study of knowledge. One of the classic questions of philosophy, to which much thought has been devoted, is how we know what we think we know. This is relevant to CBT: in therapy, the client is encouraged to ask this question in respect of their thoughts, beliefs, emotions and action. How does an individual decide on what is 'true' or 'fact', and what is a potentially inaccurate interpretation of events? In this section we briefly examine these questions, and how they have been addressed within the work of some prominent philosophers, before progressing to consider developments in the world of CBT theory and practice.

The nature of the relationship of mind and body is an elusive and complex problem. Neuroscience allows us to construct an accurate understanding of how the physical mechanism of our brain functions. However, it is much more of a challenge to explain how our physical being connects with what we identify as our subjective experience (Deary 2005). One of the most significant contributions to this debate was provided by **René Descartes** (1596–1650), who proposed the notion of mind and body dualism. Descartes suggested that there was an objective world, external to us and composed of objects and material phenomena. The inner world of the human mind, comprised of concepts such as thoughts and beliefs, was a separate strand of individual experience which existed alongside the material world. Descartes stated that the objective world operates in accordance with the laws of science, and that these laws could be identified through inquiry. He argued that this strategy could also be applied to the subjective self, and that similar laws and principles could be identified within subjective experience (Deary 2005). Descartes' ideas were highly influential in the origins of the rational and empirical movement that began with the Enlightenment and which is still in evidence today, in our faith in science. That said, there have been numerous critiques of the Cartesian view.

Immanuel Kant (1724–1804) suggested that, as opposed to perceiving a consistent objective world, our perceptions are filtered by subjective consciousness. Perception, therefore, represents an interpretation, rather than a fixed external reality. Kant does not suggest that the objective world is illusory, only that we can never gain an impression of it that is not mediated by our subjective perception (Deary 2005). In contrast to the Cartesian idea of mind–body dualism, Kant proposes a mutually influential synergy or symbiosis. This idea offers the potential for reciprocity between the concepts of 'objective' and 'subjective', as we seek ways to conceptualise the world around us while simultaneously shaping the objective world through our subjectivity.

Martin Heidegger (1899–1976) offers a further philosophical perspective which is relevant to the idea of subjectivity. Contrary both to Descartes and Kant, Heidegger argued that it was ultimately misrepresentative to talk about human beings in terms of subjects and objects. He insisted that this was an abstraction and that the best way to understand what we are is through an analysis of what we do. Heidegger discussed how we find ourselves within a world surrounded by equipment which we manipulate and navigate constantly – rather than as subjects disconnected from objects – and it is through this that we establish our understanding of ourselves through our orientation towards goals and plans. He also insisted on the fact that we must acknowledge what he called our 'thrownness' in the world. What this means is that when we begin to think about things, we do so from a point that has already been conditioned by our situation and surroundings; we have a race, a gender, a nationality, a language, and so on, and these all feed into the way we interpret the world and ourselves. Rather than seeing these as subjective prejudices, as many before him had, Heidegger insisted that these factors were unavoidable starting points not just for philosophy but for being in general, and that to pathologise them as unreliable or not objective was to seek after a point of disinterest which we could never hope to achieve.

The origins of CBT

CBT can be seen as developing from two strands of therapy: behavioural therapy and cognitive therapy. Behavioural therapy stemmed from work in the nineteenth and early twentieth century on behavioural psychology, which relied on experimentation and an empirical approach. Central to the behaviourist approach were the concepts of classical conditioning and operant conditioning. Classical conditioning is reflex or involuntary behaviour, such as salivating in the presence of food, whereas operant conditioning is influenced by the consequences of behaviour, such as being rewarded for good behaviour and punished for being bad.

During the 1960s, in the United States, Aaron Beck devised cognitive therapy as a short-term, structured problem-solving approach focusing on the relationship between the thoughts and feelings of clients experiencing depression. Beck's approach paved the way for the integration of behavioural and cognitive approaches, as it became apparent that cognitive states had an influence on what the client felt able to do (or not to do). The CBT approach recognises complex interactions between the ways in which people think, feel and behave. The combination of cognitive and behavioural approaches has led to the development of a wide repertoire of therapeutic models, each with a range of intervention strategies.

CBT Narratives: a brief introduction to narrative research strategies

The case studies presented within this book are presented as a collaboration between therapists and clients. Although the therapist is the named author, and is responsible for the overall structure of the chapter, the client has given permission for their story to be told and has also provided material (verbal, pictorial, diagrammatic) which helps to tell that story. Each client was given the opportunity to read and comment on the case study before it was submitted for publication. The purpose of this section of the chapter is to explain why this approach was adopted, and to provide some information about the research theory which influenced this choice.

Research methodology falls into two main approaches: qualitative, which examines the quality of experience and uses data such as interviews with research subjects; and quantitative, which uses numerical data derived from controlled situations such as treatment trials. The quality and reliability of research findings needs to be evidenced if the research is to be used as the basis for change, for example in treatment techniques within healthcare. Qualitative data is sometimes referred to as 'soft' data, because it is not possible to measure it in a completely objective way. It involves opinions and perspectives, which will naturally vary from person to person, be they interviewer or interviewed. There has been much debate about how to ensure consistency in qualitative research (see, for example, Mays and Pope 2000). For many researchers, a qualitative approach offers an opportunity to explore their interests in an immediate, experiential way. It is not unusual for studies to be conducted using a mixture of both approaches, which can help to address some of the concerns about validity and reliability.

Narrative research is a strand of qualitative research which focuses on the stories of its subjects. Josselson (2006) describes the results of narrative research as 'richly-detailed expositions of life as lived, well-interpreted studies full of nuance and insight that befit the complexities of human lives'. For some researchers in the healthcare professions, this approach provides a welcome contrast to a professional existence which is dominated by financial constraints and the associated need to evidence, through statistics, the efficacy of their interventions. Narrative research provides opportunities for individual stories to be explored in detail, and the meaning of experiences including health and illness. Treatment strategies can be devised based on 'the creation rather than the telling of stories', where 'therapists … help to create a therapeutic short story that becomes a meaningful short story in the larger life story of the patient' (Mattingly 1991).

Narrative and literary theory: stories and their meanings

The idea of creating stories provides a link to another form of narrative, that of works of fiction. It may seem surprising to consider works of fiction as a part of a discussion about research methods and therapeutic approaches, but there are overlaps which are worth exploring. The theory which underpins the study of literature ranges from close analysis of the text itself, known as **literary criticism**, to theories which encompass philosophical, linguistic and political concepts such as **structuralism** and **poststructuralism**. The work of writers such as Roland Barthes (1915–80) and Michel Foucault (1926–84) is worth mentioning here.

Roland Barthes' landmark notion of the 'death of the author' gives an account of reading that seeks to challenge the concept of where meaning lies. Barthes characterises the author as a godlike figure with complete authority over what their text means and how it ought to be read. He goes on to argue that this figure can have no place within literary criticism, since it serves only to limit the way in which the text is interpreted. The reasoning behind this claim stems from the way Barthes thinks about language and the written word. For Barthes, a written text is not a collection of words with a single meaning, but rather a collection of symbols which gain significance through the act of reading. The meaning is not sealed into the words by the actions of the author; rather, it is created by how the reader reacts to these words. In this respect, the author ceases to have any importance. It is within the power of the reader to create a meaning wholly independent of authorial intent. It is for this reason that, to accompany the 'death of the author', Barthes declares that this kind of understanding of writing heralds the 'birth of the reader'. Therapy is also largely conducted in words, and the idea of words holding different meanings for different people needs to be kept in mind. Many therapists will be able to describe incidents where misinterpretation has led to a rupture in the therapeutic relationship. The author does not have final say when it comes to meanings, and neither does the therapist.

Foucault's work spans a wide range of topics, including literature, politics and sociology. He examines power relationships in ways that challenge socially accepted definitions, and argues that state control over individuals has become less barbaric but more invidious in recent history: 'The power to punish is not essentially different from that of curing or educating' (Foucault 1977). This is a sobering thought for those of us who hope to help our clients to alleviate symptoms which cause them distress. In doing so, are we simply imposing our view of the world on them? And if so, who is to say which view of the world is the 'right' one? It could be argued that symptoms which lead to a diagnosis of mental illness just do not fit within the dominant ideas of our society. Those who experience these symptoms are therefore regarded as 'odd' or deviant; perhaps this is the main source of distress, rather than the symptoms themselves.

The concept of dominant voices within society highlights another aspect of narrative research which is relevant to this discussion: the question of the balance of power between the subject and the researcher. The aim of this volume is to give a voice to the young people who are the subjects of the case studies. The use of their words, artwork and images is intended to challenge the way in which books like this one speak *about* clients, rather than allowing the clients to speak for themselves. However, the fact that the voices of the young subjects of the case studies are mediated by the therapists who have written the account raises the question of who has the most control over what is said. The audience for this book is also relatively narrow. It is more likely to be read by professionals than by young people, and this is something which also needs to be kept in mind when thinking about who benefits most from the publication of these accounts. It is important that these issues are considered when reading these case studies, in the hope that readers will be encouraged to reflect on and question what is written, rather than taking what is written as fact. This mirrors the way in which those undertaking a course of CBT are encouraged to challenge thoughts and to recognise alternative perspectives.

Narrative CBT is one of the most recent developments in CBT theory and practice, often referred to as 'third wave' cognitive therapy. Rhodes (2013) provides a useful summary of the concept of narrative CBT which draws together the various influences which have contributed to the approach. These include therapeutic approaches including solution-focused therapy and systemic therapy, elements of developmental psychology, and philosophical influences such as those discussed above.

Question: What do you understand by the term 'narrative'? Can you think of ways in which narrative approaches could be helpful in therapy?

Summary

This chapter has presented a wide range of material, including some quite complex ideas from philosophy. Some of the discussion may seem to be a long way from the day-to-day reality of the therapist or the client. It is certainly not essential to have a fluent grasp of all of these ideas in order to understand the therapeutic work which is presented in the case studies which follow. However, the ability to remain open-minded, and to experiment with new approaches and ideas, is an essential feature of CBT. Furthermore, CBT formulation is a process of understanding the connections between various aspects of the experience of the client – including wider social and cultural issues, which influence therapists as much as clients. We hope that the ideas within this chapter will spark the curiosity of our readers, and encourage a lively and responsive approach to therapy.

References

Deary, V. (2005) Explaining the unexplained? Overcoming the distortions of a dualist understanding of medically unexplained illness. *Journal of Mental Health*, 14(3): 213–21.

Foucault, M. (1977) *Discipline and Punish: The Birth of the Prison*. New York: Pantheon.

James, I.A., Blackburn, I.-M. and Reichelt, F.K. (2001) *Manual of the Revised Cognitive Therapy Scale (CTS- R)*. Northumberland, Tyne and Wear NHS Trust.

Josselson, R. (2006) Narrative research and the challenge of accumulating knowledge. *Narrative Inquiry*, 16(1): 3–10.

Leahy, R.L., Holland, S.J. and McGinn, L.K. (2000) *Treatment Plans and Interventions for Depression and Anxiety Disorders*. New York: Guilford Press.

Mattingly, C. (1991) The narrative nature of clinical reasoning. *American Journal of Occupational Therapy*, 45(11): 998–1005.

Mays, N. and Pope, C. (2000) Assessing quality in qualitative research. *British Medical Journal*, 320(7226): 50–2.

Rhodes, J. (2013) *Narrative CBT: Distinctive Features*. Hove: Routledge.

Further reading

Andrews, M., Squire, C. and Tamboukou, M. (eds) (2013) *Doing Narrative Research*. London: Sage.

Belsey, C. (2002) *Poststructuralism: A Very Short Introduction*. Oxford: Oxford University Press.

Butler, G. and McManus, F. (2014) *Psychology: A Very Short Introduction*. Oxford: Oxford University Press.

Culler, J. (2002) *Barthes: A Very Short Introduction*. Oxford: Oxford University Press.

Gutting, G. (2005) *Foucault: A Very Short Introduction*. Oxford: Oxford University Press.

Hoffman, D.F. (2013) Another error of Descartes? Implications for the 'third wave' cognitive behavioural therapy. *Journal of Cognitive and Behavioural Psychotherapies*, 13(1): 115–24.

Inwood, M. (2000) *Heidegger: A Very Short Introduction*. Oxford: Oxford University Press.

3 The Cognitive Behaviour Therapy Scale for Children and Young People

Nick Wrycraft

Introduction

In this chapter we discuss the Cognitive Behaviour Therapy Scale for Children and Young People (CBTS-CYP). The scale provides the structure for the cases in this book, and has been chosen as it represents the best evidence-based approach for measuring the effectiveness of working therapeutically using a CBT approach with children and adolescents. The commentary on the CBTS-CYP includes some links to the case studies in this book. The reader is encouraged to keep these ideas in mind when reading the case studies, to help to make connections between theory and practice.

We begin by discussing aspects of CBT with children and adolescents and the challenges that this might represent. The purpose of this is to identify why the CBTS-CYP is needed and why it is necessary that a different measure is used for children and adolescents than for adults. The chapter then briefly outlines the Cognitive Therapy Scales Revised (CTS-R), the stages that it follows and the scoring mechanism that is used, before explaining the CBTS-CYP and the features of the 14 individual elements against which therapists' competence is scored.

CBT and working with children and adolescents

CBT is a time-limited, problem-focused and practical psychological approach. There are many variations in the delivery of therapy due to factors such as the specific nature of the problem, the stage of therapy, or the client's ability to engage in the process. However, there are a number of key features of CBT that are present for every course of treatment.

When working using CBT with adults it is essential to consider the client's individual needs, including culture and values, educational level, and capacity to socialise to the model. It is important to assess these needs sensitively at the beginning of therapy. When working with children and adolescents a range of developmental factors also need to be taken into account in order to ensure that CBT is delivered effectively. In order to highlight the contrasts and similarities in the treatment of adults and of young people, we have used the distinction offered by Stallard *et al.* (2014) to separate process and techiques, and have illustrated these differences in Figure 3.1.

Process (or relationship) aspects

- an effective therapeutic alliance with the client which enables the exploration of sensitive issues in an atmosphere of safety and trust
- a collaborative partnership, where problems and their meaning to the client be clearly understood and used as a basis for goal setting

CBT techniques and strategies

- jointly developing a formulation of the client's problem and how it is maintained
- a problem focused approach that accurately understands how the problem is experienced but also how solutions might address the problem
- a logical structure in the delivery of therapy and interventions
- use of techniques which encourage reflection and which, as a consequence, can change the client's mood and behaviour

Figure 3.1 Key features of CBT

Question: Looking at the features above, from the therapist's point of view, write down what might be the main challenge(s) firstly in the relationship and secondly in the process aspects of CBT.

Answer: Your answer may include the possibility of falling into a parent role when working with children or young people. This may be especially the case if the therapist has children of their own that may be at a similar age to the client. It is also possible that some of the client's cultural references and activities might be unfamiliar to a therapist from an older generation; this provides an excellent opportunity for collaboration between the therapist and client!

Concerning the process aspects of CBT, the challenges may be that the client lacks the emotional maturity, level of cognitive functioning or sense of social responsibility to appreciate the connections between factors that maintain the problem. Alternatively, the client may not feel empowered to make changes, which is also likely to affect motivation, and limit capacity to explore solutions to problems.

Question: What might be the solutions to the issues above, or those that you have identified?

Answer: If we feel that we are adopting the parent role, then this might be brought to supervision. It may be that concerns about being in the parent role arise from our own anxieties, and are baseless. Alternatively, if that propensity is a real concern, this may be managed through ongoing monitoring in supervision, taking care to reflect on interactions and to note any areas of concern in a reflective manner. If the therapist is working with clients who are of similar ages to their own children this might be an advantage in terms of understanding the particular challenges of the client's developmental stage. Similarly, age or generation differences in therapeutic relationships do not necessarily represent obstacles and may even be advantageous.

The age and stage of mental and emotional maturity, level of social responsibility and capability of the client is very relevant. In some cases there may be legal guidance such as 'Gillick competence' (see NSPCC 2015) and the Childrens' Act 1990 that provide specific criteria. In some cases, for example in older adolescents, CBT may be predominantly one-to-one and there may be limited parental involvement. In such cases, therapy relies on a high level of personal responsibility on the part of the client (for example, in the case of Stephanie, Chapter 14). When working with younger children (for example, in the case of David, Chapter 7) it is essential for parents to be very much involved within the therapeutic process.

Careful consideration needs to be given to the specific needs of children and young people in order to engage clients effectively. It is very important to ensure that the concepts of CBT are accessible and have meaning for the young person, and their family and caregivers.

The Cognitive Therapy Scale - Revised

The CTS-R was developed by James *et al.* (2001) to measure therapist competence when working using CBT with adult clients. The scale consists of 12 areas, divided into two categories (general skills and CBT-specific skills). Agenda setting and adherence are included in both categories. The individual items on the scale are listed below:

General items
Agenda setting and adherence
Feedback
Collaboration
Pacing and efficient use of time
Interpersonal effectiveness

Cognitive therapy specific items
Agenda setting and adherence
Eliciting appropriate emotional expression
Eliciting key cognitions
Eliciting behaviours
Guided discovery
Conceptual integration
Application of change methods
Homework Setting

Each of these 12 areas is then scored using the Dreyfus scoring system, which defines six levels of competence. These are outlined in Figure 3.2. In applying the Dreyfus model, therapists are scored in relation to each item of the CTS-R ranging from 0–6 on the scale shown in Figure 3.3. The maximum score that can be achieved is 72, although James *et al.* (2001) recommend reserving the highest scores only for work that is either outstanding, or carried out in highly adverse situations.

Incompetent: There are errors and behaviour falling below that expected of a competent practitioner and that lead to unhelpful therapeutic outcomes.
Novice: rigid observance of taught rules and a lack of adaption to situation specific factors, or use of initiative and discretion.
Advanced beginner: all aspects of the task are given equal and individual attention. The ability to adapt to differing situations and to exercise discretionary judgement is evident.
Competent: Tasks are connected within a conceptual overview within which plans are made and standard and routine evidence based interventions are applied.
Proficient: The therapist has a holistic perception of the client's issues, decisions are made rapidly, tasks are prioritised, and there is clear evidence of skill and ability.
Expert: Rules are not used, however the therapist has a deep insight into the client's issues and is able to apply situation specific problem solving methods. High level skills are demonstrated even in very challenging situations.

Figure 3.2 The Dreyfus scoring system levels of competence, as applied to the CTS-R

The Cognitive Behaviour Therapy Scale for Children and Young People

As more therapists undertook training in CBT, it became apparent that the CTS-R did not address key aspects of therapist performance if the client was a child or young person. The CBTS-CYP was developed in recognition of these differences. Examples of these differences include the following:

- Children and adolescents are dependent upon parents or caregivers to varying degrees; these relationships are likely to be influential in the maintenance of problems, and maybe also in devising solutions.
- Children and adolescents are developing in terms of cognitive functioning but also emotionally, linguistically and in terms of reasoning. CBT needs to be delivered at the right level in order to effectively engage the client.
- Innovative and even non-verbal methods may be used to present the CBT approach to the child or adolescent in a manner that they can relate to and understand.
- Undertaking CBT with children and adolescents and their parents needs clearer explanation than with adults.

(Stallard *et al.* 2014)

The CBTS-CYP provides a therapist competence scale intended specifically for therapists working with children and younger people. The CTS-R influenced the development of the CBTS-CYP, and although some of the elements of the CTS-R can be mapped onto the CBTS-CYP, there are significant differences (Stallard *et al.* 2014). For example, there are unique elements such as working at the right developmental level, using creativity and ensuring that the sessions are as enjoyable as possible. These features emphasise therapist competencies that can enhance the therapeutic relationship, particularly when working with children and adolescents.

The CBTS-CYP functions on the basis of concentric levels of therapist competencies. These are represented as 3 levels, as shown in Figure 3.4. There are a total of

Classifications	Score	Interpretation of scores
the item is not apparent, or there is inept performance	0	0-1 incompetent
inappropriate performance and significant problems	1	1-2 novice
competence is apparent but there are problems	2	2-3 advanced beginner
competence but some problems or a lack of consistency	3	3-4 competent
good performance of the item but with minor problem or inconsistency	4	
performance of a higher level with very limited problems or inconsistencies	5	4-5 proficient
high level performance, even in the presence of difficulties or challenges	6	5-6 expert

Figure 3.3 The Dreyfus model classification, score and interpretation

18 competencies, with four on the inner and seven each on the outer two levels. However, the CBTS-CYP only scores the outer two levels as these address the process and specific skills that are used in CBT. The inner level concerns the core philosophy of IAPT for the child and adolescent services (Roth *et al.* 2011) as opposed to competence in CBT (Stallard *et al.* 2014).

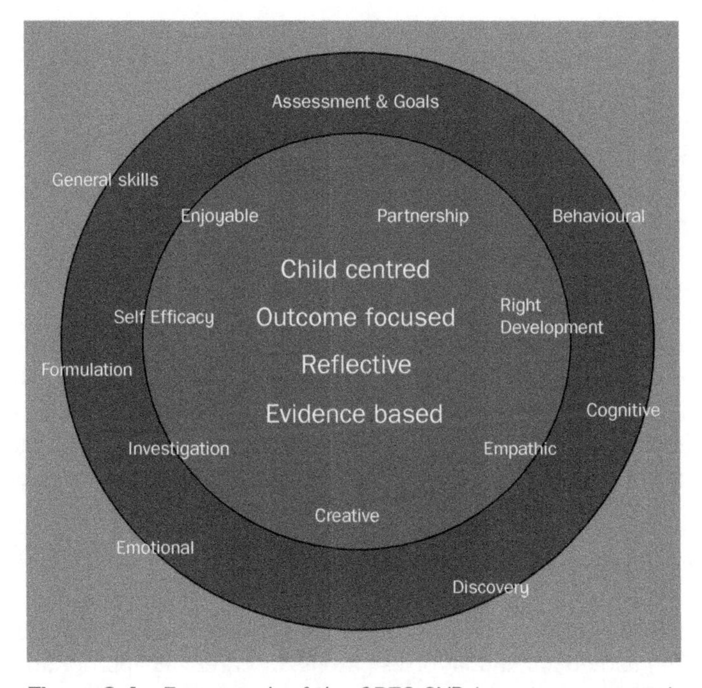

Figure 3.4 Framework of the CBTS-CYP (Paul Stallard, 2012)

In common with the CTS-R, the CBTS-CYP also uses the Dreyfus scoring system of classification, score and interpretation.

The three levels of the CBTS-CYP begin from the centre, which uses the acronym **CORE** which stands for:

C – child centred
O – outcome focused
R – reflective practitioners
E – evidence based approaches

The middle level of the framework concerns the process of CBT and uses the acronym **PRECISE**. These elements stand for:

P – partnership working
R – right developmental level
E – empathic
C – creative
I – investigative
S – self-efficacy
E – enjoyable

The final level relates to CBT specific skills, and the acronyms for these involves their being given successive letters of the alphabet from A–G as follows:

A – assessment and goals
B – behavioural techniques
C – cognitive techniques
D – discovery experiments
E – emotional techniques
F – formulation
G – general skills

Next we examine each of the 14 items within the CBTS-CYP, in order to to elaborate on the specific skills that are required at each stage. Inevitably, there is some overlap between the different attributes. In scoring the therapist's performance it is necessary to examine how features of the therapeutic relationship, such as collaboration or partnership working, are evident in relation to these individual criteria. The CBTS-CYP makes it possible to quantify subtle distinctions and to acknowledge the skills that clinicians use in adapting CBT to the individual needs of each young client.

Partnership – *collaboration and shared learning*

This element requires the therapist to encourage the development of a collaborative and respectful partnership and involves parents or carers as appropriate. Among the features that may be present are:

- Encouraging and eliciting the client's active involvement in discussion, appraising options, identifying solutions and making decisions
- Seeking the views and perceptions of parents and caregivers as appropriate
- Gaining the input and involvement of parents and carers in setting targets, planning interventions and discussing activities and experiments to be carried out at home
- Encouraging the client to give honest feedback about therapy.

It is important to make sure that the young person feels able to express their views openly, which can be tricky when their experience of adults has encouraged them to defer to the adult view (parents and teachers, for example). Stephanie's case provides examples of the way in which this can be managed successfully. In sessions, it can be useful to allow the young person some time to talk without their parents being present – although for young people like Jane, who worried about being away from her parents, this can present its own problems. Some young people are very keen to let you know their views and it can be challenging to keep the session on track!

Right developmental level – *pitch, methods, family involvement*

The therapist engages with the child or young person in a manner appropriate to their understanding and developmental level. Among the features are:

- The use of clear and non-technical language
- A balance between behavioural and cognitive techniques
- Suitable pacing of sessions to enhance the client's level of understanding
- Using both verbal and non-verbal techniques
- Involving parents and carers in treatment sessions as necessary.

These issues are relevant to all of the case studies in this book. Specific examples of the use of non-verbal techniques can be found in Stephanie's case, and in Lily's case (Chapter 9). In both instances, drawings were a helpful adjunct to the talking parts of the session, helping in a variety of ways – for example, as a means to externalise anxiety. Eleanor's trips outside the clinic could also be seen as a non-verbal strategy.

Empathy – *acknowledgement, warmth and genuineness*

The therapist demonstrates empathy to the child or young person and their parents or carers as appropriate. This may be apparent through:

- Showing interest and concern in the form of active listening, feedback and summaries
- Responding empathically and recognising distress, anxiety or excitement

- A respectful, open and caring approach
- Empathising with parents or carers concerning their own issues, and the effect on their ability to support the child or young person.

Again, these are core features of the accounts of therapy presented in this book and there are examples to be found in each case study.

Creative – *verbal and non-verbal techniques*

The therapist creatively adapts CBT in order to ensure that the approach feels relevant to the child or young person, and, as appropriate, to parents or carers. This may be evident through the following features:

- A range of verbal and non-verbal methods that facilitate understanding and engagement
- Innovative use of various media, such as talking, drawing, questionnaires, metaphors, role-plays and puppets to illustrate ideas and concepts (Stephanie's Manga drawings are a good example of this)
- Flexibly adapting the concepts of CBT to the child's specific perspective
- Using the child and young person's preferred media, for example computer, drawing, writing.

Robert's therapy (Chapter 11) was conducted almost exclusively outside the clinic, demonstrating the flexibility of the approach and the way that it works with 'real-world concerns'. The balloon experiment, and the videos we made to consolidate Robert's learning, provided a good example of the way that fun can be employed to ameliorate anxiety.

Investigation – *discovery, reflection*

The therapist applies a curious and open approach that promotes guided discovery and reflection. This may be apparent through:

- Engendering an approach of collaborative inquiry, where the cognitions, beliefs and assumptions of the child or younger person and their family or carers can be objectively evaluated
- The child and young person being actively involved in the design of experiments
- Facilitating the child and young person to think about alternative explanations of events
- Helping the child and young person to reflect on the findings of experiments.

Self-efficacy – *building on strengths and ideas*

The CBT approach encourages self-efficacy and positive attempts to change. This may be apparent through:

- Drawing attention to the strengths and positive coping resources of the child or young person and their parents or carers
- Assisting the child or adolescent and their parents or carers to recognise the skills and strategies that have proven to be effective in the past
- Helping to develop the child/adolescent's and parents/carers' ideas and strategies for coping
- Providing positive feedback and encouragement for the use of new skills by the child or young person and their parents or carers.

Enjoyable – *interesting and encouraging*

The therapist makes the session interesting and engaging. This may be apparent through:

- The materials and approaches that are used, including a balance of activities and the use of humour (Eleanor's trip to the beach (Chapter 8) involved all of these)
- Keeping sessions to a suitable length of time (for younger children, having a break within the session, and/or playing a game as a reward at the end of the session, can be helpful)
- Balancing the session between task-focused content and developing the relationship
- Making the session relevant to and actively incorporating the child's interests in the content.

Assessment and goals — *ratings and diaries*

The therapist identifies clear goals for interventions and makes appropriate use of diaries, questionnaires and rating scales. This may be apparent through:

- A thorough assessment of the problem, involving information from other settings
- Negotiation of the desired outcomes of interventions and the times and dates to review progress
- Using a variety of methods to assess symptoms, emotions, thoughts and behaviour such as diaries, tick charts, thought bubbles and rating scales
- Making reference to goals and targets when planning activities and to rating scales and other assessments when considering progress.

Behavioural techniques – *awareness, triggers, techniques of change*

Various behavioural techniques are used that promote change. This may be apparent through:

- The use of behavioural techniques, for example activity scheduling, developing hierarchies, graded exposure and response prevention (see Robert's case, Chapter 11)
- Offering a clear rationale for the use of behavioural techniques
- Identifying and carrying out reward and contingency plans (some of the tasks set will be challenging and quite hard work – for example, in OCD. What to do when things do not go to plan is an important factor to consider, and rewards for hard work can be a source of encouragement)
- The use of modelling, problem-solving, role-play and skills training
- Offering praise and positive feedback, encourage involvement, highlight important points or develop plans.

Cognitive – *awareness, identification, challenge, cognitive reframe*

The use of a variety of cognitive techniques that promote change. This may be apparent through:

- Promoting cognitive self-awareness through, for example, thought records and bubbles. ('What's going on in your head? Are there words, pictures, or both?')
- Encouraging the identification of cognitions that are helpful, and those that are unhelpful. Using analogies can be useful here – for instance, imagining the difficult thoughts being the kind of thing that a bully might say, and the helpful thoughts being the kind of thing that your best friend would say.
- Identifying important dysfunctional cognitions.
- Promoting reflection and the generation of alternative thoughts, through, for example, considering alternative perspectives ('What would you say to your best friend if they were worried about this?'), attending to new information ('Have you considered all the possibilities here? Could there be other explanations?'), and continuum work, which challenges 'all or nothing' thinking.

Discovery – *experiments*

The therapist uses a range of methods to promote self-discovery and understanding. This may be apparent through:

- The therapist using Socratic questioning and taking alternative perspectives
- Providing rationales for behavioural experiments, and involving appropriate family support in their planning
- Carrying out behavioural experiments to test beliefs, assumptions and cognitions
- Collaboratively agreeing and planning session tasks and home activities to promote self-discovery
- Encouraging reflection on the self-discovery acquired through experiments.

Emotional – *awareness, identification, management*

The therapist uses a range of emotion-focused techniques to promote change. This may be apparent through:

- Supporting the child or young person in identifying a range of emotions
- Promoting the child or young person's capacity to distinguish between different emotions, through, for example, emotional recognition work and identifying significant bodily signals
- Supporting the child or young person to develop emotional management skills through for example controlled breathing, guided imagery and relaxation.

Formulation – *integration of CBT model*

The therapist facilitates an understanding of the problem that illustrates links between cognitions, emotions, events and physiological responses. This may be apparent through:

- The therapist offering a clear and logical rationale for the use of CBT
- Developing a collaborative formulation identifying the links between particular events, thoughts, emotion and behaviour supported by theory and assessment measures
- The therapist demonstrating an understanding of the contribution of significant past events and relationships in the origin of current problems
- Offering an explanation of activities, goals and targets in relation to the formulation
- Incorporating the role of parents or carers in the child or young person's problem(s), where appropriate.

General skills – *session planning and organisation*

The therapist has prepared and is calm and organised in the session. This may be apparent through:

- Effective preparation of materials and resources that are required for the session
- Responding appropriately to the child or adolescent's behaviour during the session
- Ensuring that there is an agenda, specific goals and a structure to the session
- Efficient timekeeping that allows for the completion of tasks
- Ensuring that sessions are effectively paced and adapted to the needs of the child or young person
- The ending of therapy is prepared for and a relapse prevention plan is in place.

Learning task: When you have read the case studies, reread this chapter and try to identify which of the areas identified within the CBTS-CYP are demonstrated.

References

James, I.A., Blackburn, I.-M. and Reichelt, F.K. (2001) *Manual of the Revised Cognitive Therapy Scale (CTS- R)*. Northumberland, Tyne and Wear NHS Trust.

NSPCC (2015) A child's legal rights: Gillick competency and Fraser guidelines. Available at: http://www.nspcc.org.uk/preventing-abuse/child-protection-system/legal-definition-child-rights-law/gillick-competency-fraser-guidelines/ (accessed 12 January 2015).

Roth, A., Calder, F. and Pilling, S. (2011). *A competence framework for Child and Adolescent Mental Health Services*. Available at: http://www.ucl.ac.uk/clinical-psychology/CORE/child-adolescent-competences/CAMHS%20Competences%20Framework_V1%20(2).pdf (accessed 12 January 2015).

Stallard, P. Myles, P. and Branson, A. (2014) The Cognitive Behaviour Therapy Scale for Children and Young People (CBTS-CYP): Development and psychometric properties. *Behavioural and Cognitive Psychotherapy*, 42(3): 269–82.

4 Ann – Depression

John Harrison

Biography

Ann (not her real name) is a 20-year-old woman who had a history of self-harming behaviour when we met 5 years ago. Prior to this, Ann had no contact with mental health services and was to all intents and purposes a fit and active individual.

This chapter examines the process undertaken by Ann and me as we aimed to use a cognitive behavioural therapy approach to deal with her self-harming behaviours. With Ann's consent we will look at the stages we followed in her treatment and use some of her own words to describe how the treatment felt to her. I will then look at what we did in the light of what is known about the use of CBT within self-harm management before offering my own perspective on how things went.

Ann was 16 when we first met. She was undertaking an apprenticeship, having left school that summer. She was a small, slightly built young woman who described cross-country running as one of her real passions. Ann had been self-harming in her room when a friend had walked in and discovered her. The friend was shocked to see that Ann had cut the top of her arms with the blade from a disposable razor. A tearful Ann confirmed that this was not the first time she had done this, and revealed scars from previous cutting on the inside of her thighs.

An appointment with a general practitioner followed. While Ann expressed no suicidal thoughts, she did state that she would find it difficult to stop self-harming. The general practitioner thought a referral to mental health services would be best and a meeting with a psychiatrist was made. After this initial consultation, it was felt that she would be a candidate for CBT and I was assigned to meet with Ann and discuss how we could best address the problems that had led to her referral. Ann and I worked together over a number of months for 12 sessions, each of which lasted about an hour.

As I write, Ann has completed her apprenticeship with another organisation and now works in the food service industry. This chapter will not only allow insights into how CBT can be used to deal with self-harm behaviours but also identify some of the causes for one particular young person.

Process

My first meeting with Ann took place in my office. I recall that she was quiet and withdrawn, and I did my best to put her at ease. I told Ann that what I needed to do was first of all listen to what she had to say. While she was initially reluctant, Ann was eventually able to talk about herself, how she felt that she was 'getting things wrong all the time', and this led to feelings of low self-esteem and self-loathing. We also talked about her childhood and who was at home and what she enjoyed doing. She spoke of her love of running and we were able to establish that this was a pastime that we both enjoyed doing. Ann was able to talk about her close-knit group of friends and how she had tried to hide her self-harm from them, and how worried she now was that they might exclude her from the group as the act of self-injury had become widely known. This allowed me to lead into a few questions about her self-harm. These included what her self-harming meant to Ann and what had led to her last act of cutting in particular. Ann was able to articulate that the acts of self-harm came from her own sense of not being good enough. Her most recent episode of self-harm had been precipitated by an incident in college. A mix up in her cooking had caused Ann's dish to be incorrect, and she felt that she had once again failed due to her 'clumsy and daft ways'. As a result Ann felt that she did not deserve her place on the apprenticeship and that others were judging her harshly. This in turn had led to her ruminating on other aspects of her life such as her parents' divorce and how she had failed to make any close friends on her new course. These thoughts would then be the trigger for her acts of self-harm. For Ann, the act was not only her way of 'teaching myself a lesson and to stop being so bad at things' but also of prolonging her negative feelings as she felt that she did not deserve to be happy. Afterwards, she would feel ashamed at what she had done and often promised herself that she would not self-harm again. However, she confessed that the act of harming herself was difficult to give up as 'I always get things wrong and do wrong just by trying to be right'.

I thanked Ann for letting me listen to her story and said that I felt it would be good if we met again in order to help her tell me more about her feelings and how these could cause her to self-harm. Ground rules for the remaining sessions were established. I told Ann that I was here as her therapist and that she could contact me in the clinic if things got too difficult. I explained that she could leave a message out of working hours (she never did) and that I would contact her as soon as I could. It was important that Ann understood that I could not provide crisis support; in a crisis, she would need to contact her GP. Practical issues such as the time and location of each session were also mentioned, and I closed by asking Ann to purchase a note book and to bring that with her to the next meeting.

Our second session saw Ann and me establish further ground rules, and we discussed the goals of the coming sessions. I asked Ann to keep a journal of her thoughts and to use the notebook to write down when she felt the urge to self-harm and what events might have triggered this. I never asked Ann to stop her self-harm, though we did look at alternative ways of dealing with her emotions. This session also led us to look at activities that would help her when the need to self-harm occurred. Ann spoke of her love of cross-country running and we both expressed how good running made us feel. Ann was able to talk about how running gave her a sense of getting away from her problems and using the time to empty her mind of her bad thoughts about herself. I encouraged her to look at other things she could do, such as phoning friends and watching television with her mother. I felt that these events would help Ann build up some resilience to the negative thoughts she had about herself.

The initial sessions that followed kept this same pattern. I would always begin by asking Ann about her mood and from her journal we were able to begin to identify what we called the triggers for her self-harming behaviours. The journal often provided a way that we could begin our sessions as Ann would, on occasion, be reluctant to talk and this gave us the entry point to see what had happened in the last 7 days. The journal was also useful in the sense that it allowed Ann to see that there were positive events in her life and times when she felt good about herself and the things that she could do. As she said, it made her realise that not everyone had negative thoughts about her and that she did have a very good relationship with her mother and that love did exist in her life.

As a result of these sessions, patterns began to emerge in which certain situations would allow her to see when the negative thoughts could lead to self-harm. These were often around her time at college, when she felt that she was not as able as the other students. For Ann, these other young people were both capable and confident in their capability, and she could not help but compare herself unfavourably to them:

> Everybody else just seems to know what to do. I feel clumsy and worry that what I make is just not as good as theirs.

We looked at alternatives to dealing with these moods. Ann was able to speak about playing music, and I suggested that doing this could help her when the need to self-harm became too great. Combining music with running was Ann's suggestion, and we devised a playlist that she could listen to do deal with these bad days. I was particularly pleased in one session when Ann noted that she had run back from college whilst listening to her headphones:

> it gave me a sense of breaking free from the rubbish day that I had. Instead of sitting on the bus and just thinking about how bad college had been, I could clear my head.

I told Ann I was delighted that she had come up with this idea and that she had been able to see what had caused her to feel bad and by herself had found a way to overcome them. We then looked at the pros and cons of both the thoughts that made her feel down and the ways in which she was able to deal with them.

It was in these sessions that Ann confessed to avoiding college on some occasions as she felt that that these were 'the triggers' that made her self-harm. I asked her to write in her journal what these thoughts were like, and she described her sense of failure and loneliness on these days:

> I dread even getting up on them days. That feeling that not only am I wasting my time but everyone's. Who is going to want to eat what I make, it is nowt like the others. I just feel rubbish and that all I do is rubbish too.

Again, I was able to make use of Ann's journal as she had described times when she had cooked for her family and how much they had enjoyed what she made. This allowed me to ask Ann to challenge her negative beliefs about her own abilities by comparing these events. She was able to acknowledge that it was the thought of college itself rather than her abilities that caused her problems. I suggested that this proved that she did have the ability to do well and that it was possible that others were not comparing her unfavourably to the rest of the students in her class. Whilst she was initially unable to accept this, we did agree that it was something that she could think about over the coming days and we would discuss it again in our next session.

It was agreed that Ann would prepare and cook a meal for a group of friends, based on the work that she had done in college, and that she could invite some people from her course. Ann expressed her anxieties about this but went ahead and held a dinner party in her own home. This process was undertaken to deal with the emotional avoidance that Ann was displaying and to improve her mood tolerance within stressful situations. We were able to see that even the most negative emotions Ann had about her abilities would be reduced in time and that she did have the ability to allow these intense feelings to pass.

Skills

Once we had identified a number of issues and negative thoughts that affected Ann, the therapy began to move more towards developing the skills that would allow her to deal with them. It was evident that a pattern emerged of her emotional and cognitive reasoning towards an event and the behavioural actions that followed. It was important that we developed some form of response that would support her in the long term.

By using her journal and through our discussions, Ann was able to identify what she saw as her main problems. Her perception that she was failing at college was the greatest of these, compounded by her belief that she was not worthy of doing well as she was an unlovable person who failed at all she did. We were able to label these as her 'big hills' (a running analogy) that she would have to overcome by putting in a bit more effort just as she did on her runs. My aim as therapist was to help Ann develop these skills in her own time. I would simply act as a guide who could direct her as to which way to go, but the work would be hers.

As with all new elements of our therapy sessions, Ann expressed reluctance and voiced her inability to deal with what was taking place. I explained to her that she had already began to solve problems as she had taken the first step. This was putting her problems into words, something that I said she had done well even from our earliest sessions together. This process of problem-solving is a well-established element of CBT and meant that Ann's responses to problems could be structured and monitored within our sessions.

After the problem had been put into words, the next step was to devise some plans to tackle it and to select one to put into practice. The plan had then to be activated before its evaluation. We were able to practise these within our sessions before Ann implemented them on her own. These were very much based around the idea of helping Ann confront the negative behaviours that could lead to her self-harm. The first of these was based on her reluctance to go to college on certain days. Together, we formulated the idea of Ann getting up to have breakfast with her mother on those mornings when she would often just stay in bed. This not only ensured that Ann was ready to leave the house but also meant that she would be supported and could talk through her anxieties with her mother before facing what the deal had in store:

> It is good to talk through things with Mum. She may not fully understand what is going on, but I know she cares and it's that bit extra that helps, isn't it?

We had already established that Ann's self-harm often followed a negative day at college and would take place when she thought her mother was not at home. While her running after college had helped, it was something that she did alone, and we agreed that on other occasions a different approach was needed. Again, we talked the issue through in our sessions and followed the five-point plan[3] to devise a way of overcoming these issues. It was agreed that Ann would ensure that she arranged to meet a friend after college and go home via their house. This would give Ann the chance to allow her intense emotions to pass in an environment where self-harm would not be possible. These occasions also helped reduce the isolation that Ann felt before self-harming. A common feature of self-harming behaviour in young people is the feeling perceived or otherwise of being alone (Nijman and Campo 2002). Ann spoke of how these visits with friends helped her a great deal, giving her time to 'let off steam'. She arranged to meet a friend once a week who wanted to begin running as a way of keeping fit. For Ann, this was an empowering experience – here was somebody who sought her advice and who, she could support, rather than being the one who needed to rely on others:

> It's dead weird isn't it? Here is [name] who I always saw as well confident and popular and there's me who's dead daft telling her how to run proper!

I suggested to Ann that the running sessions were an indication that her ability to communicate with others was really improving. Her self-harm, though known among her peer group, was not something that was discussed. Similarly, in her conversations with her mother, self-harm was not something that was mentioned. When Ann's mother had learned of her daughter's self-harm, she had reacted badly and fluctuated between blaming Ann and then herself. This had compounded Ann's feelings of low self-worth and led to the topic becoming taboo at home. During our sessions we were able to reflect on this and agreed that a good position would be one in which Ann could talk about self-harm with her mother in a non-judgemental environment. Whilst this did not happen overnight, due to Ann's reluctance to 'set her Mum off', she was able to articulate the need for her mother to listen without passing judgement.

Another area of concern was Ann's poor communication with people in college. Despite being in a close peer group at school, Ann had failed to make any real friendships at college and described her days as 'lonely and degrading'. I was able to encourage Ann to challenge the beliefs that she was not someone who deserved to be at college, and who failed to live up to the high standards that she felt her peers had set. Increasing Ann's social network was an important element of her therapy. In order to equip Ann with the cognitive skills to confront these negative thoughts, we needed to give them a name and see how they could be overcome. Ann was able to concede that there were some aspects of college work that she was stronger in than some of her peers. Whilst there were some students who excelled at all aspects of the course, this was not the case for everybody, and some struggled. Initially this was counter to Ann's self-perception and it took a long time for her to admit that her feelings of shame were

---

3. The five-point plan is based around the five areas of CBT: situation, thoughts, emotions, physical feelings, and actions.

based on her beliefs rather than those of others. The chance to work in pairs or small groups often arose and Ann would often try and distance herself from others and work alone. I suggested that she volunteered to work with a student who had difficulty with a certain dish, but Ann was unwilling to do this ('What? So we can be rubbish together and get it twice as wrong?'). Again, we looked at this as one of her negative schemas and used the plan we had devised to approach it. By our tenth session, Ann had been able to work with another girl in her class; this had led to a shared lunch break and Ann speaking to other students. While I reflected that I was delighted and that I saw this as a sign of real progress, Ann felt that she was just being humoured and that the others would talk about her once she had left. These feelings of isolation never fully resolved themselves and Ann continued to see time in college as a painful experience that left her with a good deal of negative self-perception.

The final two therapy sessions that Ann and I shared took place at monthly intervals following our tenth meeting. These sessions were very much concerned with evaluation and follow-up. The sessions themselves were a chance to look towards the future and to evaluate how much Ann had learned about her self-harm and how to prevent future episodes. The most important aspect of our penultimate meeting was Ann's disclosure that she had decided to leave college. While this could have been seen as a backward step, Ann was able to articulate that she felt our time together had led her to seeing the need for a fresh start:

> I know it sounds like I am running away but that is nowt like what is happening. In the past it would be me just going along with failing because that was what I did. Now it's new me, new start.

Ann's intention was to enrol at another catering college a short distance away and put what she had learned about herself into practice. I felt that this was a real indication that Ann was taking a positive step in being the kind of person she deserved to be.

Our final session saw Ann reflecting on what she felt had worked and what she had found most difficult. Ann was able to accept that there were still aspects of her thinking that it could be helpful to address. There were days when she felt her self-confidence was low and that the Ann of old was back. On these occasions the urge to self-harm was there, but she was able to implement protective strategies. Whilst self-harm remained a concern for Ann, she was able to see that it had been many weeks since her last act of self-injury and our final session was a positive one. Our final act was to draw up a list of what had worked for Ann during her therapy. We put these in order of importance and agreed that what had worked best were the strategies that Ann had developed for herself.

Ann's viewpoint

Ann's perception of her therapy is an important aspect of the process (Slee *et al.*, 2007). For Ann, her life had seemed to have hit a negative impasse and this generated feelings of low self-worth. Her peer group at school had been important for her; they had helped her come to terms with her parents' divorce and she felt that she had suffered loss as a consequence of starting at college. For her, self-harm had become a way of dealing with this:

> You just feel rubbish. That all the fun had gone out and that there is no way a thing is going to be better again. You know, just what's the point? You are rubbish, so treat yourself as rubbish. No one cares when you cry so just cut and cry alone.

Ann's initial reluctance to engage in therapy was born of these negative beliefs, coupled with her fear of being seen as mentally ill. Her mother's response to the discovery of Ann's self-harm had led to arguments and dire warnings of the future. As a consequence Ann saw her therapy as the first process in a diagnosis that she would carry with her:

> There was no way. I mean no way, that I was talking to this bloke who has me down as mad. I know loads of people that cut, there's masses of stuff in magazines. I don't want to be down as mad, I'm sad, it's different.

What was noticeable was the fluctuation in Ann's engagement over the course of therapy. While the sessions are mentioned in brief in the body of this chapter, there was not a clear, linear path. Some weeks not only saw limited progress but an actual decline in Ann's attitude toward her therapy and her life in general. Her journal entries reflected these low points in her journey:

> Some days are low days and all the running is not going to sort it out. Some days dragging myself here and dealing with you are too much. Why ask me how it went, you know the answer?

These setbacks were overcome by the development of skills such as identifying and challenging negative thoughts, and a more positive outlook was attained for the most part. Ann's final sessions were tinged with anxiety for what the future would hold as well as the belief that she would eventually be able to lead a life free of self-harm:

> What I want in the end is to be a happier person and not be angry about that [happiness]. What I want is my share and it will be me that will have to get it.

Therapist's reflections

The most important aspect of my therapeutic relationship with Ann was to develop a non-judgemental understanding of her self-harming behaviour. It was important for me to see Ann not just as someone caught in a negative cycle of behaviours but as someone who might eventually go on to carry out a fatal act of self-harm. The correlation between self-harm behaviour and eventual suicide is well established (Hawton *et al.* 2003). At the same time, it was vital that I did not ask Ann to stop her self-harming behaviours as the act itself could be the very thing that was keeping her from carrying out even more destructive behaviours (Rudd *et al.* 2006). What I needed to establish for Ann was the point that she was not just another client I saw but that I was her therapist who would help her deal with the problems she was having at the time.

CBT as an intervention in the management of self-harm is designed to deal with the negative cognitions that lead to self-harming behaviours, and the behavioural difficulties that can pre-empt them (Alford and Beck 1997). Whilst I had worked with a number of self-harming individuals in the past, what struck me about Ann was that her self-harm seemed very much to be based around her perceived failures at catering college. I felt that these had very quickly escalated into negative self-perception and isolating behaviours. The contrast to her outlook at school was quite stark, and I felt it was important that we dealt with this as soon as possible. Also, I did feel that there was a good deal of deep-seated resilience that could be tapped into. Ann coped well with her parents' divorce and had made much of her peer support network. That we were able to develop a plan to visit friends after a difficult day in college was ideal in combatting the isolation that is an integral part of self-harming behaviours.

While we made use of the strengths from Ann's past, our sessions were also about looking at the future. This meant making sure that the problem-solving techniques that we developed together would help Ann in the long term and that self-harm would be seen as less and less like an answer (Hawton *et al.* 1998).

By the end of our time together, Ann saw me as very much part of her 'old world' that was inhabited by a vulnerable, younger version of herself. I was very happy to go along with this and felt that Ann had developed a new resilience. What is also pleasing is that Ann was able to see the value of her time with the community team I worked in and that she sent updates of how well she has done in the time since we first met.

Glossary

Self-harm. Self-harm is a term used to describe an event in which an individual injures or harms herself. The methods for self-harm vary according to the individual and can include cutting, hair-pulling or the ingestion or insertion of substances or objects. For some people the act can be a way of dealing with stressful situations and keeping negative emotions under control. For others it can be in response to psychotic episodes, where the self-harm can have a highly ritualised aspect (Hill 1995). It is important that each individual has their act of self-harm taken seriously and that they are treated with compassion and understanding. Whatever the reason for the act, self-harm is one of the most frequent causes of hospital treatment, with over 150,000 admissions each year (Royal College of Psychiastrists 2006).

References

Alford, B. and Beck, A. (1997) *The Integrative Power of Cognitive Therapy.* New York: Guilford Press.

Hawton, K., Arensman, E., Townsend, E., Bremmer, S., Feldman, E. and Goldney, R. (1998) Deliberate self-harm: systematic review of efficacy of psychosocial and pharmacological treatments in preventing repetition. *British Medical Journal*, 317: 441–447.

Hawton, K., Zahl, D. and Weatherall, R. (2003) Suicide following deliberate self-harm: Long term follow up of patients who presented to a general hospital. *British Journal of Psychiatry*, 183: 537–542.

Hill, K. (1995) *The Long Sleep: Suicide and Young People*. London: Virago.

Nijman, H. and Campo, J. (2002) Situational determinants of in-patient self-harm. *Suicide and Life-Threatening Behaviour*, 32: 167–175.

Royal College of Psychiatrists (2006) *Better Services for People who Self-Harm: Quality Standards for Healthcare Professionals*. London: RCP.

Rudd, M., Mandrusiak, M. and Joiner, T. (2006) The case against no-suicide contracts: the commitment to treatment statement as a practice alternative. *Journal of Clinical Psychology*, 62: 243–251.

Slee, N., Arensman, E. Garnefski, N. & Spinhoven, P. (2007) Cognitive behavioural therapy for deliberate self-harm. *Crisis*, 28: 175–182.

Further reading

Shea, S. (2002) *The Practical Art of Suicide Assessment: A Guide for Mental Health Professionals and Substance Abuse Counsellors*. Hoboken, NJ: Wiley.

Van Heeringen, K. (ed.) (2001) *Understanding Suicidal Behaviour. The Suicidal Process Approach to Research, Treatment and Prevention*. Chichester: Wiley.

Young, J. Klosko, J. and Weishaar, M. (2003). *Schema Therapy: A Practitioner's Guide*. New York: Guilford Press.

5 Carly – Substance misuse

May Baker

This case study has been written from the author's different experiences in her field of practice, but the story is brought together under one person's voice.

Biography

Carly is a 19-year-old woman who is currently in treatment with a community drug team. Her story begins when she was assessed and accepted at a city centre inpatient drug detoxification unit (IDDU). For purposes of confidentiality a pseudonym is used (Nursing and Midwifery Council 2008).

Carly has been known to drug services in this area for 3 years. She was initially seen in the outpatient community clinic where she attended appointments every 2 weeks to see the nurse facilitator in relation to her drug use. When she first came into services she was living with her mother, who is a sex trade worker. Carly has lived with her mum all her life but has never known her father. She has an ambivalent relationship with her mother and does not feel particularly close to her. She has used heroin since the age of 16. She states that there was no particular reason why she started to use heroin, only that she hung around with some people who used. At times her story of how she began using changed, depending on who she spoke to. Carly also uses cocaine on a recreational basis. She does not see this as a problem and only uses when she is out with friends. She smokes approximately 10 cigarettes a day and states this is more of a problem than her 'coke' use. She does not use any other drugs including alcohol.

Carly's physical health is fairly good, with no history of any physical problems. Her early milestones were met and she attended school regularly. She left school at the age of 16 with two GCSEs. She sees this as a remarkable achievement as she was hanging around with lots of boys at the time and says she was hardly ever in school. Towards the latter months of her studies she started using drugs. On leaving school she quickly became engrossed in her heroin use, which escalated out of control. She was using up to 1 gram of heroin daily. This was smoked from foil; she says she has never injected as she is scared of needles. About 1 year ago she became involved with a much older man whom she continues to see. She says this man is her friend and is the only one who really cares about her. She has a platonic relationship with him and he buys her presents and clothes. His name is Eddie and he is 45 years old; he has his own flat where she lives on and off. Her main residence is her mum Sandra's house, but she tries not to spend too much time there. She is very disapproving of her mum's work, even though she has been around this all her life. She finds her mum supportive in financial terms, but not emotionally. Her mum thinks her relationship with Eddie is 'disgusting' and has tried to persuade Carly to break her friendship with him, but to no avail.

Carly has been admitted to the inpatient unit to refrain from illicit heroin and to establish a therapeutic dose of maintenance methadone. This will stop any withdrawal symptoms and encourage her to be independent of street heroin. Her drug regime has been maintained at 50 mg methadone mixture oral daily. She appears to have stabilised on this amount for the last 5 days and has regained some normality. Carly will progress to fully detox using the drug lofexidine. Her physical and mental health will be monitored and she will be given the supportive medication when necessary (British National Formulary, 2014).

Process

My first meeting with Carly was disjointed and strained. We initially met when she was being assessed for the IDDU and she was under the influence of heroin. She was unable to fully respond to the assessment and was not coherent in her thinking. I was aware of this and had to ensure that she was not only mentally but physically able to take part in the assessment process (Ashcroft 2011). The assessment was therefore postponed to a later date. This annoyed Carly as she thought she was being rejected for a bed in the unit. She became very emotional and started to cry and sob. It was difficult to calm her, and she needed lots of reassurance that the assessment was not cancelled but put off to another day. It was apparent at this stage that Carly appeared quite fragile and would need a supportive and simple approach. I offered her another appointment the next day and said if she wished she could bring along a friend or her key worker. I told her I would phone her the next morning to confirm her attendance. She appeared relieved that she would be seen so quickly and left the unit composed and grateful that she would soon be given help. I also had to reiterate that she would have to attend the assessment in a sober state and not 'out of it'. I decided I would ring her the following morning prior to her appointment.

On reflection I thought that perhaps I had succumbed to Carly's emotional breakdown and given her preferential treatment by offering her something which other service users do not automatically get. The usual procedure for clients who attend under the influence of drugs or drink is to be sent another appointment in line with the existing waiting times. It is not normal practice to offer a second appointment so quickly. I did, however, try to rationalise my behaviour with the thought that she was a young vulnerable woman who needed help now and not when the next available appointment was, which was in 6 weeks. I tried to think of working collaboratively with her and felt that her engagement in the process was of paramount importance at this point (Simpson and Brennan 2009). I wanted to work in partnership with Carly to ensure that she attended the initial assessment and so begin the process of working together.

The following day, I called Carly at 10 a.m. to remind her of her appointment at 11 a.m. Her response was clear and she appeared upbeat. Her attendance at the IDDU was completely different from our initial meeting. She attended on her own and she appeared slightly embarrassed but quite calm. She was composed and eager to tell me how much she needed this detox.

After the assessment, which lasted for an hour, I asked her what she wanted from our service. The main point she stated time and again was not to come off heroin but that she needed help. She said that she was useless and that her life was 'crap' and that it was all her fault that she was like this. I did try to clarify what this meant, but at this point it was not clear. She did, however, agree that in order to begin the process of receiving help, she would need to detox. After consultation with her key worker and consultant at the community drug team, an arrangement was made for her to be given the next available inpatient bed (Rassool 2011).

Carly entered the IDDU within a week and her stay was scheduled for 3–4 weeks. This would offer enough time for her to be detoxed from heroin and to think about and begin a plan for relapse prevention.

My partnership with Carly commenced also at this time as I had completed her assessment and played a pivotal role in her treatment and welfare while she was in the unit. I felt a strong sense of empathy for her as she was around the same age as my daughter, but had clearly experienced a different side to life. Her experiences from a young age had moulded her psyche and behaviour. As the days progressed her emotions became erratic. At times she would be jolly and happy, sharing jokes with others and teasing staff. On other occasions she would be despondent and inconsolable. She had very low self- esteem and thought of herself as a failure. Her detoxification played a large part in her emotional disturbance, but by the end of the second week she seemed more aware of her behaviour and some focus began to emerge.

At this stage I did wonder what would become of Carly; she did not appear ready to embrace the outside world, although she was due for discharge within the next week or two. She was almost drug-free and her plan to prevent relapse had barely been mentioned. Her only thought was to return to live with Eddie, staying with her mum when she needed to.

I had built up a good working relationship with her and I know that she trusted me – perhaps this was because she may have seen me as a mother figure. She knew I had a daughter her age and we discussed things like clothes and music and TV programmes. She was very keen to find out more about my home life and wanted to know which university my daughter attended and what she was studying. At this point I had to be clear with Carly about our relationship and how we could work together. It was important not only for Carly but also for me that boundaries were in place and that we respected each other's privacy. I stated that we should only disclose what we felt comfortable with. At first she felt a bit put out as she was a very open person who told everyone her business. However, once I explained to her that this was to help her and protect her then she seemed fine (Hewitt *et al.* 2009).

Carly was unsure what she wanted when she left the unit. She knew that she would be drug-free but did not know how she could maintain this. She thought that she would just hope for the best. She had been drug-free before, stating that she went 'cold turkey' about 2 years ago and managed to stay off heroin for about 4 months. She did, however continue to use cocaine when she was out with her friends. I really tried to understand what it must be like for her and to envisage how she perceives things around her, especially relationships. These seem to be quite superficial and based on her needs and what she wants. She does not appear to have any real friends whom she can trust and confide in or who really care for her. On her own admission she says most of her friendships are based on and around drugs. Eddie was the only person who really cared about her. My understanding of Eddie was somewhat different and I tried to think of a way in which I could get Carly to examine and think about her relationship with Eddie. I did not want to frighten or judge Carly in a way that could lead her to retreat from our relationship, which really had just begun to develop. However I did want her to be able to leave the unit with hope and opportunity so that she could change things for the better and be more in control of her own life (Wardell 2013).

I spoke with the consultant psychiatrist and other members of the team to elicit their views on my idea for undertaking cognitive behavioural therapy with Carly. I had not at this point asked her if she would be interested in doing this, as I wanted to make sure the team thought that this process could be a move forward for her. Most of the team members thought that it was a good idea but were not sure if she would stick with it for any length of time as they perceived her as 'flighty' and 'manipulative'. On the other hand, they also thought that this could be an ideal opportunity for her to make changes that centred round her real needs and perhaps could help her to gain some sort of control over her future. It was agreed that I would approach Carly to explain the process of CBT and ask her if she would be interested. The plan would be to commence the first two sessions whilst she was still in the unit and then carry this into the community when she was discharged.

Carly was delighted that I wanted to be her therapist and I think she saw this as an extension of friendship that would continue after she left the unit. At this point I had to spend some time with her explaining what my role would be and what would be expected of her. I tried to get across in straight terms that this was something that would make her think a lot about her behaviour and aspects of it that she wanted to change. It may not always be a good thing in that it could be distressing at times. She was not put off by this and still wanted to do it.

Skills

Our first meeting for CBT was scheduled for the end of the third week. As I already knew Carly quite well and understood her habits and her outward persona, I believed that the sessions would need to be manipulated to make them serve her needs. At this time, I was also aware of how little I had disclosed of myself. This may have been unintentional on my part, but I did recognise that the balance of power was in my hands. To develop a true therapeutic relationship and encourage discussion and disclosure, I knew that I would have to be much more open with her (Baughan and Smith 2013).

I decided that, as an intelligent and insightful person, Carly had to be given information on the process of CBT and then this could either be the catalyst for her to embrace the technique or to reject it as a tool for her development. Therefore the first session was really more of a teaching session with her asking lots of questions about CBT and how it works (Simmons and Griffiths 2009). She was fascinated by this and had never really been aware that her thoughts and feelings could be linked to how she behaved.

I tried to identify our common link and what made us like each other. This was much easier for Carly to do as she said I was easy to talk to but 'didn't take any shit'. I was not quite sure what she meant by this, but she did articulate that what she meant was that I could see through people when they were not being true or were covering up. I asked her if this was a good trait and she said that was why she got on with me, because I could see that she was suffering as a person and did not just see her as drug addict. This made me think of my own behaviour and how I must come across to others. I wanted to explore why she did not think that her drug taking was a big problem to her and she gave a very open and honest reply. Carly found that using heroin managed in some way to block out any of her feelings of hopelessness; she liked the way the drug took away all her pain and just made her 'kind of numb'. It allowed her not to think, and this then made it easier to function in her own world. She said that what she thought about herself always made her feel 'worthless and a nobody'. This is why using heroin helped. From the first time she took it she knew that it seemed to saved her from her own thoughts – thoughts that always resonated how stupid and useless she was. I wanted to explain to Carly how important an effect our thinking has on our feelings and behaviour. I explored this by explaining Beck's (1976) CBT model. Carly could recognise how some of her feelings made her feel physically unwell at times and she felt nervous and anxious around some social situations. She could see how this worked when we put this onto paper.

This made her think about her own situation and her use of drugs. She said she used heroin so that she did not have to face up to anything. She acted silly and superficial, threw tantrums if she did not get her way, and argued with her mum just to wind her up. Most disturbing was her belief that she did not deserve any friendships. She really thought that real friends were for special people who worked hard and had lovely families and were clever and bright and had a future. I wondered at what age Carly had started to think this, and she stated it was 'as long as she could remember'.

We did not use the term 'homework' during our work together, but decided that work between sessions would be a project, which Carly related to. She liked school when she was really young and loved to do projects and lots of independent work. She was clearly a bright girl and I wondered if she had ever considered further education as part of her future. Her two GCSEs were in art and history. She thought this was a bit of a dream as her life was in 'such a mess'; she also didn't think that Eddie would approve.

I wanted to keep to a tight schedule with defined areas. I was very much aware that Carly had many issues with her life and did not want to open up too many areas in which she would feel overwhelmed and unable to cope. I therefore let her take the lead and asked her to put a 'wish list' together. I think at this point Carly really felt empowered and set about this with gusto.

This approach uses CBT but links into solution-focused therapy (SFT), which is a reliable tool as an adjunct to CBT (McAllister, 2007). Beck (1976) describes core beliefs and assumptions, and he states that people can have strong beliefs in what they are thinking even if there is no evidence to support this. Carly's core beliefs are based in negativity. She states she is a failure, she is worthless and hopeless. These negative automatic thoughts are usually triggered by an event or situation and can provoke significant anxiety. Assumptions are usually identified as an *if–then* approach. For example, Carly assumes that if she tried to go to college then people would find out that she is a drug addict and would judge her as a 'nobody'. She has such low self-esteem that when we work together to elicit her negative automatic thoughts, I can show Carly how these thoughts are being maintained by her belief in them. She has no proof to explain why she believes in these thoughts. I then turn this around and challenge her belief. What are these thoughts based in and where is the evidence to support this? For instance, Carly constantly states that she is useless; however, when I list the numerous things she has achieved, and describe to her what she wishes for and what dreams she has, she starts to think about the words she is saying and the match between her achievements and her dreams. She does see that it is her perception of the situation and not always what others see. This makes her laugh and it is almost as if the penny has dropped. I try to roll with this, and get her to look at her strengths and achievements and to stop dwelling on the negatives (Miller and Rollnik 1991).

These sessions continued for some weeks.

Client's viewpoint

At first Carly was not entirely sure whether the CBT was really what she needed; however, she was sure that she wanted and needed to speak to someone on a regular basis in order to clear matters in her head. I managed to convince Carly that what she was describing was really CBT. She also agreed that talking and breaking things down had managed to help her see where she was going. This was not without its obstacles for Carly, as she had had a deep conviction of self-preservation from a very early age. She stated that opening up and actually speaking about her issues was the most difficult thing to do. She said this was easy with me as she knew I would help and would not let her down. The weekly appointments that were arranged after her discharge from the IDDU were rather gruelling for her at first. She missed the first appointment due to illness but when she eventually attended on a more regular basis she started to explore the real issues behind her drug use and how she was going to cope with these and try to move her life forward.

Carly soon talked about her father and why she had never known who he was. This had made her bitter from a young age. 'I remember asking my mum why I never had a dad', she explained. Her mum's reply was cutting: 'We're better off without him and don't talk about it again'. Carly spoke of the few occasions when she tried to find out more about her dad. She said she always got the same answer until she was in her teens when her mum was much more confrontational about the matter. She clearly did not want to speak about the subject and told Carly to never speak to her again about it or she would be thrown out of the house. At this point Carly knew that the matter was closed. However, this still didn't stop her thinking about it and so her thoughts and dreams tended to revolve around her missing father. She did recognise that she liked Eddie because he was older but did not go any further in relation to him as a father figure. She seemed to see him as more of a friend who looked after her but said she did not confide in him. Towards the end of our sessions I did wonder if Carly had indeed 'opened up the can of worms' that she did not know how to control, but she said she felt an element of empowerment (Grant, 2009). She said she looked at herself differently and felt that life could be different if she really wanted it to. She thought that it was unbelievable that she still hadn't gone back to using heroin since she had left the IDDU, and saw this as an enormous achievement. She thought this was about me being there for her and did not really see how she had managed this entirely by herself. Her real aim now was to find her dad.

Therapist's viewpoint

My belief in Carly was somewhat subjective as I really liked her as a person. This seemed rather strange to some of my colleagues as they saw her as manipulative and childish. However, what stood out for me was her intelligence and vulnerability. I thought that this was a young woman who had been given no chances in life and had tried to make the best of her situation. I did not see her having the kind of strong mother–daughter bond which I had with my daughter, and I believed that her behaviour was a product of her upbringing and social circumstances. However, I did not condemn or blame her mother for her lifestyle. As far as I knew, Carly didn't lack any material things and had always had a safe warm home. However, the only person who could have given her love and security was her mother and it seemed she was rather cold and distant with her daughter. The attention and approval she craved just was not to be realised at home. This perhaps was the real reason why she liked Eddie so much, as she saw him as someone who accepted her for who she was. However, Carly had pondered and thought about Eddie and how he fitted into her life. She was beginning to think that her life needed to move in a different direction and that Eddie in some way was stifling this as he wanted to take care of her. However, what the evidence actually revealed was that he wanted to control her. Only Carly could have come to this conclusion as she was the one who, with my help, analysed what her relationship with Eddie had become. This made things more difficult for her as she knew what she really wanted to do but felt as yet that she could not make the break with Eddie. She believed that she was just too weak and that she needed him whilst she looked for her father. This could have been Carly's self-preservation kicking in, and I acknowledged her bravery in doing so.

Conclusion

The CBT sessions continued for another 2 months and at this stage Carly had come to a crossroads. She cited her main achievements as growing up and standing on her feet; being proud of who she is; knowing she has a father whom she is searching for; and of course staying off heroin. The path forward for Carly was still very shaky. She was a very vulnerable young woman who could quite easily fall back on her heroin security blanket if life became fraught and more difficult again. I think the most important thing that she can rely on is that she has managed to grow as a person and accept herself in a much more positive way. Her whole emphasis on life changed and she started to believe that things could and should be better for her. She believed in her own recovery and finished the sessions full of hope. All she needed was the opportunity to continue to grow and fulfil what she wanted from life.

The reality at times can be somewhat different, and I know that she was re-referred 18 months later by her GP to the community drug treatment team as she had started to use heroin again. This explains how difficult the addiction cycle can be and how exposed people are to relapse. I would hope that she has the capacity and strength to re-enter treatment and quickly turn around her relapse, and if she can, she may see this as not a negative but as a blip that she needs to learn from. The road forward for

Carly is not yet easy but with support and compassion she may manage to take more positive steps towards it.

Glossary

Drug addiction. A cycle of addiction that involves taking and being dependent on drugs.
Heroin. A highly addictive drug made from morphine which is extracted from the opium poppy.
Methadone. A synthetic opioid, used as a medicine to treat opioid addiction.

References

Ashcroft, J.R. (2011) The importance of physical health assessment. In D.B. Cooper (ed.) *Introduction to Mental Health – Substance Use*. Oxford: Radcliffe Publishing.

Beck, A. (1976) *Cognitive Therapy and the Emotional Disorders*. New York: International Universities Press.

Baughan, J. and Smith, A. (2013) Caring as a two way process of giving and receiving. In J. Baughan and A. Smith, *Compassion, Caring and Communication: Skills for Nursing Practice*, (2nd edn). Abingdon: Routledge.

British National Formulary (2014) Lofexedine hydrochloride. In *Medicines Complete* [online]. Available at: https://www.medicinescomplete.com/mc/bnf/64/PHP3230-lofexidine-hydrochloride.htm (accessed 13 November 2014).

Grant, A. (2009) Freedom and consent. In P. Barker (ed.) *Psychiatric and Mental Health Nursing: The Craft of Caring* (2nd edn). London: Hodder Arnold.

Hewitt, J., Coffey, M. and Rooney, G (2009) Forming, sustaining and ending therapeutic interactions. In P. Callaghan, J. Playle and L. Cooper (eds) *Mental Health Nursing Skills*. Oxford: Oxford University Press.

McAllister, M. (2007) Helping other people to be solution-focused. In M. McAllister (ed.) *Solution Focused Nursing: Rethinking Practice*. Basingstoke: Palgrave Macmillan.

Miller, W. and Rollnick, S. (1991) *Motivational Interviewing: Preparing People to Change Addictive Behaviour*. New York: Guilford Press.

Nursing and Midwifery Council (2008) The Code. London: NMC.

Rassool, G.H. (2011) Service provision and interventions. In G.H. Rassool, *Understanding Addiction Behaviours: Theoretical and Clinical Practice in Health and Social Care*. Basingstoke: Palgrave Macmillan.

Simmons, J. and Griffiths, R. (2009) *CBT for Beginners*. Los Angeles: Sage.

Simpson, A. and Brennan, G. (2009) Working in partnership. In P. Callaghan, J. Playle and L. Cooper (eds) *Mental Health Nursing Skills*. Oxford: Oxford University Press.

Wardell, J. (2013) Strength and diversities: a substance misuse perspective. In A. Hall, M. Wren and S.D. Kirby (eds) *Care Planning in Mental Health: Promoting Recovery*. Chichester: Wiley Blackwell.

6 Charlotte – Type 1 diabetes

Vineeta Gupta

Charlotte was referred to psychology as she was described as being very fed up and frustrated with diabetes. As a consequence, her diabetes control was not good.

Charlotte is 15 years old and was diagnosed with diabetes at the age of 3. She describes having phases when she struggled with diabetes more than others. She went on an insulin pump when she was approximately 13. This is reported to have helped her quality of life, but challenges remain.

Formulation

We did a timeline and saw correspondences between times when diabetes was difficult and times when life was generally difficult. It appeared that the transition to secondary school was a particularly challenging time. Many children struggle with the change from primary school to secondary (Young Minds 2012). Changing to a much bigger environment, with high expectations of autonomy and less close relationships with teachers, is a difficult time.

In addition, developmentally this is a time of entering adolescence. The challenges of adolescence are well documented in terms of developing self-identity, egocentric tendencies and transfer of core relationships to peer group rather than family (Newman and Newman, 2003).

For younger people with diabetes, this poses particular difficulties. There is an expectation that the young person will become more independent with diabetes management as there is potentially less support available at secondary school. Also young people begin to socialise independently away from their parents, therefore knowing how to manage diabetes safely is very important. Crucially, at this age, peer groups and identity become extremely important and it is common for young people with diabetes and other chronic health conditions to want to feel the same as their peers (Suris *et al.* 2004). However, this comes at a time when the physical effects of puberty such as hormones and growth spurts can cause many fluctuations in insulin requirements, making it difficult to maintain stable blood sugar levels anyway.

For Charlotte, dealing with peer group pressure was a significant issue. Friendship dynamics meant she did not feel confident and safe to be open about her diabetes and therefore did not carry out her diabetes management around others; she was not doing regular blood testing or giving herself insulin when required:

> I hid it, I didn't want anyone to see my pump or injection, I'm self-conscious anyway and I don't like the attention when people are looking at me or ask what I'm doing or being mean about something I'm wearing. They would look at my pump and blood test kit and think 'what's that?'

Charlotte described feeling very isolated with her diabetes and felt her peer group did not understand and were judgemental about it. The fear of judgement was making her feel low in mood and angry. Furthermore, Charlotte lived in a rural area, making socialising outside of school harder; this increased her feelings of isolation:

> *Charlotte:* I hate people who judge, there's no need for it ... I've been shocked that people can't accept that there are people with diabetes ... I can't understand how they work
>
> *VG:* How does that make you feel?
>
> *Charlotte:* If someone says something nasty then I get annoyed, they don't have diabetes, they don't have to deal with it, they don't know what it's like, I think that's one of the reasons why they put hate on it, they don't know what it's like.

Part of the formulation and assessment phase involved socialisation to the CBT model and psycho-education. As is common in therapeutic work, there was an overlap between the formulation and intervention. With diabetes there are a number of physical effects on the body which can impact on psychological factors. For example, we discussed how stress releases adrenaline which affects the amount of glucose in the body. Therefore stress can cause blood sugar levels to go higher (Diabetes UK 2014). Furthermore, poor diabetes control can lead to impaired cognitive function which can make the pragmatics of remembering the diabetes regime even more challenging (Christie and Martin 2012). This is exacerbated by the fact that anxiety also has an impact on attention and concentration (Sage *et al.* 2008). Not to mention that frontal lobes in the brain which are involved with memory and attention are not fully developed in adolescence (Johnson *et al.* 2009).

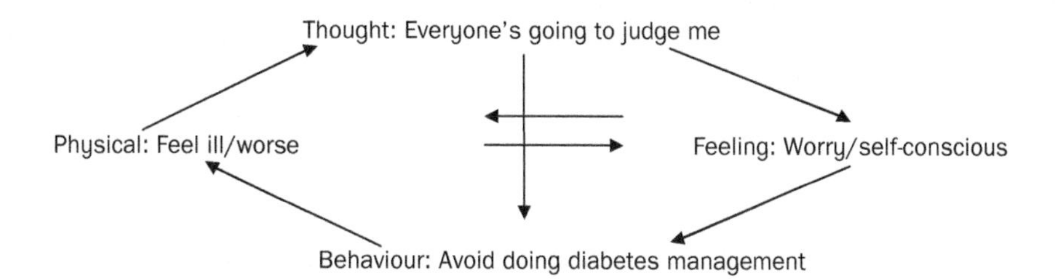

This is really hard and can cause other patterns to develop:

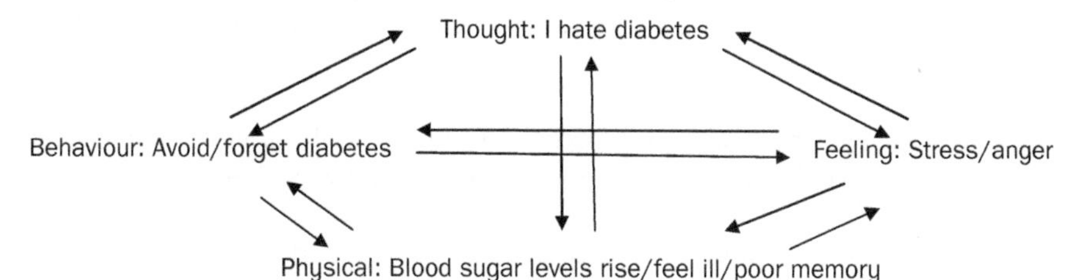

Figure 6.1 Charlotte's initial formulation

Through our work we were able to identify a vicious circle, as shown in Figure 6.1. As Charlotte observed:

> I was self-conscious about doing [the blood tests], it's not a nice feeling to think people are looking at you, but then you feel even worse because you're not doing them and you're going high and feeling groggy and tired and that in itself isn't good. It's like one bad feeling leads to another.

Charlotte's main issue was that she did not like carrying out her diabetes management in public or school, therefore her diabetes levels were not within recommended parameters. Our work involved identifying the beliefs underlying her reluctance. Charlotte had said that friendship issues had not been easy and there had been many dynamics to manage. She felt uncomfortable carrying out diabetes care in the presence of her peer group because she felt worried that other people would judge her. This is not an uncommon fear; there is much written about shame and diabetes (Archer 2014). There is still a lack of understanding about diabetes in the general public, particularly Type 1 diabetes. Many patients and families report negative experiences and stigma being attached to the diagnosis. For example, patients report receiving comments about weight and lifestyle and suggesting it was their fault they have diabetes because they eat too much sugar. This is, of course, factually incorrect – Type 1 diabetes is not linked to lifestyle or weight issues.

Patients have also reported negative reactions towards blood testing and injecting, with incidences of bullying and taunting by other children, for example accusing diabetes patients of being drug addicts as they inject. This negative perception can be reinforced by adults and institutions. Clinical anecdotes from diabetes professionals have spoken of schools that have not allowed children to do blood tests or inject in class due to health and safety concerns, with some insisting a child can only inject or test in the toilets. I wonder how this makes children feel? It could reinforce their negative feelings about diabetes and confirm beliefs that it is something to be ashamed of and not to be visible in public. Thankfully, through better provision of services and raising awareness this is beginning to be addressed.

Empathy

At this point I tried to empathise with Charlotte as much as possible. I talked about my experience of working with other young people with diabetes and how it was natural for patients to struggle at times. I hoped this would help her to develop trust in me, so she felt like I understood her issues. I also wanted to normalise her thoughts and feelings. She said:

> I think it was hard not having anyone to talk to about how I was feeling or someone who knows what I'm going through . . . it was nice to talk to someone.

I empathised on how difficult it must be to have to carry out diabetes tasks every day. We talked about how 'outsiders' may perceive diabetes as simple – they may say 'just take your insulin', but the reality of managing it in real-world situations every day is quite different. Individuals have to plan and consider diabetes for all aspects of their life, for instance eating, drinking alcohol, exercise, exams, sleepovers, festivals. This can become very draining and frustrating, especially in addition to all the usual challenges of adolescence.

Goals

We started our work together in January. After the initial assessment phase we discussed the goals and agreed that these should focus on helping Charlotte to be more confident and open with her diabetes. Charlotte was due to finish her GCSEs and start at a new college in September. We talked about the benefits of starting college without the constant worry of diabetes and feeling physically well. We therefore agreed that a good goal to aim for was for Charlotte to feel comfortable and confident with her diabetes by September.

We decided we would use a graded hierarchy approach. This uses a step-by-step procedure for breaking significant goals down into a series of small and achievable tasks. This is in line with the principles of SMART goals (Specific, Measureable, Achievable, Realistic, Timely). I explained that if you were low in confidence, experiencing success was very important. A success, no matter how small, would reinforce the belief that 'I can do this', whereas a failure would reinforce the belief that 'this is too hard and overwhelming'.

We talked through the model of anxiety, and I explained that anxiety rises when we feel scared or threatened. Often when people get anxious they avoid or escape the situation, which causes the anxiety to drop; however, this is provides temporary relief and in the longer term increases anxiety, as you learn that it was avoiding the situation that brought the anxiety down and the original fear remains.

Charlotte and I agreed on a hierarchy. I asked Charlotte to think about the ultimate goal and rate the anxiety out of 10. The initial goal was 'to get the pump and blood test kit out when you need it'. Charlotte rated this as 8/10 on anxiety (Figure 6.2). We then worked backwards and considered each step. Charlotte reported this as helpful:

> having smaller goals to get to the big goals, that helped. Taking small steps to get to the big step. … It was good to split it up rather than do it all at once, it helped to set a goal for next month and work your way up.

We agreed that Charlotte would need strategies to help her manage the anxiety at each step. Using the vicious circles examples described in Figure 6.1, we identified that Charlotte's negative thought 'everyone's going to judge me' was a barrier. I explained that having a positive thought or statement can help to combat the negative one. Such positive self-talk could be used in conjunction with simple relaxation techniques to help the physical symptoms of anxiety. Charlotte found deep breathing the most helpful relaxation technique. When it came to identifying positive self-talk, Charlotte struggled initially. When we talked it through, she decided that perhaps she was 'overthinking' the situation and should focus on action. Therefore her positive self-talk became 'Don't think, just do it!'

Step	Anxiety Rating	Time Scale	Helping Strategy
Get pump and blood test kit when you need it.	8/10	May	
Talking to people who don't know I have diabetes		End of April/Start of May	
Testing– not hiding behind bag	7/10	After Easter	Ask to mum to help if there: "Oi, injection!" Don't think, just do It! Deep breathing (relaxation)
Doing pump without hiding it	5-6/10	Before Easter	
Talking about it with people you know	4/10		
Start getting pump out		March	

Figure 6.2 Charlotte's hierarchy

Collaboration and family involvement

A key aspect of the hierarchy was that it was a collaborative process between Charlotte, myself and family members. Negotiating each step required input from all three of us; Charlotte and her mum suggested steps based on the pragmatics of their everyday life. Charlotte talked openly about her anxiety levels about each step, and I facilitated the process to ensure each stage felt safe, appropriate and that Charlotte had strategies to cope with each step.

Charlotte managed the hierarchy extremely well and successfully mastered each step. She reflected that it had been very useful:

> It was really helpful [to have a hierarchy] because I used to hate getting my pump out in public. That used to be the biggest pain and worry but because I started with getting my pump out, I could work it into everyday life, getting it out when I'm in a shopping centre shopping or when I'm at the bus stop, even if there weren't people around it still helped because it was still in public and I just worked my way up from there.

Charlotte felt having her mum as support was a helpful part of the process:

> Sometimes I felt scared and mum helped because she'd tell me to do it and I'd do it, so we'd combine, she'd say 'oi, do your injection!' and I'd do it without thinking about anything.

We discussed the fact that her mum had most likely tried this strategy in the past without success, yet being ready for change and using strategies within a framework and plan was key.

Furthermore, some of the deep breathing relaxation exercises were helpful:

> Sometimes it's helpful just to calm you down ... it stops you getting into a panicky state of mind ... [for example] at school around my friends and stuff, around people that I didn't necessarily like who are more likely to be bitchy.

Creativity

Although my role is to be primarily focused on the diabetes, I believe part of the formulation and intervention is to place diabetes in context with other aspects of life. I felt that Charlotte was generally struggling with her identity. Identity development is a normal part of adolescence. However, if you have a chronic illness, there is a danger that your identity becomes dominated by your condition. I encourage young people to consider the difference between 'I'm a diabetic' and 'I'm a football fan with diabetes'.

Charlotte was finding this difficult. She was also finding it difficult to occupy herself due to living in a rural area. Consequently, she had much time to ruminate on negative thoughts. Therefore, alongside the diabetes-specific intervention, I suggested that Charlotte make a scrapbook about herself and her interests:

> I wrote about my animals and the hobbies I enjoyed doing, and music I like, the food I like, it was helpful when my diabetes was getting me down to look at it and think 'it's not all about [diabetes], try and remember you've got all these points as well.

This exercise seemed to tick a number of boxes; it would occupy her, it was practical and it would get her to consider other aspects of her life. Furthermore, it was enjoyable. Through our sessions we had spoken about her creative side and I thought she would enjoy a project like this:

> *Charlotte:* I did a page if I was feeling down as well, if I wasn't feeling great I'd make a page and that would distract me from how I was feeling.
>
> *VG:* How often would you look at it or do a page?
>
> *Charlotte:* At that time because I was self-conscious I would do a page every couple of days. Less now, I haven't looked at it for weeks because I don't need to now.

Blood testing

Charlotte progressed through the hierarchy well. She was successfully using her pump in public places much more and was seeing the benefits. However, blood testing was still a big issue and Charlotte was finding this a bigger hurdle to overcome.

We discussed what the barriers were, and Charlotte said she struggled to remember consistently. Taking into account the effect of diabetes and anxiety on memory, this seemed a reasonable explanation for the problem. We agreed that Charlotte would try some simple solutions such as placing reminder notes in key places (for example, on the dog's food cupboard). However, when we reviewed this strategy at the next session it had been unsuccessful:

> You need to sort your feelings out first. Sticking notes up was probably helpful for a day or two, but I forgot about them and they blended into the background.

In hindsight, as a therapist, I wonder if I could have done things differently here? One of the challenges of working in a physical health setting is being the only mental health professional in the team. The narrative of multidisciplinary teams in physical health can be to find solutions and to 'make people better as quick as possible'. This can stem from a combination of strategic pressure to produce results and also caring about patients and wanting the best possible health outcome for them. However, the danger of this approach is to move too fast for the individual and to be too solution-focused. As a mental health professional, embedded and immersed in a physical health team, it is possible to be drawn into this way of working. It is not to say mental health professionals should never be solution-focused, but it is vital to keep the balance, through reflection and supervision. This is not only for the benefit of clinical work, but also to keep a clear sense of professional identity.

Methods

At this point, I decided to take a step back and change my approach to understand the blood testing situation better. I used Socratic dialogue to understand more of the underlying thoughts and feelings. Socratic dialogue uses questions and statements to explore the content and meaning of a patient's experience. When Charlotte was discussing her anxieties about testing in front of her friends, I used 'probe questions' to drill down further into her thoughts and feelings. Probe questions are questions which ask patients for their perception of the worst-case scenarios (Wells 1997).

By this stage Charlotte had started to become more comfortable using her pump in front of her friends, but testing was still difficult. I was curious to know why:

> *VG:* Why is testing different to using the pump?
> *Charlotte:* It's more noticeable.
> *VG:* Can you tell me a bit more about that? How?
> *Charlotte:* They'll say something about the blood and they'll say something about the noise.
> *VG:* And what worries you about that?
> *Charlotte:* They'll ask questions.
> *VG:* What worries you about them asking questions?
> *Charlotte:* That I might get angry.

VG: And what's the worst that could happen?
Charlotte: Then they'll ask why I'm angry and I'll get even more angry.

This led to a productive discussion about her angry feelings. Charlotte said she was frustrated at the lack of understanding about diabetes and assumptions people make.

We discussed a possible alternative perspective, which was the difference between people making judgements and natural curiosity. I wondered if previous negative experiences had led her to the belief that when people ask about diabetes they are all being judgemental. I tried to normalise curiosity by asking her to put herself in the others person's shoes:

VG: What would you do if someone said they had asthma and had an unusual inhaler to take – would you look at the inhaler?
Charlotte: Yes.
VG: How long do you think it would keep your attention for?
Charlotte: Not very long.
VG: And what would it make you think about them as a person?
Charlotte: Nothing really.

However, although I was keen for Charlotte to challenge her thoughts that most people are negative and judgmental about diabetes, it was also important to acknowledge that bullying and prejudice do exist in society, and as a therapist it felt wrong to ignore the possibility that sometimes negative reactions may occur. Through our sessions we began to discuss values which are part of identity development. We had a discussion about prejudice generally and discussed challenges many people face in the world, such as racism and homophobia. We talked about Charlotte's thoughts and what she thought of people who were prejudiced. Charlotte was very clear that prejudice made her angry, and this was a strong part of her value system.

We discussed how to manage negative reactions. At this point it was helpful to have input from Charlotte's family (mother and older brother) who were able to encourage and reinforce the fact that the opinions of prejudiced people were not opinions that should be respected or listened to. We also talked about how Charlotte was currently letting the anxiety of prejudiced people affect her life – perhaps stopping her reaching her goals.

Then we discussed a new hierarchy so that Charlotte could test her beliefs and discover evidence for herself. The aim was to challenge her belief that 'all people will judge': this all-or-nothing thinking was an obstacle to Charlotte doing her blood tests. The new hierarchy was similar to the pump hierarchy, and involved small manageable steps of doing blood tests in public places. Charlotte decided she wanted to start talking about diabetes more and being more open about it, consequently one of her steps was putting a photo of her blood-testing kit on a social media site. She followed this with a series of mini experiments, each of which was slightly more challenging than the last: doing blood testing whilst walking to the bus stop, in town, in a small supermarket, in a large supermarket, and finally the canteen at college.

Cognitive and behavioural changes

Charlotte was successful in increasing the amount of blood testing she did in various places. I was curious to know how she achieved this:

> *Charlotte:* I tried not to think about any bad thoughts that other people might have. I'm not scared of it, of doing a blood test, of thinking 'oh that's blood and people don't like blood'. Then I'm going to get bad thoughts about, oh it's blood, and getting bad reactions. But not thinking about it makes you worry less.
> *VG:* So it's actually stopping your thoughts before they get carried away?
> *Charlotte:* It's kind of like a spider diagram and blood test in the middle and branches off with different thoughts, but now its stops with just blood test in the middle.

We talked about her belief that 'all people will judge' and whether this had shifted. Charlotte's confidence levels grew and she was able to talk about her diabetes with new people when she started college. Charlotte explained that on her first day at college she had mentioned her diabetes to another student, who had appeared unperturbed and had remarked that she 'didn't judge or anything'. This reaction reassured Charlotte. I reminded Charlotte of her worry about others judging her:

> *VG:* That links to one of your circles which is everyone's going to judge me and I wonder what you think now?
> *Charlotte:* I don't think they do, they might think about it like new gossip for about 5 minutes but then it's old news and something else has caught their interest.
> *VG:* When did you learn that?
> *Charlotte:* Not that long ago, our teacher asked us to go around the room and say something about yourself and I said I have diabetes. She said 'oh right' and then moved on and no one said 'what?' or anything, they didn't care. It was good as I got it out there so I don't have to worry about hiding which is a comfort.

This was a significant shift in thoughts. Charlotte shifted from 'most people will judge' to 'most people don't care'. This more balanced thinking enabled Charlotte to be more open about her diabetes, which had a number of positive knock-on effects.

I was also interested to know how Charlotte felt about the individuals who may make negative remarks:

> I just think that's their issue and not mine and they can think what they want. I'm less concerned about what they say, I just do it and if they want to say something they can say it to my face. I'd rather deal with it than have my foot cut off because I've got a problem with it.

This shift gives me great hope for Charlotte's future. The fact that she is attributing negative reactions to others, rather than internalising anxiety, will give her extra resilience in the future. There is a danger that individuals with low confidence and low self-esteem could adopt a personalisation thinking style, that is, they could blame themselves for negative reactions from others. This type of thinking style is more likely to lead to increased feelings of shame and inadequacy about diabetes.

Reflecting on work and progress

Vicious circles

I was curious to know which aspects of therapy were useful. I asked about the process of identifying and drawing vicious circles:

> It was helpful because it showed me how I'd made a change when thinking about people judging me ... I don't care and that felt a lot better.

This made me realise that this intervention was not just about diabetes. Successfully going through the hierarchy had been an achievement in itself which had boosted Charlotte's self-esteem:

> since I got on top of my diabetes I'm more confident in myself as well and less shy ... my mum says I'm a lot more confident as well, I wouldn't really notice a difference but she did and my friends. ... I did feel proud of myself for being able to do it ... it's about being an individual as well ... I wasn't being a sheep to society.

Charlotte's thinking pattern had changed to that shown in Figure 6.3.

Family relationships

In addition, Charlotte reports having better relationships with her family:

> I feel a lot less tired, I think I'm getting on with my family a lot more, if I was groggy and tired I'd be more aggressive and now because I'm not we're getting on a lot better.

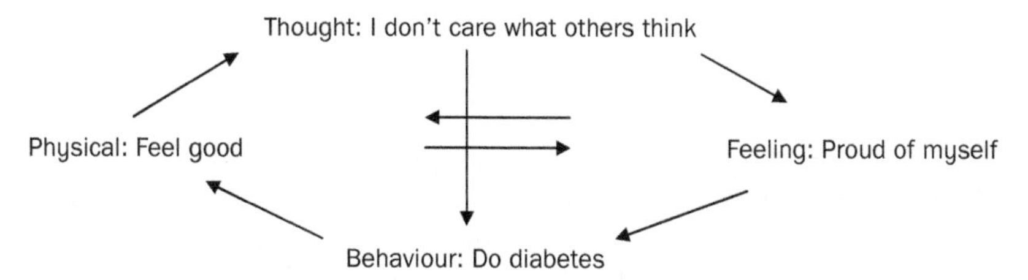

Figure 6.3 Charlotte's reformulation: a positive maintenance cycle

It is not uncommon for family relationships to improve with increased diabetes adherence. The impact of a chronic illness on the whole family has been well recognised and the need for psychological support to be available for the whole family is acknowledged (Altschuler 1997). For a parent, the anxiety of a child who is not adhering can be extremely stressful. Families can find their relationship becomes dominated with conflict about diabetes.

Positive reframing

Charlotte said that a key aspect of change was trying to reframe the negative thoughts about diabetes. Focusing on any positive aspects of diabetes was helpful in maintaining her mood and good relationship with diabetes:

> There's part of me which still hates it and wishes I didn't have it, but I try and see it as a good thing because it makes me special and unique to everyone else because I've got this and I've got a special machine which gives me insulin. That helps because it puts diabetes onto the good side then everything seems OK.

It was also helpful for Charlotte to reframe her thoughts about anger. We discussed how anger can be a positive emotion if used constructively. Many of the key equality movements over the last century (women's rights, racial equality) would not have happened without the anger and passion of individuals who believed in the cause.

Charlotte has become keen to educate others about diabetes and was considering doing a presentation to fellow students.

Other strategies: friends

Charlotte said it was useful to give friends a chance to adapt to diabetes as well:

> It's not easy for them to think, oh I can't react to that, you have to give them time. It's kinda like giving a dog a chew toy for 5 minutes then it's like that's it now, I can't play with it anymore, I can't react to it anymore … they get used to it.

Charlotte's increased confidence has improved her friendships, as observed by herself and her mother. They feel that her new relaxed attitude makes her seem more approachable and friendly to others.

Conclusion

Charlotte has become a much more confident young person who is more accepting of her diabetes. She acknowledges that challenges remain and she could still make improvements to her diabetes management, but she now has the skills and attitude to do it. Her relationship with her diabetes has changed; she has worked really hard at fighting the negative thoughts and feelings and even sees positive aspects of diabetes,

Tips to other patients from Charlotte's perspective	Tips to other professionals from VG's perspective
Don't shy away from doing it, its fine. It's better to live life being healthy and happy and not having to worry about blood tests all the time.	Don't underestimate the physical impact of poorly controlled diabetes. It can make you feel awful. The physical symptoms are an integral part of the formulation.
People don't care that much. They're more worried about what they might look like or what's happening on the news or across the road.	If they have poor control, consider your intervention carefully, take into account they are tired, feeling ill, and likely to have poor memory and concentration.
Try and bring it into everyday conversation. If you're meeting up somewhere or talking about going somewhere, it's saying 'wait a minute I've got to do a blood test' then your mind's better that you've done it and your friends get used to it as well.	Get to know their diabetes regime well, it helps with empathy. Check their understanding about diabetes, don't assume because they've had it for years that they understand it.
It's really helpful to not think about diabetes as a bad thing all the time and think about it in a good way. You can choose the colour of your pump and belt, it can get you out of a few things and it makes you unique rather than different.	Don't just focus on diabetes; it's often just one piece of the jigsaw. Take a history, talk about life before diabetes.
You're not the only one with problems; everyone's got their own problems.	Use the system, friends and family can be helpful. Involving others in the strategies can help them feel more supported. Equally is there anything you can do to help the system adapt? E.g. Education, Support.
Give psychology a try. Go in with an open mind, and think that some ideas might not help but try them out and don't just throw them away and forget about it, give it a go.	Consider developmental stage carefully. Are the presenting diabetes problems mirroring or exacerbating age appropriate issues?

Figure 6.4 Tips for patients and professionals

especially aspects which fit with her value systems – for example, being an individual and not a 'sheep'. In 8 months I watched her change from a shy, self-conscious girl who was battling with her diabetes demons, to a confident, more assured person with strong values, a young person who described recently skipping though a shopping centre, swinging her pump around shouting 'I have diabetes!'

We have summarised our work together in a series of helpful tips (Figure 6.4) which we hope will be useful for patients and therapists alike.

References

Altschuler, J. (1997) *Working with Chronic Illness.* Basingstoke: Macmillan.

Archer, A. (2014) Shame and diabetes self-management. *Practical Diabetes,* 13(3): 102–106.

Christie, D. and Martin, C. (2012) *Psychosocial Aspects of Diabetes. Children, Adolescents and Their Families.* London: Radcliffe Publishing.

Diabetes UK (2014) Hypers. http://www.diabetes.org.uk/Information-for-parents/Hypos-and-hypers/Hypers (accessed 12 November 2014).

Johnson, S.B., Blum, R.W. and Giedd, J.N. (2009) Adolescent maturity and the brain: The promise and pitfalls of neuroscience research in adolescent health policy. Journal of Adolescent Health, 45(3): 216–221.

Newman, B.M. and Newman, P.R. (2003) *Development through Life: A Psychosocial Perspective.* Belmont, CA: Wadsworth/Thomson Learning.

Sage, N., Sowden, M., Chorlton, E. and Edeleanu, A. (2008) *CBT for Chronic Illness and Palliative Care.* Chichester: John Wiley.
Suris, J.C., Michaud, P.A. and Viner, R. (2004) The adolescent with a chronic condition. Part I: developmental issues. *Archives of Disease in Childhood,* 89: 938–942.
Wells, A. (1997) *Cognitive Therapy of Anxiety Disorders.* Chichester: John Wiley.
Young Minds (2012) *The Transition from Primary to Secondary School; How an Understanding of Mental Health and Emotional Wellbeing can Help Children, Schools and Families.* http://www.youngminds.org.uk/Transitionfromprimarytosecondary.pdf (accessed 10 November 2014).

7 David, Sai and Alan – Home coaching with a preschool child and his parents

Jeannie Gordon

This chapter is an account of the Incredible Years home coaching programme (Webster-Stratton 2011) I delivered to a young child aged 3 and his parents over a 6-month period. Using case notes and the parents' words, I describe how the home coaching programme was implemented, and the changes and outcomes observed by both the parents and myself. The names of both child and parents have been changed.

Biography

David's father referred himself and his wife for parenting support. David is 3 and lives with his father Alan, aged 35, mother Sai, aged 35, and two stepsisters, Rita, aged 14, and May, aged 16, from his mother's first marriage. The family live in a small three-bedroom house on a large estate; David shares a room with his parents. The house is untidy, but clean. Alan does full-time shift work and Sai is a full-time mother.

David's parents have been married for 5 years. Sai and the father of her two daughters were divorced over 10 years ago after a very difficult marriage where incidents of severe domestic violence led to the daughters' father being imprisoned; he is not allowed any contact with the family and does not live in the UK. Following the divorce, Sai moved from Thailand to the UK. She communicates daily with her sisters via the internet. Alan has little contact with his own family and describes his father as a violent man.

Alan and Sai stated on their referral form that they were very concerned about David's head-banging, his lack of speech and his behaviour when frustrated, when he would get into rages and hit Sai (but not Alan). They also were concerned that he had no routine at bedtime.

David attends preschool twice a week. The preschool is also concerned about David's speech. He has been referred for speech therapy and has additional support in nursery for his poor language. The preschool has no concerns regarding David's behaviour.

David was a premature baby, and Sai described the birth as 'OK'. She stated that she misses the support of her sisters. David was bottle-fed and reached the normal physical development milestones. Alan's work took him to Afghanistan shortly after David's birth so he was absent during David's early life.

Alan and Sai both have a history of mental health difficulties and at the time of referral were both receiving cognitive behavioural therapy from the local adult mental health service. Both had been diagnosed with depression and were on antidepressant medication. Both had also been diagnosed with post-traumatic stress disorder (PTSD). Sai believes the violent personal assaults she suffered at the hands of her former partner are the cause of her PTSD. Alan believes his PTSD was due to military combat while on active service in Afghanistan.

Early meetings: engagement, empathy, collaboration

On my first visit David did not look at me or want to have any social interaction with me. He ran to the sofa, sat back and banged his head on the back of it (he did not hurt himself, as it was cushioned). I observed him repeating this behaviour throughout my visit. He would stop, look to see if one of his parents was watching and then continue. His parents would continually tell him to stop, but David continued. All attempts at distraction failed and I noted that the parents were using negative comments such as 'stop banging', 'don't do that' and 'you need to stop'.

Alan and Sai described David's routine. David was put to bed between 10.30 and 11.00 p.m. They stated that it was this late because David liked to sleep in the afternoon. David was still taking bottles, day and night, despite being over 3. He also wore nappies, and Alan and Sai were not considering potty training. David was not clear in his speech and was unable to string a sentence together. David would point and grunt to get his needs met. Alan and Sai shared that the family general practitioner had stated that David may have autistic traits.

While observing David, I noted that he picked up the iPad and stopped head banging whilst he played on this. The TV was on in the background throughout the whole of my visit. In the corner of the room there were overflowing boxes of toys, some broken; the front room was chaotic and disorganised. I briefly met both stepsisters, who came in, said hello and went to their bedrooms.

The parents completed the initial assessment forms and we also completed an ecological genogram. This is a simple graphical chart which facilitated a visual representation of the significant people and relationships in David's life. This, I believe, was the start of our collaborative relationship. I used open (Socratic) questioning approaches to ensure clarity of understanding, empathy, and to develop a therapeutic understanding of the issues presented (Miller and Rollnick 2002).

Together we established achievable goals for David and also collaboratively set personal goals for Alan and Sai. I felt it was important to spend time listening to their best hopes, communicating my compassion for their situation and for the difficulties they faced as parents while being very clear about the realistic expectations. I believe a fundamental aspect of the intervention involves truth in the therapeutic alliance. In addition, Alan and Sai must feel their needs are being met in some way before being able to engage fully. I needed to have a holistic view around David's presenting difficulties, therefore an ecological perspective for case conceptualisation and formulation was necessary (Bronfenbrenner 1979).

From my observations and from the family history, my initial formulation was that David had signs of attachment difficulties. I considered that in David's early years both parents had emotional struggles which were compounded by the ongoing effects of PTSD.

Individuals with PTSD tend to have a high level of anxiety and arousal. Symptoms include difficulty sleeping, impaired concentration, and being easily startled. Affected individuals tend to have a high level of irritability and may experience an exaggerated concern for their own safety and the safety of their loved ones. Parents with PTSD can therefore tend to be overprotective. Irritability and low frustration tolerance can make a parent seem hostile or distant, which can lead children to question their parents' love for them. Research undertaken with the families of Vietnam war veterans revealed that children of veterans with PTSD are at higher risk of behavioural, academic and interpersonal problems. Their parents tend to view them as more depressed, anxious, aggressive, hyperactive and delinquent compared to children of non-combat Vietnam veterans who do not have PTSD. In addition, the children are perceived as having difficulty establishing and maintaining friendships. Chaotic family experiences can make it difficult to establish positive attachments to parents, which can make it difficult for children to create healthy relationships outside the family. Research also indicates that children may have particular behavioural disturbances if their parent participated in abusive violence (atrocities) during combat service (Rosenheck and Fontana 1998).

Additionally, PTSD in a parent can have an impact on the child's development (Murray and Cooper 1997) physically and psychosocially. A strong linear relationship has been reported between maternal PTSD symptoms and severity of eating and sleeping issues at 18 months in premature infants (Pierrehumbert *et al.* 2003).

During the early home coaching sessions I shared my thoughts openly with Alan and Sai and invited them to reflect, discuss and add to my formulation. They both agreed that they loved David very much but were often so consumed with their own issues and feelings that they were too tired to emotionally connect with David. It was just easier to put the TV on or give him the iPad. They were aware that they did not interact enough with David; however, they were also very quick to blame each other. They referred to the differences in their own upbringing and culture.

I recommended the Incredible Years home coaching programme and explained my rationale for this based on three factors. The first was the programme's extensive validation history (e.g. Webster-Stratton 1994; Webster-Stratton and Hammond 1997). The second was that the key content and process components fitted well with our local community and service values. The collaborative nature of the therapeutic relationship, and the expectation that families will choose behaviours consistent with their values to teach their children, are specific examples of this. The programme has been used successfully with diverse populations, suggesting that the approach transfers well across cultures (Reid *et al.* 2001, cited in Webster-Stratton 2011). Finally, Bowlby's attachment theory (Bretherton 1992), has elucidated the importance of the affective nature of parent–child relationships. The foundation of the Incredible Years programme focuses on building warm and nurturing parent–child and teacher–child relationships through child-directed play, social and emotion coaching, praise and incentives.

I used a drawing of the thoughts, feelings and behaviour triangle (Stallard 2011) to explain the principles of CBT in the home coaching programme, and to link it to the parent–child relationship. I gave a general example in relation to playing with children (Figure 7.1). I explained that through discussion, instruction, practice and education parents would be able to understand how they feel, think and respond to their child and that this would enable them to make positive changes, as illustrated below in Figure 7.2.

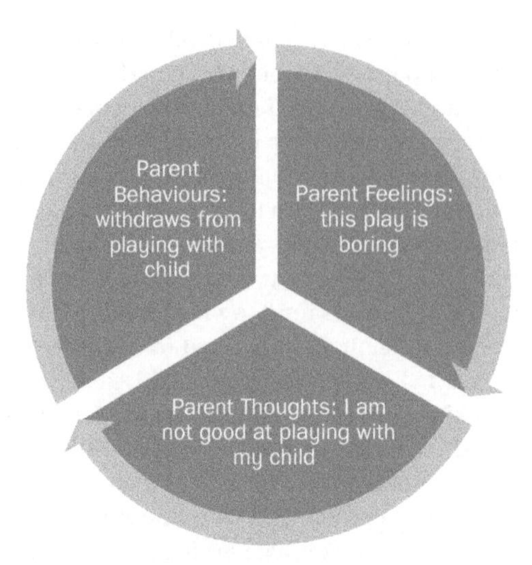

Figure 7.1 Understanding the problem: links between thoughts, feelings and behaviours

The home coaching programme model was selected because David's father is a shift worker and could not attend regular Incredible Years parenting groups. David's mother is Taiwanese and did not feel confident enough in her use and understanding of English to attend a group on her own.

The home coaching programme is a one-to-one home-based model of the Incredible Years group programme, which is a well-designed and comprehensive intervention

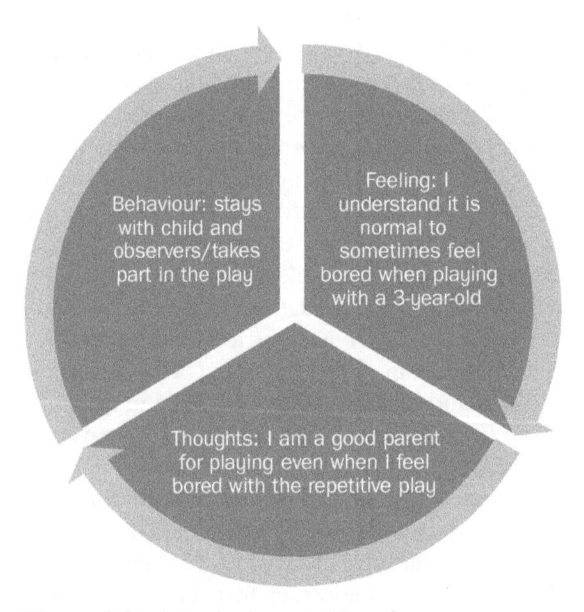

Figure 7.2 Introducing positive changes

package with a strong theoretical basis. It was originally devised to treat early-onset conduct problems in young children and was then revised to address conduct problems by promoting social competence universally. Children who display high rates of antisocial behaviour or aggression are at risk of developing conduct problems (Webster-Stratton 2011). The short-term goals are:

- Improved parent–child interactions, building positive relationships, parent–child bonding and attachment
- Improved parental functioning, less harsh and more nurturing parenting, and increased parental social support and problem-solving
- Prevention, reduction and treatment of early-onset conduct behaviours and emotional problems
- Promotion of child social competence, emotional regulation, positive attributions, academic readiness and problem-solving.

The long-term goal is the prevention of conduct disorders, academic underachievement, delinquency, violence and drug abuse.

It normally takes a minimum of 13 visits to cover all the topic areas in the home coaching programme. Each session is lasts 1½ hours. Longer interventions can be offered to families with complex problems. The professionals (interventionists) are referred to as home coaches, and use the same collaborative approach, techniques and materials for teaching parenting skills as those used in the standard group administration. These include watching video vignettes, discussing effective strategies, role-playing, and assigning practice activities for completion between sessions.

I delivered the home coaching programme with David and his parents over 15 sessions, providing extra sessions in order to adjust the pace of delivery according to Alan and Sai's level of understanding and their success with practice activities. All sessions were delivered in the home. Topics covered in the home coaching programme included:

- Child-directed play, strengthening children's social skills, emotional regulation and school readiness skills
- Using praise and incentives to encourage cooperative behaviour
- Positive discipline – rules, routines and effective limit setting
- Positive discipline – handling misbehaviour.

These topics are standard parts of the Incredible Years programme.

Skills: methods for cognitive and behavioural change

Video modelling and live modelling

Video modelling is a cost-effective training method that has been extensively used in the Incredible Years programmes (Brestan and Eyberg 1998). This method is based on Bandura's theory of observational learning (Bandura 1989, cited in Webster-Stratton 2012). It was proposed that participants would model positive behaviours by observing the interactions demonstrated in the videotapes (Webster-Stratton 2004). The study undertaken by Singer and Singer (1983, cited in Webster-Stratton 2011) showed that children who watched a television programme that promoted prosocial behaviours exhibited significantly greater desirable behaviours.

In the session the parents are shown short DVD scene clips (called 'vignettes') of parent–child interactions at home during dinner, play, and other key family times (Webster-Stratton and Reid 2007). The parents reflect with the home coach on their observations of the vignette and collectively discuss, explore ideas and problem-solve. Some of the scenes are positive, some are negative, which enables parents to recognise that there is no perfect teaching or parenting (Juffer *et al.* 2008, cited in Holmes and Farnfield 2014). The home coach facilitates the parents' learning by asking how the concepts illustrated in the vignettes might apply to their own situations.

Role-play

In the session, following a vignette and discussion, the parents are encouraged to practise the skill. Role-playing with the support of the coach allows participants to understand key concepts (Webster-Stratton 1990). Through role-play parents learn how it feels to use appropriate strategies in interactions with their child. Experiences of success are very important, as this improves the motivation to use these skills. Positive achievements can also boost self-esteem (Emler 2001).

Following a vignette which showed a parent undertaking descriptive commenting (where the parent describes what the child is doing), Alan and Sai came up with words they could use when describing what David was doing in play. Alan and Sai then role-played a scene where they used descriptive commenting words in 'mock' play time with the home coach. This learning was successfully transferred to their interactions with David.

Home practice

Homework and exercises are given to participants to try out the newly learnt skills and to apply the knowledge to real-life contexts (Webster-Stratton & Reid 2007). The main exercise is for parents to play daily with their child. Encouragement is given for the parents to record this play experience; an example of a typical record sheet is reproduced in Figure 7.3.

David and Sai were also given the Incredible Years audio book for parents to support their understanding of the programme content and rationale.

Process and leadership skills

There were times when one or both parents were low in mood, stressed and upset with each other, and I had to be mindful of my role. They had an excellent CBT therapist and I had to remember that when I was with Alan and Sai it would have been easy to

Home Activities

RECORD SHEET: PLAY TIMES

Remember to Build Up Your Bank Account

Record times you spent playing with your child, what you did, and any reaction you noticed in yourself or your child.

Date	Time Spent	Activity	Child's Response	Parent's Reaction
29 July 2013	Few hours	Went to Food Festival.	[redacted] seems happy. Playing with his friends. Enjoy his food and pointing few things he saw at the festival.	~~Tell~~ Discribe him what he saw – like birds, people rolling boats, dogs and Ice cream
30 July 2013	40 mins in afternoon	Play with mini pool. And watering the flowers.	He's talk about the slide at swimming pool. He's ask me to fill the water in pot.	I ~~tell~~ praise him as he watering the flowers. Telling story about he swimming at public pool.
1 July 2013	20 mins twice a day	Playing tents and throwing and catching ball.	He seems happy. He's giving idea how to play tent (cooking and play ball in tent)	Play together. Following his intruction. Giving praise.

Figure 7.3 Record sheet

be drawn into the personal marital issues, and not address the issues relating to David. The guidelines for the programme delivery contain session protocols and a fidelity checklist; this facilitated me in maintaining the goals in relation to outcomes for David, and keeping this at the forefront of the agenda for the session.

Creativity, self-efficacy, discovery, fun

We started the first programme topic by discussing child-directed play. Play and giving special time to a child are the foundation of the Incredible Years programme. I connected this to the concept of the 'attention rule'. Children love attention and will work to get it. They especially like it from parents. Attention can be positive (praise, play) or negative (criticising, mocking, shouting). If a child does not get positive attention, they will work to get negative attention, because it feels better than no attention at all. To aid the parents' understanding I related the concept to David's head banging:

David plays quietly = no attention

David head-bangs = parents shout = David receives attention

I explained that the ongoing negative attention (shouting) that David receives from the head-banging is the maintenance factor. To stop the head-banging behaviour the parents need to stop the maintaining factor and give positive attention to the behaviours they want, that is, to ignore, where safe, his head-banging, and to praise him when he is interacting appropriately. If parents actively participate in play they give their child positive attention and thus the child will have less of a need to resort to negative behaviours to gain attention.

Child-directed play is a useful tool in enhancing attachment and positive relationships between adults and children (Webster-Stratton and Reid 2009). This kind of play can also enhance children's social competence and self-efficacy. In the session, through watching vignettes and though live practice, the parents were encouraged to foster David's imagination by following David's lead in the play. For example, if David turned the car into a plane the parents were instructed to give minimal comments such as 'now the car is in the air' and asked not to criticise the direction of the play (for example, not to say things like 'cars don't fly'). Alan and Sai were also encouraged during play to praise and encourage the positive behaviours they wanted to see from David. A behaviour they want is for David to talk more, so in play they were encouraged to comment when he used words. Phrases such as 'David said car' and 'David using his words' might be used, for example. This can help promote a child's sense of perceived competence and self-worth (Webster-Stratton and Reid 2009). This skill is referred to as descriptive commenting, and it shows the child that adults are paying attention to the child's positive behaviours. At the same time, this process teaches the child important vocabulary.

The positive attention encourages the child to continue playing. As David had speech delay, the parents were also encouraged to use academic coaching to teach him skills such as counting and names of objects. Academic coaching is a form of descriptive commenting where the parent gives a verbal commentary on the child's actions and the things they are playing with, such as colours, shapes and numbers. This form of coaching develops language skills. By my third visit I noticed a significant improvement. David greeted me by walking to me and handing me a toy he was holding. During the session David's head-banging was reduced to about 10 minutes.

I observed that David responded extremely well to detailed praise and attention, particularly from his mother. Both parents had taken all the principles and learning outcomes from the first week and acted on them. Sai, in particular, was doing child-directed play every single day.

Through discussion of child-directed play we were able to discuss David becoming more independent. This led to discussions around a bedtime routine and potty training. I became aware that Sai was napping in the afternoons for 2–3 hours with David. Her napping may have been related to her poor sleep pattern, a common symptom of PTSD. Sai agreed to stop her own nap in the afternoon to encourage David not to have a nap, and we said that we would monitor this over the next 3 weeks.

While we were practising academic coaching I observed a huge change in David. I was on the floor with both parents as we worked on a skills practice following the vignettes. David came over and expressed a real interest in our activity. Through coaching prompts from me, both parents started academic coaching with David. David responded very well, formulating the words as the parents pointed to colours. For example, Alan picked up the purple cup and said 'purple cup', and David immediate modelled this by saying 'purple'. The parents were very surprised at David's response and this encouraged them to do more.

On the fourth visit David greeted me, smiled, but was still not able to say hello without prompting. There was no head-banging at any point during the session. David looked healthier and the parents said they had stopped all naps. David now had a bedtime routine, going to bed between 7.00 and 7.30 p.m. Through prompting and recommendation from earlier sessions, Alan and Sai had introduced bedtime routines and reading stories to David. David would listen to two stories and then stay in bed and go to sleep.

One of the other fundamental changes Alan reported was that when he came home from work that week David ran up to greet him for the first time and held his arms out and seemed to want his father's attention. Alan put this down to the regular playtime David was having. The parents had also reorganised the front room and thrown away old toys; they had also introduced outdoor toys and more fun creative play such as putting a small tent in the front room as a den for their son.

Alan and Sai were still concerned about David's feeding and his poor diet. With the support of the programme they felt they could successfully reduce his bottles during the day. They informed me that the family's norm is to have meals sitting on the sofa watching the TV. With a lot of encouragement from me, and reminders of their success in introducing a bedtime routine, they felt they could start a mealtime routine. They agreed to a set period of time when they would turn the TV off during mealtimes.

At this point I gave them the toddler book and had marked out the pages on routines such as a mealtime routine. Alan and Sai also started potty training with David, and he responded extremely well to all the changes. He had started using the potty and did not mind not having the TV on at mealtimes. This encouraged the parents to start thinking about having family mealtimes and investing in a dining table.

At session 6 the parents were so excited to tell me when I arrived that David had spoken his first sentence. He was not only using academic words (for instance, 'blue car') but also putting in emotional words and social coaching words, for example, 'David is happy' and 'please can I'.

The session content moved on to the topic of rewards systems, to shape behaviour and introduce limit setting. As the sessions progressed I moved the session times to tailor the timing of the day where the parents expressed most difficulties in order that we could maximise role-play practice in the session. I felt this would embed the skills, and give me an opportunity to praise the skills employed, thereby enhancing Alan and Sai's sense of success.

One example of these techniques was demonstrated during a teatime session. I observed David refusing to sit at the table, at which point Sai offered a sticker as a reward to David if he managed to eat sitting up at the table for an agreed period of time (a visual timer was used as a prompt). David responded straight away and sat at the table, and Sai praised David for sitting at the table. David then left the table and started to run about, and in response Sai practised a 'when–then' command. This is when a clear command is given in relation to something the child wants or requests, for example:

> *Child:* Can I have a snack?
> *Parent:* When you take your coat off then you can have a snack.

Sai used the when–then command to remind David of the behaviour wanted and the reward system, telling him: 'When you have finished your tea then you can have a sticker'. David responded by sitting at the table. This observation gave me reason to praise Sai in detail on the skills she used. She reflected on how difficult it was to keep remembering to use all the skills learnt, but how the small changes she was making helped her feel more in control.

In later sessions we focused on independence for David, including introducing potty training at home. Sai was still using nappies at home for when David needed a poo, despite the fact David was able to use a toilet both at home and at preschool. David was also still using a bottle for all drinks and even though he was now sitting at the table for meals, Sai had a tendency to feed David. Sai struggled to follow through on encouraging David to develop independent skills, and I spent some time exploring her reasons for this. We examined the need for David to have school readiness skills such as using a pencil, a fork and spoon, have basic social skills, and be able to use the toilet. Sai explored her own social isolation and her need for 'social readiness', and she started to explore the links which she took to her CBT sessions. Sai started working part-time at a care home, which enabled her to pay for driving lessons. Following Sai's positive changes, Alan reflected that he felt his job was not helpful to his stress level and was making moves to seek alternative employment.

Family's experiences of the home coaching

Both Alan and Sai said they felt it was very helpful having a 'coach' to work through the steps of the programme with them. They felt the process made them feel respected and that I had understood them and their situation. They said they felt I had worked in partnership with them and that they had control over what happened in the session. They stated that the parenting skills, which were in fact 'life' skills, were helping them to cope with their own problems more effectively.

They felt the core skills learnt were child-directed play, distraction skills, how to communicate better, and a better understanding of David's needs.

They also reflected on the discussions they had had about their own PTSD and depression in relation to their parenting roles. Sai said she had gained a greater understanding of how the trauma of her previous marriage may have affected how she interacted with David when he was much younger. Alan was more accepting that the events in Afghanistan and the long absence from David when he was a baby had a link to both his depression and David's attachment to him.

David is too young to verbalise his experience, but he was able to express his joy when playing with his parents, and on the last session he said 'goodbye sticker lady' to me without prompting. That made me smile all the way home.

My reflection and reformulation of the home coaching

From the first meeting to the last session, a period of 6 months, the outcomes were extremely positive. A pre- and post-assessment measure was the Strength and Difficulties Questionnaire (SDQ; Goodman 1997). The SDQ is a brief child mental health questionnaire for children and adolescents aged between 2 and 17 years. It asks questions about 25 attributes, some positive and others negative. These 25 items are divided between five scales: emotional symptoms, conduct problems, hyperactivity/inattention, peer relationship problems, and prosocial behaviour. The total difficulty score of the SDQ (range 0–40) is a fully dimensional measure, with each one-point increase in the total difficulty score corresponding to an increase in the risk of mental health disorder.

David showed a reduction on the SDQ from a pre score of 24 to post score of 9, a significant positive clinical outcome. This result provides initial support for the home coaching programme.

Both parents had accepted help and both had received supportive counselling and CBT from partnership services, and I feel the success they had with other professionals enabled them to trust the intervention right from the start.

I felt the key to the success was having both parents present in the sessions. Alan and Sai were very willing to change and were insightful. They were very aware that they needed to change some of their behaviours, and that unless they changed theirs, David would be unable to change his.

The home visiting also enabled me to tailor the programme to the family's needs and David's developmental stage.

Even though by the end of the sessions I was pleased with the positive outcomes and changes, I was concerned whether the parents had the ability to maintain the skills and positive interactions with David. My worry is that without ongoing support Alan and Sai may lose motivation and revert to old habits, or their own mental health issues could recur. Sai and Alan's PTSD and depressive symptoms can adversely affect the development, and possibly the safety, of David. Growing up with parents with mental health problems could have a negative impact on David's adjustment into adulthood. As a result of David's exposure as an infant to his parents' symptoms of depression, he may, as he grows older, have impaired cognitive and socio-emotional development. Attachment difficulties can also cause problems in interactions with others and in the development of personal independence. Children who have had these experiences also have a higher risk of being diagnosed with depression later in life (Honey 2003).

References

Brestan, E.V. and Eyberg, S.M. (1998) Effective psychosocial treatment of conduct-disordered children and adolescents: 29 years, 82 studies, and 5,272 kids. *Journal of Clinical Child Psychology*, 27, 180–189.

Bretherton, I. (1992) The origins of attachment theory: John Bowlby and Mary Ainsworth. *Developmental Psychology*, 28, 759–775.

Bronfenbrenner, U. (1979) *The Ecology of Human Development*. Cambridge, MA: Harvard University Press.

Emler, N. (2001) *Self-Esteem: The Costs and Causes of Low Self-Worth*. York: York Publishing Services for the Joseph Rowntree Foundation. http://www.jrf.org.uk/publications/self-esteem-costs-and-causes-low-self-worth (accessed June 2014).

Goodman, R. (1997) The Strengths and Difficulties Questionnaire: a research note. *Journal of Child Psychology and Psychiatry*, 38, 581–586.

Holmes, P. and Farnfield, S. (eds) (2014) *Routledge Handbook of Attachment: Implications and Interventions*. New York: Routledge.

Honey, K. (2003) A stress-coping transactional model of low mood following childbirth. *Journal of Reproductive and Infant Psychology*, 21, 129–143.

Miller, W. and Rollnick, S. (2002) *Motivational Interviewing: Preparing People for Change* (2nd edn). New York: Guilford Press.

Murray, L. and Cooper, P.J. (1997) Effects of postnatal depression on infant development. *Archives of the Disabled Child*, 77 (2), 99–101.

Pierrehumbert, B., Nicole, A., Muller-Nix, C., Forcada-Guex, M. and Ansermet, F. (2003). Parental posttraumatic reactions after premature birth: Implications for sleeping and eating problems in the infant. *Archives of Disease in Childhood: Fetal Neonatal Edition*, 88, F400–F404

Rosenheck, R. and Fontana, A. (1998). Transgenerational effects of abusive violence on the children of Vietnam combat veterans. *Journal of Traumatic Stress*, 11, 731–742.

Stallard, P. (2011) *A Clinician's Guide to Think Good – Feel Good: Using CBT with Children and Young People*. Chichester: John Wiley & Sons.

Webster-Stratton, C. (1990) Enhancing the effectiveness of self-administered videotape parent training for families of conduct-problem children. *Journal of Abnormal Child Psychology*, 18(5), 479–492.

Webster-Stratton, C. (1994) Advancing videotape parent training: A comparison study. *Journal of Consulting and Clinical Psychology*, 62, 583–593.

Webster-Stratton, C. (2004) *Quality Training, Supervision, Ongoing Monitoring, and Agency Support: Key Ingredients to Implementing the Incredible Years Programs with Fidelity*. University of Washington. Available at: http://bit.ly/1KIzzo3

Webster-Stratton, C. (2011) *The Incredible Years Parents, Teachers, and Children's Training Series: Program Content, Methods, Research and Dissemination, 1980–2011*. Seattle: Incredible Years Press.

Webster-Stratton, C. (2012) *Collaborating with Parents to Reduce Children's Behavior Problems: A Book for Therapists Using the Incredible Years Programs*. Seattle: Incredible Years Press.

Webster-Stratton, C. and Hammond, M. (1997). Treating children with early-onset conduct problems: A comparison of child and parent training interventions. *Journal of Consulting and Clinical Psychology*, 65, 93–109.

Webster-Stratton, C. and Reid, M.J. (2007) Incredible Years Parents and Teachers Series: A head start partnership to promote social competence and prevent conduct problems. In P. Tolan, L. Szapocznik and S. Sambrano (eds) *Preventing Youth Substance Abuse: Science-Based Programs for Children and Adolescents*. Washington, DC: American Psychological association.

Webster-Stratton, C. and Reid, M.J. (2009) Parents, teachers, and therapists using child-directed play therapy and coaching skills to promote children's social and emotional competence and build positive relationships. In C.E. Schaefer (ed.) *Play Therapy for Preschool Children*. Washington, DC: American Psychological Association.

8 Eleanor – Anorexia

Alison Coad

Background

Eleanor is a 21-year-old woman who has a five-year history of anorexia nervosa. Prior to receiving a diagnosis of anorexia, Eleanor had been diagnosed with obsessive-compulsive disorder (OCD) at the age of 13. (Appendices providing further information on anorexia and OCD are provided at the end of this chapter.)

This chapter attempts to capture some of the detail of our work together. With Eleanor's help, and with contributions from her in her own words, we hope to describe the ways in which we set goals, measured progress and revised our strategies as circumstances changed. This will include an account of the challenges faced by Eleanor following her discharge from the clinic, and the difficulties which she continues to experience at the time of writing. As a clinician, I will try to identify the ways in which our work together was shaped by cognitive behavioural theory, and the ways in which my practice grew and developed around Eleanor's particular needs. Supporting evidence from the relevant literature will be incorporated into the discussion.

Eleanor was admitted as an inpatient to a specialist eating disorders clinic when she was 17. By this point, Eleanor's weight had dropped to a dangerously low level (her body mass index was 13.5). and her parents had acknowledged that they could not manage her illness at home. As the clinic was 50 miles from Eleanor's family home, it was not possible for Eleanor's parents and sibling to visit her more than once each week.

The clinic offered an intense programme of therapeutic support which focused on improving food and fluid intake, reducing compensatory activities such as over-exercising and purging, and helping Eleanor to develop more realistic expectations of herself and her body. Therapeutic groups addressed issues such as body image and anxiety. Each patient also received one-to-one therapy with a qualified psychological therapist. Eleanor was offered the opportunity to work with me, as I had experience in working with younger clients and I was also able to offer CBT.

Eleanor and I worked together for over 2 years. At the age of 19, she gained a place at the local further education college and completed an access course which gave her the qualification she needed to apply to university. At the time of writing, Eleanor is part-way through her degree studies and is living in a shared house with a group of mature students.

Early meetings: engagement, empathy, collaboration

Our first therapy session took place in Eleanor's bedroom at the clinic – not the usual procedure, as therapy sessions tended to take place in a therapy room set apart from the main building. Reflecting on this point, it seems fitting that our first encounter should have taken place on Eleanor's territory, and that she had the option of inviting me in or of shutting the door. This was the first step in making our relationship collaborative. When we have reflected together on this first meeting, Eleanor recalls that she was 'howling' in distress; I have a memory of Eleanor weeping, and a very clear sense that the worksheets and notepad in my bag were not going to be useful for this encounter. The bag stayed closed, and I spent an hour with Eleanor trying to gain a sense of what it felt like to be Eleanor on that day at that time. The mental guidelines provided by my training in CBT took a back seat, and I worked with the key aspects of process at the forefront of my mind: engagement, empathy and collaboration were crucial. Between us, we did our best to find a vocabulary that might help us to describe what was happening for Eleanor. This involved an attempt to describe distress using imagery of colour, texture and shape. Distress was 'large, dark and spiky'. This was the start of a process of identifying feelings. By the end of the session, things were calmer, and we agreed to meet again to continue our conversation.

We met on a weekly basis and it quickly became clear to me that Eleanor was not a candidate for 'standard' CBT techniques – thought records, challenging negative automatic thoughts, looking for evidence all felt restrictive and impersonal. I wanted to understand the feelings part of Eleanor's experience, so that between us we could conceptualise her experience – the collaborative formulation which is so important as the basis of treatment in CBT (Kuyken *et al.* 2011). As our relationship developed over the course of Eleanor's admission to the clinic, the collaborative aspect of our work became increasingly significant. It became apparent that we shared a number of interests – reading, films and education among them. Occasionally, when Eleanor's recent experiences were too painful for her to bring to therapy, we would discuss these shared interests. Over time, they provided metaphors for experiences which provided a 'safe' way for us to talk about painful emotions such as fear, anger and grief. They also highlighted our common experience – the fact that the relationship between us was multi-layered and was not exclusively focused on our roles as 'therapist' and 'client'. Eleanor's love of literature reminded me of my own fascination with the subject. English literature was my favourite subject at school – my first degree, which I gained at the age of 21, was a BA in English and History. In the first year of our work together, when Eleanor was still very unwell physically, she was unable to concentrate well enough to read a novel. However, she remembered the pleasure that stories had given her as a child and we talked about this, using the idea of a narrative of Eleanor's early life to help us to gain an understanding of characters and events. Family history became less of an anxious muddle, and we began to hypothesise about the way that Eleanor's difficulties might have evolved. Eleanor made reference to these connections in the personal statement that she submitted as part of her application to university:

> My earliest memories of literature are of my grandfather re-telling the tales of Kenneth Grahame's *Wind in the Willows*, transporting me from my fear of darkness and of sleep, into calming and imaginative dreams.

I was reminded of aspects of my own experience – the anxiety about academic ability, the mixture of fear and excitement around the prospect of going to university – and I described these feelings to Eleanor, which encouraged her to explore her own responses.

The line between the professional and the personal in the therapy relationship was something which needed to be managed very carefully. Empathy was a very important part of the relationship, and my respect and affection for Eleanor was very clear to me (and, from our discussions, it was clear to Eleanor too). It was my responsibility to manage these sensitive aspects of the relationship to ensure that Eleanor felt safe. Although I often felt a parental concern for Eleanor, I needed to maintain a professional stance to ensure that I did not create a dependency. Eleanor and I discussed these issues in our sessions, particularly towards the end of therapy when it was apparent that Eleanor would be discharged home for the summer prior to registering at university. Conversations about the forthcoming changes in Eleanor's life involved elements of self-disclosure on my part, both about my own experiences of leaving home to go to university and about my experience as a parent of a child who had left home for university the year before. We discussed these 'overlaps' openly, which helped us to maintain the spirit of collaboration and the boundaries that we each needed to maintain our 'positions' in our relationship (Minuchin 1974). These discussions helped Eleanor to recognise that many aspects of her experience were not a direct result of illness. Having grown up with obsessive compulsive disorder and anorexia, it was very difficult for Eleanor to know how to recognise which experiences were a normal part of development. It was important to me to be able to recognise that although I believed that Eleanor and I had developed a clear shared understanding of her situation, this did not mean that I always understood what was happening for her. I needed to remain alert to the ways in which familiarity can lead to assumptions. Eleanor's ability to articulate her experiences – a skill which developed at remarkable speed once she started college – kept me on my toes. If I didn't quite 'get' what was going on, she would be able to point me in the right direction.

Creativity, self-efficacy, discovery, fun

As Eleanor improved physically, her concentration also improved and she was able to think about resuming her education. This was a delicate process, fraught with anxiety. Eleanor's low self-esteem and perfectionist tendencies – already thoroughly activated by her daily challenges with food and body image – were very much in evidence as she began to think about taking a place in a class at the local college. She worried that she had missed too much of her education, that she would be hopelessly behind compared to the other students, and that they would all think that she was weird, fat or ugly. At this stage in therapy, I had started to wonder about the value of a weekly therapy session within the clinic. How could more talking help Eleanor to prepare for a life outside the clinic, and how could she begin to rehearse life situations unless we tested some of them out? In my work at the local child and adolescent mental health service clinic, I had often taken young people out of the clinic to help them practise social skills, or to encourage them to challenge negative thoughts and beliefs through behavioural experiments. I had also used this strategy when young people were clearly uncomfortable in the clinic environment, and needed a neutral environment such as the local coffee shop to help them to feel less like a patient, and more like a human being. I wondered if Eleanor would benefit from some time with me outside the clinic. Part of our work on Eleanor's life narrative had included images of relaxed family occasions at the seaside and in the countryside. Could we recreate some of those relaxed feelings if we were able to spend time at the beach, or on a country walk? I proposed the idea to clinic staff. It was met with surprise, as no other therapist had suggested this before, and there was already an established protocol for support staff to accompany clients going out for a snack or lunch. Was there a conflict of roles here? It was something of an experiment, but approval was given and Eleanor and I ventured out for a morning at the beach. This was a turning point in the therapeutic relationship. I chose a quiet local beach, lent Eleanor a camera, as she wanted to make her own record of the experience, and we headed off.

The trip took around 3 hours, which immediately challenged the idea of a 'therapy appointment'. Once outside the clinic, we were both aware of the fact that we had left the boundaries of the therapy room behind us. What if we ran out of things to talk about? Did this really count as 'therapy' or was I just trying to give Eleanor (and myself) a bit of a break from the clinic environment? And how would we negotiate snacks (usually a formal process taken at the table in the clinic, and overseen by nursing and support staff)? These thoughts – my own anxious predictions about my practice, a point which I have only identified as a result of writing this case study – were managed between us. We did not run out of things to talk about: we had already established a lot of common ground and a mutual respect which made us comfortable in each other's company. The concern about whether this was 'therapy' was quickly dispelled as the benefits for Eleanor were obvious. The environment reminded Eleanor of happy family days out, when she had been able to enjoy an ice-cream without guilt. She was able to recognise the sharp contrast to her current situation, in terms of her relationship with food, but was also able to connect to feelings of safety, belonging and pleasure. The contradictions in this experience helped Eleanor to recognise that recovery is a mixed and at times circuitous process. The desire for certainty, which is such a familiar feeling for sufferers of OCD and anorexia, was something which needed to be seen for what it was – an unattainable state. This was the occasion when Eleanor first ate in my company. It was a painful process for her, as she was able to see that part of the safety of our relationship had been based on the avoidance of the thoughts and feelings that linked to eating. The challenge of eating her cereal bar was managed by telling me about her thoughts – 'I feel so greedy' – and acknowledging how difficult this was. We did not try to find an answer to the problem, or to make it go away, but we did name it. The fact that we then continued our conversations without any change in rhythm provided some evidence for Eleanor that she could show this part of herself without it resulting in rejection. It also proved to her that she could tolerate feelings of shame without having to punish herself – a pattern which she was able to identify when we worked together on the material for this case study. This point is explored further in the following sections, which describe the ways in which the CBT aspects of our work came together.

Skills: methods for cognitive and behavioural change

Following the success of our 'active therapy' sessions, I found myself wondering about the ways in which standard cognitive behavioural techniques might be helpful. Although I was not following a formal treatment protocol, I was mindful of the ways in which thoughts, feelings and behaviours formed patterns for Eleanor. I wanted to find a way to use techniques such as identification of thoughts and feelings, and to help Eleanor recognise how automatic thoughts can link to behaviours. What I did not want to do was to over-formalise our sessions, and set up expectations which might trigger Eleanor's need to 'get things right'. Our early therapy sessions included some work on the identification of feelings, but it was some time before we focused on cognitions and beliefs. The foundation for this work developed gradually, as the therapeutic relationship became more secure. Guided discovery (also termed 'Socratic dialogue') offered a way for us to explore Eleanor's anxieties. This mode of conversation gave me the opportunity to be curious without taking up the position of 'the expert'. Eleanor and I explored ideas together, checking things out as we went along. If either of us was unsure about our understanding, we were open about this, and did our best to clarify meanings. Our mutual interest in literature provided a useful vehicle through which Eleanor was able to verbalise her experiences – as shown by this quotation from Eleanor's application for a university place:

> I have learnt the importance of speech and words when trying to communicate with someone having difficulty expressing emotions. Literature represents a lot more to me than a subject I study; it has become my saviour and my route to freedom.

Having reached a point where it was possible for Eleanor to identify some of her thoughts and feelings, we spent time looking at the ways in which thoughts affected Eleanor. It was often difficult for Eleanor to discuss the content of her intrusive thoughts. In common with many OCD sufferers, Eleanor attributed special meaning to this process (Rachman 1997); she also experienced what Salkovskis (1985) describes as 'an overinflated sense of responsibility'. One our early behavioural experiments related to testing out the power of thoughts. Eleanor's challenge was to articulate some of her anxious thoughts – to speak them out loud, in spite of her fears about the potential consequences (would the thoughts come true?). Some of the thoughts related to Eleanor herself, and involved illness (specifically cancer) and death; some related to harm coming to Eleanor's loved ones. It took a lot of courage for Eleanor to speak about these issues with me, and her discomfort within the sessions was evident. What these discussions did, over time, was to prove to Eleanor that she was able to pay less attention to distressing thoughts and images. It also increased her ability to tolerate uncertainty.

The behavioural part of our work initially focused on Eleanor's responses to distress, such as self-harm and emotional outpourings (for example, the 'howling' described in Eleanor's account of our first meeting). Food and food-related behaviour did not form part of our early work together, which may seem odd given Eleanor's diagnosis; this aspect of our work will be discussed in more detail in the next section.

The 'real-world therapy' described above paved the way for cognitive and behavioural change. These sessions took place as Eleanor prepared to enrol at the local higher education college, and they became a part of the transition from life as an inpatient to life as a student. Eleanor's ability to manage unhelpful patterns of thinking was developing rapidly. As her confidence grew she found that she was able to undertake challenges that had seemed impossible a few months earlier – writing essays, presenting papers to her fellow students, and forging friendships. College provided regular opportunities to challenge anxious predictions; it also provided a peer group, which helped Eleanor to normalise her responses to challenging situations.

Eleanor's experiences during her year at college provided her with an accelerated phase of teenage development. She experienced her first romantic relationship, became part of a close group of friends, and went through the highs and lows of an intense academic programme. During this year, discussions about Eleanor's discharge from the clinic were a constant theme. It was evident that Eleanor was no longer in need of inpatient treatment, but the question of appropriate accommodation for her raised some difficult questions. Eleanor's relationship with her parents had become very difficult following their decision not to allow her to return to the family home on discharge from the clinic. This was a painful choice for all involved, and was made on the basis of previous experiences which suggested that neither Eleanor nor her parents were ready to live together as a family at this time. Eleanor had made great progress with the meal plan prescribed within the clinic, but still experienced high levels of anxiety when faced with food choices. Eleanor's parents did not feel able to contain that anxiety, and were concerned that she would relapse if she were to move back into the family environment. Not surprisingly, Eleanor experienced this as a painful rejection, and she and her parents became estranged for a number of months. The grief she experienced as a result of the change in her relationship with her parents was very much apparent in our sessions, although it still proved difficult for Eleanor to put her feelings into words. Over time, Eleanor's belief that her parents had rejected her changed as she began to appreciate the ways in which their decisions had enabled her to develop independence. Eleanor's older brother was a key figure in her life at this time, and it was he who maintained a link to the family, providing stability and security. Rebuilding family relationships was a key long-term goal, which evolved gradually over several months.

Formulation and reformulation

The account of Eleanor's progress from our first meeting to our recent work together on this case study is not a straightforward success story. There have been many positive events, but some problems are ongoing, as the formulation and reformulation diagrams show (see Figures 8.1 and 8.2). Fears of 'not being good enough' are still troublesome at times. Negotiating the weeks at home prior to her departure for university, Eleanor experienced fears that she would somehow 'not be good enough for mum and dad' and that she would end up 'going mental'. The fact that she was able to verbalise these fears helped her to recognise the contrast between past episodes of crisis and her feelings and behaviours at this time. She was able to use this learning to help her to manage the effect of the breakup of her relationship with her first boyfriend. As Eleanor observed in an email:

> The whole relationship and then its break up has been driving me crazy and affecting me quite badly. I have been thinking everything that happened over and over until I convinced myself of its meaning, I have been in torment over

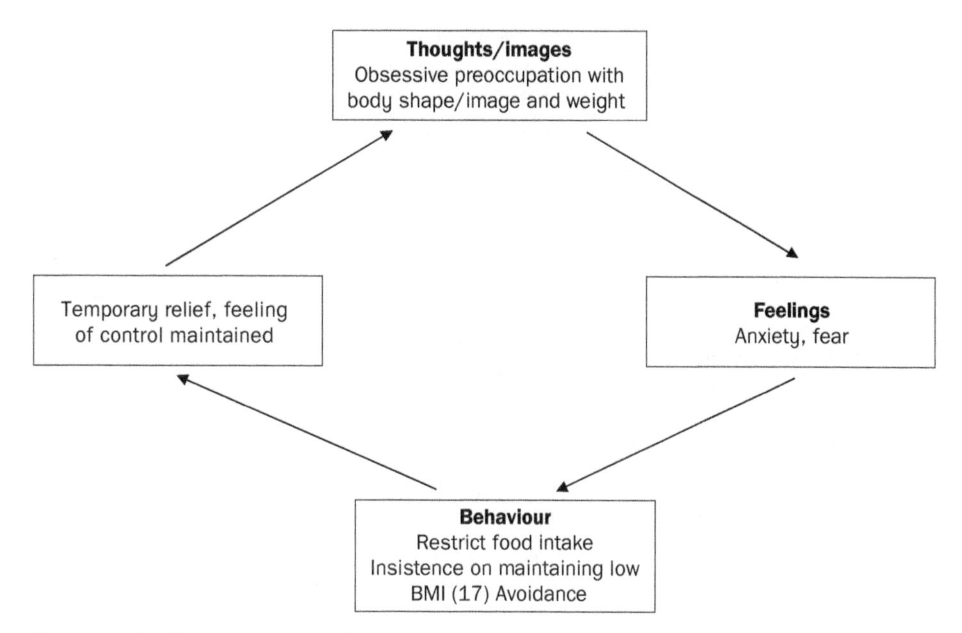

Figure 8.1 Eleanor's initial formulation

> what I did wrong and why I wasn't good enough. I think I was thinking that for the first time I had been myself and showed myself to him but then it ended in destruction so came to the conclusion I wasn't good enough after all and started to hate myself again.

Eleanor managed her distress by seeking support from her parents, and by practising mindfulness meditation ('to get myself out of my head'). Her understanding of her thoughts and feelings enabled her to establish a more positive cycle, which is illustrated in Figure 8.2.

Intrusive thoughts have also continued, although Eleanor is able to recognise the thoughts as 'brain activity':

> my brain will go to thoughts of killing myself in awful ways – a really extreme shock to shut off those awful feelings. It's a bit of a relief for a few minutes … My brain's trying to find a solution to things and it comes up with these horrible thoughts.

Eleanor also worries about relapse – 'the biggest fear for me is ending up in hospital again' – but she is able to balance that worry with the pleasure of her life outside the clinic:

> I'm also having amazing moments … before I left the clinic I felt a bit depressed, and anxious, but also excited about not having all these rules and restrictions all of the time. [Now I can recognise] the good moments … I love my parents … [and I can see] the amazingness of life and the world.

Relevant Childhood Data
Father had alcohol problems
Mother diagnosed with depression
Anxious, 'clingy' child – separations difficult
Remembers feeling thirsty, and never being able to drink enough water to satisfy that thirst

Core Beliefs
I'm not good enough
I must be exceptional to be accepted

Conditional Assumptions/Attitudes/Rules (if ... then ...)
If I am perfect, then I am acceptable
If I am thin enough, then I am perfect
If I demonstrate my needs, then I am unacceptable
If I make mistakes, then I am defective

Coping Strategies
Restrict my food intake/use food to suppress emotions
Avoid activities which could prove that I am not perfect
Seek lots of reassurance

Situation Mealtime at the clinic	Situation Going to college	Situation Being at university
Automatic Thought If I eat what they are telling me to eat, I will get fat	Automatic Thought I can't cope with the work	Automatic Thought I can't cope as well as the others
Meaning of Automatic Thought If I get fat, I will be ugly and imperfect and therefore I will be rejected	Meaning of Automatic Thought I am stupid	Meaning of Automatic Thought I'm weird/different
Emotion Anxiety, fear	Emotion Anxiety, anger with self	Emotion Fear, anxiety, sadness
Behaviour Restrict food intake	Behaviour Work extra hard, put myself under lots of pressure	Behaviour Use food to suppress feelings, (which triggers overeating and then compensatory behaviours)

Figure 8.2 Eleanor's final formulation (based on Beck, 2011)

Looking back over the work we have covered together, there are three main phases. The first was getting to know each other, and building a relationship of trust and respect. The second was the more active and experimental phase, when we took therapy outside the clinic. This was a key point in our relationship, which Eleanor has identified as a significant shift in her treatment. Therapy became a more active part of Eleanor's life within the clinic, and the life which she was creating for herself in the world outside. The third phase, which is ongoing as we continue our contact through the work on this case study, involves a mixture of the things we have learned together. Eleanor has used techniques such as mindfulness (Kabat-Zinn 1994) to help her to tolerate intrusive thoughts, and to slow down her automatic responses to those thoughts. She has identified some of the unhelpful beliefs about herself, the world and others (Beck 1970), which kept her trapped within a cycle of painful behaviours. Eleanor was also able to identify some clear goals, and to begin to work towards them. Managing family relationships differently was an important goal. Returning to education was another significant target, which was achieved with great style – Eleanor gained a distinction at college and was offered a place at university to study English literature.

None of these goals would have been attainable unless Eleanor was able to stay well physically. Anorexia continues to present challenges for Eleanor and the fact that new symptoms have emerged has led to uncertainty and confusion. In the early days of her admission, Eleanor recalled that eating was an enormous challenge and that she had to work very hard to maintain her food intake. Following her discharge from the clinic, she recognised that her relationship to food was very different:

> A lot of stuff has always been attached with food … I had to force myself to eat to get my life back … [now] part of me is scared of not being allowed [food] … denying myself, thinking of it as a punishment. I almost want to comfort myself, and not be punished again..

These concerns led to new symptoms – bingeing and purging – which Eleanor struggled to understand in the months following her discharge. It was difficult for Eleanor to disclose this information to me, as she felt so ashamed:

> it's gone a bit out of control and it's freaking me out a bit … I feel quite ashamed about it, and I feel freaked out about it because I've never had that issue before and it just makes you feel like an awful person.

We realised that Eleanor was concerned that I would judge her negatively – just as she had feared that I would consider her 'greedy' if she were to eat in my presence. Once this fear was recognised, Eleanor was able to challenge her negative thoughts. She quickly came up with evidence, from her experience of our relationship, that I would be unlikely to judge her negatively. She was then able to test out her anxious prediction by describing her symptoms (bingeing and vomiting) and observing my response. Eleanor became more relaxed following this discussion and she was able to identify the ways in which thoughts, feelings and behaviours had produced a new vicious cycle:

> I'll allow myself to have a biscuit, but then I know I can go to the toilet afterwards. It's kind of a relief, because I'm allowed to eat it, but I don't have to worry about anorexic thoughts … it's sort of a way to allow myself to eat and not feel so guilty.

As Eleanor also realised, this behaviour created more anxiety, which kept the cycle going:

> The anxiety becomes unbearable ... it just keeps rising and rising ... it feels like I could just go mental ... it's like a constant ringing that gets more and more piercing. I feel like I'm going to explode.

Eleanor has found ways to manage these symptoms safely. She has sought help from professionals as and when she needs it. She maintains a healthy weight and is able to function well in her academic and personal life. Most significantly, Eleanor is able to make decisions about her needs which enable her to deal with things at her own pace. Throughout our therapeutic relationship, we worked in a way which encouraged Eleanor to make choices about how and when to move forward. At times, I realise that I was too directive, suggesting challenges before Eleanor was ready for them. It also became clear to me that using standard therapy tools, such as worksheets, did not suit Eleanor. Our work was based much more in reflective conversations, which enabled Eleanor to reach her own conclusions about what helped her and what was likely to make things more difficult for her. Practical experiments, including trips out of the clinic and 'rehearsals' of important events such as presentations for college, helped Eleanor to prepare herself for the life that she wanted. Formal measures were not used during treatment, and so evidence of effectiveness is purely qualitative; but Eleanor has achieved a number of significant goals.

Conclusion

Eleanor's case is an unusual one in a number of ways. The fact that we were able to work together over such a long period of time is undoubtedly one of the reasons why we were able to achieve so much. The closeness which developed between us would not be comfortable for some patients or professionals. That said, the respect between us, and the mutual understanding, ensured that the relationship was close but contained. It has been a part of a much bigger piece of work offered by the clinic, which gave Eleanor the skills to move into young adulthood.

Eleanor's experiences have given me a much better understanding of the meaning of recovery. We continue to work together, although our agenda is more often related to literature than anorexia. I am indebted to Eleanor for her willingness to share these experiences.

Appendix

Anorexia nervosa: how is it diagnosed?

A diagnosis of anorexia nervosa is made according to the criteria provided in publications such as the *Diagnostic and Statistical Manual of Mental Disorders* (DSM) which is published by the American Psychiatric Association (APA) and updated on a regular basis. The most recent edition is DSM-5, which was published in 2013. The criteria have been revised in this edition to remove reference to food 'refusal' 'since that implies intention on the part of the patient and can be difficult to assess' (APA 2013). The current criteria are as follows:

1 Restriction of energy intake relative to requirements leading to a significantly low body weight in the context of age, sex, developmental trajectory, and physical health.
2 Intense fear of gaining weight or becoming fat, even though underweight.
3 Disturbance in the way in which one's body weight or shape is experienced, undue influence of body weight or shape on self-evaluation, or denial of the seriousness of the current low body weight.

Obsessive-compulsive disorder

It is recognised that patients diagnosed with anorexia nervosa have a higher likelihood of experiencing other disorders such as depression and OCD. Research shows that OCD is often diagnosed alongside anorexia [REF]. The DSM-5 diagnostic criteria for OCD are as follows:

1 Recurrent and persistent thoughts, impulses or images that are experienced at some time during the disturbance as intrusive and inappropriate and that cause marked anxiety or distress.
2 The thoughts, impulses or images are not simply excessive worries about real-life problems.
3 The person attempts to ignore or suppress such thoughts, impulses or images or to neutralise them with some other thought or action.
4 The person recognises that the obsessional thoughts, impulses or images are a product of his or her own mind (not imposed from without as with thought insertion) (APA 2013).

References

American Psychiatric Association (2013) *Diagnostic and Statistical Manual of Mental Disorders* (5th edn, DSM-5). Washington, DC: American Psychiatric Association.
Beck, A.T. (1970) The core problem in depression: The cognitive triad. In J.H. Masserman (ed.) *Depression: Theories and Therapies* (pp. 47–55). New York: Grune and Stratton.
Beck, J.s. (2011) *Cognitive Therapy: Basics and Beyond* (2nd edn). New York: Guilford Press.
Kabat-Zinn, J. (1994) *Wherever You Go, There You Are: Mindfulness Meditation in Everyday Life*. New York: Hyperion.
Kuyken, W., Padesky, C.A. and Dudley, R. (2011) *Collaborative Case Conceptualization: Working Effectively with Clients in Cognitive-Behavioral Therapy*. New York: Guilford Press.
Minuchin, S. (1974) *Families and Family Therapy*. Cambridge, MA: Harvard University Press.
Rachman, S. (1997) A cognitive theory of obsessions. *Behaviour Research and Therapy*, 35(9): 793–802.
Salkovskis, P.M. (1985). Obsessional compulsive problems: A cognitive behavioural analysis. *Behaviour Research and Therapy*, 23: 571–583.

9 Lily – Obsessive compulsive disorder

Sarah Rogers

In this chapter we meet Lily, a 10-year old-girl with obsessive compulsive disorder (OCD) and Tourette's syndrome (TS). Lily's case highlights the complex nature of OCD and ways in which cognitive behavioural therapy (CBT) interventions can be adapted to meet the needs of children. Lily was keen for others to understand her lived experience of OCD, and she provides insight into her thoughts and feelings about the disorder and the therapy she received. My reflections on the process of therapy are detailed throughout, and an update on Lily's progress is given at the end of the chapter.

Background

Lily lives with her mother Helen, stepfather David and younger brother Joseph. She has positive relationships with her parents and extended family, and she enjoys being an older sister. Lily attends a mainstream primary school in the city and receives good support from her teachers. She has good friendships and also enjoys many activities, including gymnastics, using her Heelys (skate shoes) and making items from loom bands.

Lily was referred to the local child and adolescent mental health service (CAMHS) following parental concerns about her excessive worrying. As a result of the complex nature of Lily's presentation, several assessment appointments were offered in a CAMHS outpatient clinic. It was important to understand the presenting difficulties from the perspectives of Lily and her parents: joint and separate appointment times were offered to allow Lily a private space to talk, and Helen and David the opportunity to openly discuss Lily's difficulties and their concerns about parenting. Discussions revealed a number of interrelated difficulties:

- Lily was experiencing persistent worries, many of which were related to her relationship with her mother. Lily worried that her mum might leave her, that her mum might get ill or die, or that her mum might not love her. She engaged in a number of behaviours in order to minimise these worries, such as washing her hands or demanding that mum repeat a certain word, phrase or facial expression in a precise way. Lily would become tearful and distressed if these actions were not carried out correctly.
- Lily had a number of motor and vocal tics, and these were becoming more problematic. Lily struggled to control squeaks, twitches and body jerks and she was becoming distressed as a result.
- Lily's worries and tics were leading to heiightened stress, resulting in more generalised difficulties such as problems with sleep and low mood. Prior to the start of therapy, Lily frequently reported that she wanted to die. Looking back,

Lily remembers believing 'there is something badly wrong with my brain'. She felt scared and often thought 'I can't live like this, it's too hard'.

- The impact of these combined difficulties on the whole family was significant. Lily's parents found it difficult to calm her down when she was stuck in habits, rituals, or persistent tics. It was also hard for them to disengage from Lily's requests to copy her or do things in a particular way, due to the amount of distress this caused. Overall, it was becoming almost impossible to undertake routine daily activities.

Further assessment by a consultant psychiatrist led to diagnoses of OCD and TS. Statistics show that it is common for OCD and TS to co-occur: 20–30 per cent of individuals with OCD also experience tics and 5–7 per cent have a confirmed diagnosis of TS (OCD-UK 2014).

Research evidence (O'Kearney *et al.* 2010) and clinical guidelines (National Institute of Clinical Excellence 2005) indicate that cognitive behavioural interventions should be a first-line treatment for all children with OCD (moderate to severe impairment). Interventions should include the use of exposure and response prevention (ERP) and involve the child's family. If there is not an adequate response to CBT, then the inclusion of a pharmacological intervention should be considered. As this chapter will show, Lily's care encompassed all of these aspects.

Early contacts

It was important, during our early contacts especially, to fully consider Lily's ability to understand and engage in a cognitive behavioural approach. This meant being thoughtful about Lily's chronological age, developmental level, use of language, and her position in the family system around her. Lily was initially scared and reluctant to talk about her problems because she believed that I would laugh at her. In our early work we spent time normalising these fears and instilling hope that change was possible.

Assessment

In order to initiate conversations about Lily's problems, we began our first meeting by looking at the Spence Children's Anxiety Scale (Spence 1998) together. The aim of this was to explore the worries that Lily was experiencing and to demonstrate that she was not the only person with such difficulties. This proved to be a useful engagement task and enabled Lily to talk openly about her difficulties and elaborate on areas that caused her distress. Scores from the questionnaire revealed that Lily had significant difficulties with separation anxiety, worries about physical injury, and obsessive compulsive symptoms. I went on to ask Lily what she would choose if she had three wishes: she identified two wishes. which were 'to make all the things I do and the worries go away' and 'to never get ill again'. Lily reported being 10/10 certain that she wanted to change and 7/10 confident that she could change with some help. Given a range of options, she identified that talking, playing and artwork were things she was comfortable with.

During our second one-to-one meeting, we focused on her worries in more detail. Lily took the lead in drawing a spider diagram and listed hand-washing, intrusive thoughts (e.g. mum is going to die), saying 'night night' in a certain way, and squeaking at bedtime as particular problem areas. She explained that she felt blamed by her family for doing each of these things, which resulted in feelings of frustration, lots of tears, and worrying even more.

During early sessions it seemed important to understand and differentiate the symptoms of OCD and TS, so Lily could see that her experiences were not her fault and that particular behaviours could be targeted and changed. This included age-appropriate conversations about the disorders, why people get these problems, how many people get these problems, and what can be done to make things better. Work also included a timeline of events: Lily identified that her worrying began at age 6, her 'habits' at age 9½ and uncontrollable squeaks at age 10. Looking back at her earliest experiences, Lily remembers a constant fear of getting sick and some episodes of squeaking. She recalled her mum getting annoyed and this upsetting her because she thought she could not help it. Lily reports that it was a relief finding out that she had OCD, that her thoughts and feelings were not her fault, and that there was something that could help.

Identifying maintenance cycles

While it is helpful to have a good working knowledge of the theoretical models of OCD (e.g. Salkovskis 1985; Salkovskis *et al.* 1998), in my direct work with Lily it was more important to work collaboratively on simple formulations of difficulties that she could easily relate to. We quickly established that Lily was able to understand the concept of getting stuck in cycles, so our first and subsequent analyses of her difficulties took the form of circular diagrams, such as that shown in Figure 9.1.

As the combination of OCD and squeaking (tics) was causing Lily and her family the most anxiety and distress, we first worked on understanding the link between the two problems. We drew cycles out on the whiteboard and then on paper. One example

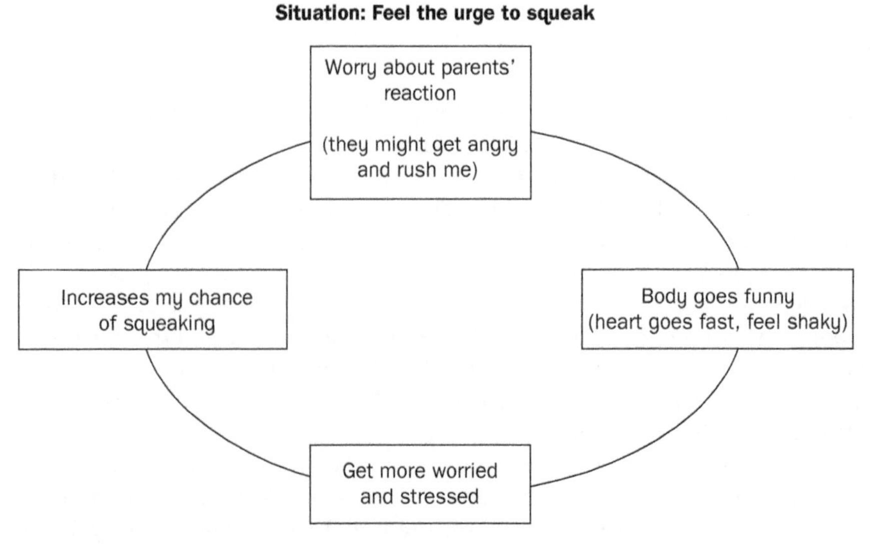

Figure 9.1 Initial formulation: vocal tics

was of Lily leaving school at the end of the day. Lily reported that she often needed to squeak at the end of a long day but worried about squeaking in front of her parents because of the reaction she might receive. Lily worried that adults would rush her, and as a result she would not be able to do the squeaks correctly and finish them. While worrying, physiological symptoms became apparent and she noticed that her heart was beating quickly and that she was starting to shake – this made her feel stressed as well as worried. The stress, unfortunately, increased the severity of her squeaks and, in turn, maintained the worries about squeaking in front of her parents – thus creating a vicious cycle. Lily found this formulation helpful and she requested that we share this with her parents, feeling hopeful that they would understand better and therefore react differently. Lily began this process of feedback by writing her parents a letter:

> Dear adults
>
> This letter is about my squeaking and worrys. I have lots of different worrys. I worry about home time when schools over and at bed time about my squeaking. When I get worried my heart beats really fast and I get shaky.
>
> Sarah and I think that I can't stop my new squeaks. It feels there, there all the time. I worry about me doing my squeaks when I meet my mum or dad or my nanny. I worry that when I start my squeaks its not as easy to stop. I worry about when my mum or dad might get annoyed with me for doing my squeaks.
>
> When I worry about all of these things and I get panicky I end up squeaking even more. I find it really hard to stop.
>
> Thank you for listening from Lily xxx

Once Lily began to feel confident that her parents understood her struggles, we began to look at how OCD alone was getting stuck in cycles – Lily called these repetitive cycles 'OCD attacks'. This ensured we all understood the problems in the same way and that there was a clear rationale for change. Figures 9.2 and 9.3 illustrate examples of Lily's OCD cycles. In each, a trigger situation resulted in Lily experiencing an obsessional thought, which led to uncomfortable feelings that she felt she could not deal with. Lily found the only way to escape the uncomfortable feelings was to do as OCD said, resulting in the compulsive behaviours of verbal rituals or tapping. On other occasions compulsive behaviours included hand-washing, facial expressions, or seeking repeated responses from her parents.

Lily showed good insight when looking at these cycles in detail, and could see that the cycles needed to be broken somewhere in order to reduce OCD. This led us into a variety of 'child-friendly' cognitive behavioural interventions, offered on a weekly basis.

Interventions

Evidence for the efficacy of cognitive behavioural interventions in childhood OCD has increased in recent years. There is a growing literature on adapting CBT techniques when working with children (Friedberg and McClure 2002; Fuggle *et al.* 2013; Graham

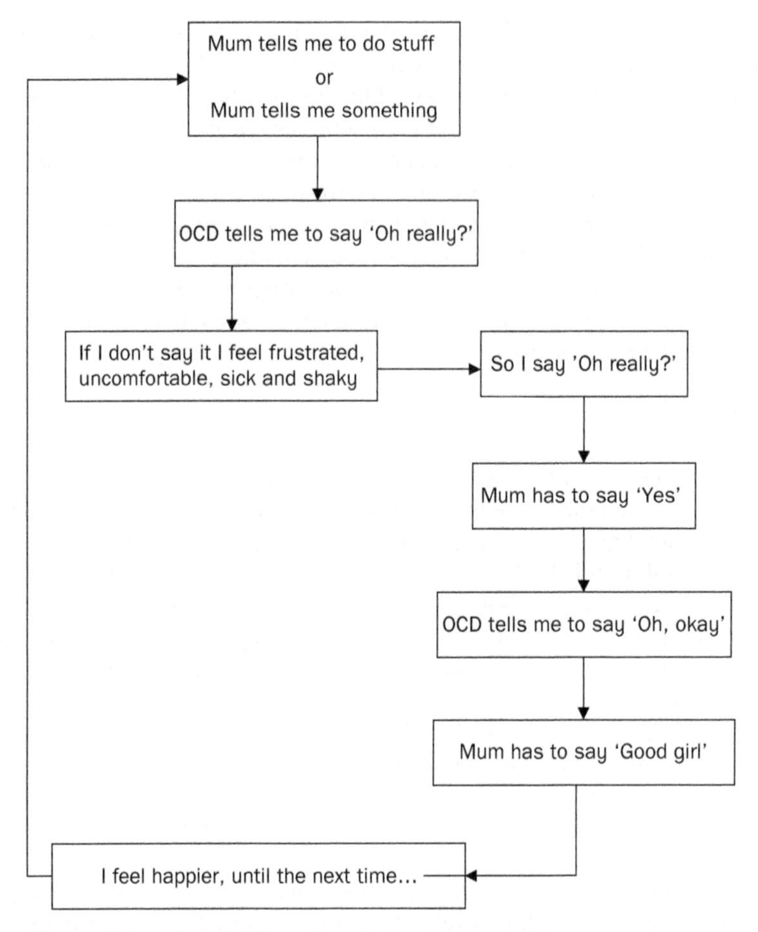

Figure 9.2 Lily's OCD cycle: obsessive thoughts

and Reynolds 2013; Seiler 2008; Stallard 2002) as well as working with CBT for OCD more specifically (Derisley *et al.* 2008). Sound empirical knowledge and good clinical intuition were important when working with Lily's complex presentation: Lily experienced both good periods and difficult periods throughout our work together, so the content and pace of sessions varied according to her individual needs.

Awareness

During early sessions, attention was paid to Lily's experience of anxiety, as obsessional rituals enabled her to avoid uncomfortable feelings. This began with psycho-education about physiological symptoms of anxiety. We spoke about the flight, fight or freeze responses using a caveman and tiger story, and then explored Lily's understanding of the story by drawing a picture of a character (whom she named Bob) on the whiteboard. Lily helped me place arrows on Bob to indicate where his bodily feelings of anxiety would be.

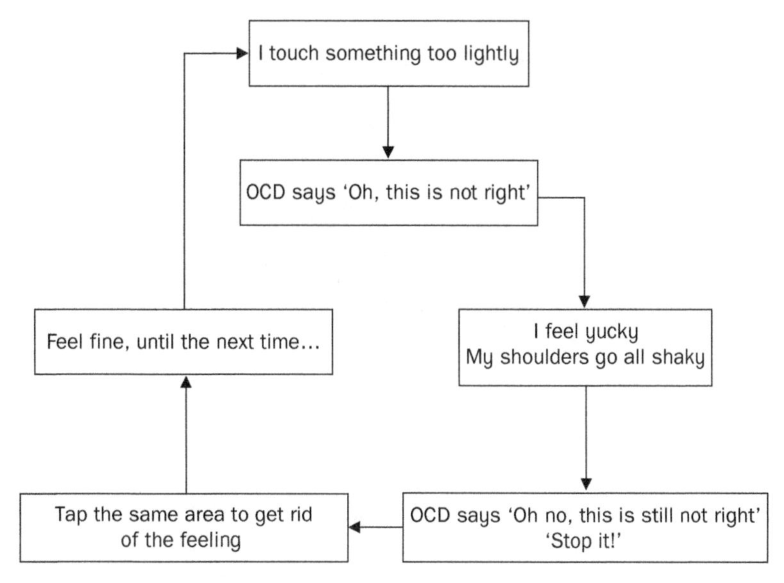

Figure 9.3 Lily's OCD cycle: compulsions

Next, Lily was introduced to a graph depicting the rise and fall of anxiety each time a worry was triggered but then avoided (through rituals). We talked about the rationale for ERP, such that Lily would be asked to face an anxiety-provoking situation, sit with the uncomfortable feelings that it evoked, and refrain from engaging in her preferred (compulsive) response. This would enable her to learn that the feared outcome was unlikely to come true. Lily was able to help me draw new lines on the graph to indicate what was likely to happen to anxiety as it was faced more frequently – a reduction in the height of the anxiety curve and a reduction in the time taken to recover from a physiological response.

Perhaps the most important aspect of our work together at this stage was externalising the concept of OCD to help Lily understand that she was not to blame and that she was not defined by her diagnosis. Lily was encouraged to think about what her OCD looked like. Lily drew a round-faced character (see Figure 9.4) which looked quite sinister. She described seeing lots of colours and similar faces, and explained that he would tell her to think things that made her feel bad. She called this character 'Horrid Henry'. Lily was able to put the blame on Henry and described him as mean, horrible and evil. Henry became a core part of our therapeutic intervention.

In conjunction with my sessions with Lily, her parents were also included in work aimed at understanding OCD, seeing the links and the differences between OCD and TS, and understanding the rationale for future ERP interventions. Consideration was also given to common family responses to OCD, such as that family members often engage in behaviours that are offered to support the individual with OCD (e.g. washing their hands too frequently or repeating a phrase) but inadvertently maintain the OCD cycles. As Lily's family were frequently being drawn into complex rituals or reassurance-giving, it was important to offer them support and encouragement. They were

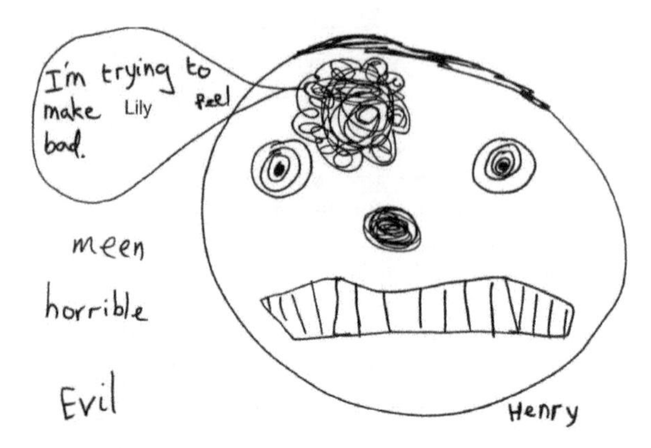

Figure 9.4 Externalising OCD: Horrid Henry

also given permission to disengage from Henry's requests while containing the distress this caused Lily. It was important for Lily's family to verbalise their dilemma about whether her behaviour was on purpose or whether she could not help it. This parental support was offered in parallel parent sessions (with a colleague) as well as interwoven in sessions offered to Lily. Helen reported that this work was helpful and that she was able to learn what to say to Lily during an OCD attack.

Pharmacology

It became necessary, quite early on in our work, to consider medication for the OCD and TS symptoms. While Lily and her family were highly motivated to engage in a process of change, Lily was too anxious and upset to effectively engage in exposure work. To give a sense of Lily's level of distress at this stage in our work, it is helpful to explain a typical scenario on an appointment day. Lily would often arrive at the clinic screaming and crying as she came in from the car. This was usually triggered by Helen refusing to engage in a ritual because they needed to be on time for the appointment. Lily would continue this behaviour in the waiting area until I was able to meet her for the appointment. Lily would look to Helen for reassurance and try to engage her in a series of verbal and facial expression rituals. Even if Helen did engage, Lily would become extremely upset if these rituals were not carried out correctly. On bad days it would take several minutes to calm Lily and support her in being apart from her mother. While Lily was then able to converse with me in the clinic room, our interactions were often impeded by tic sequences that would last for seconds or minutes at a time.

Lily met with the consultant psychiatrist who prescribed medication for TS and, at a later date, medication for OCD. Over a period of several weeks there were signs that the medication was helpful: Lily was able to leave Helen more quickly with minimal anxiety, she was calmer and more able to focus in our sessions, and her parents were noticeably more relaxed. Looking back, Helen reports that 'medication was needed to open up the gateway for therapy'.

Discovery – introduction of experiments

In many of our sessions, Lily and I would often begin by reviewing a problem and drawing this out in a circular diagram. This started with reviews of small problems, where a single behaviour would need to be repeated: for example, mum says something ('We're here', 'We're going now', 'Hello', 'Night night'), Henry tells Lily it has not been said right, mum has to say it again, and so it repeats. As sessions progressed, we looked in more detail at complex cycles with multi-layered repetitions or sequences (such as the cycle demonstrated in Figure 9.2). Lily was able to see that Henry was in control of these cycles and that she needed support in being able to break the chain of events.

This seemed an appropriate time to introduce the idea of setting up behavioural experiments in order to begin challenging Henry. Behavioural experiments are activities that test out the validity of thoughts in everyday situations. For Lily, this was testing out whether she could tolerate uncomfortable feelings and learn that nothing bad would happen to herself or family members. Lily was aware that Henry was often in control of what she was doing and she wanted this to change. Initially, a hierarchy of goals (in this case using a picture of a ladder) was drawn up, with items increasing in perceived difficulty: for example, reducing the 'night night' routine, 'hello' and 'goodbye' routines, and disengaging from repetitions of vocal sounds and facial expressions. As sessions progressed, it felt more important to select goals according to the needs of Lily and her family rather than stick rigidly to the hierarchy. Sometimes problematic situations occurred at home which required the family to choose and work on goals more flexibly and independently. On some occasions Lily really struggled with the combination of her OCD and TS symptoms and it was often helpful to set tiny achievable goals in order to maintain her motivation. At other times Lily was in high spirits and was keen to choose completely new goals and set up experiments to challenge Henry. All of these experiments involved non-engagement in compulsive behaviours (and exposure to difficult thoughts and feelings), varying responses to the ones dictated by Henry, or delaying responses over increasing amounts of time.

To set up an experiment, Lily was invited to identify a way in which she could challenge Henry. For example, Lily chose to refrain from saying 'Oh really' as she could see that if she did not say this, the rest of the verbal ritual would not have to be carried out. Lily's mother was encouraged to refrain from responding to Henry and engaging in the ritual. Most importantly, Lily and her mother were to unite against Henry and keep reminding each other of why they must do these very difficult experiments – essentially to see if Lily could manage the difficult feelings that Henry evoked and establish that no harm came to anyone. To encourage Lily, reward charts were set up and stickers were awarded each time she defeated Henry throughout the day (see Figure 9.5).

Creativity and fun

In order to achieve the goals set out in the experiments, sessions also involved creative methods for skills-building, allowing Lily to challenge thoughts and change unhelpful behaviours while managing distress.

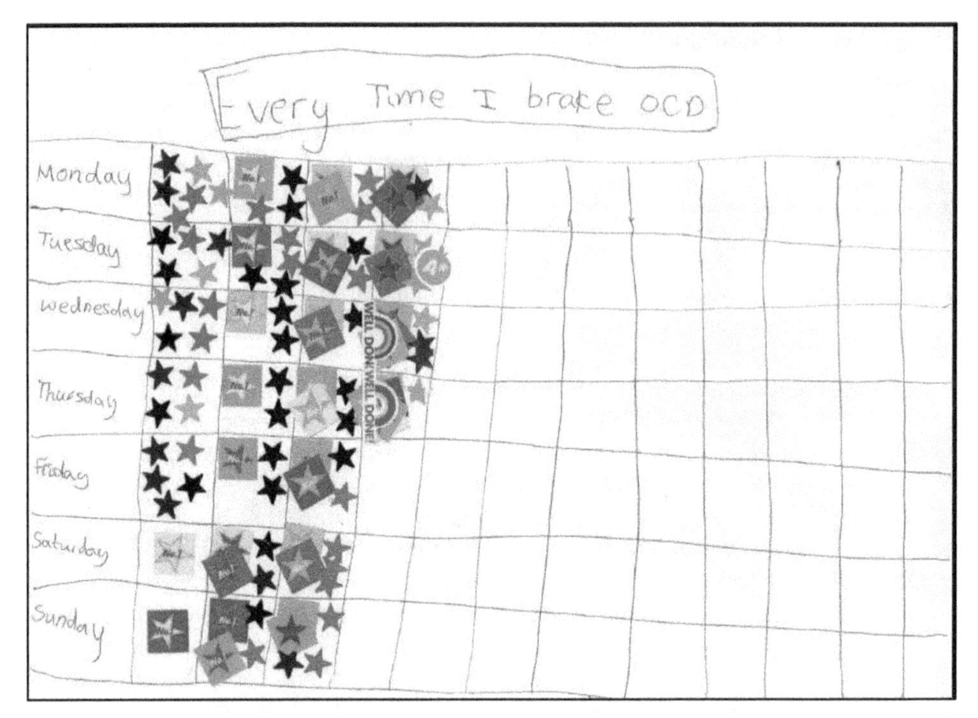

Figure 9.5 Lily's reward chart

Gaining a sense of control over Henry was, perhaps, the first and most important aspect of all our work. This began with an activity-based session where Lily was encouraged to externalise her feelings towards Henry. Lily drew pictures of Henry and demonstrated her feelings of anger and frustration towards him in several different ways. She practised shredding him, shrinking him (on the photocopier), screwing him up and putting him in the bin, drowning him in a cup of water, ripping him, stamping on him, punching him, and drawing all over him to make him look silly. This was the most animated I had seen Lily since we began our work together. Lily and her family continued to implement these ideas at home and it was regularly reported that Lily had managed to 'drop-kick Henry into the next county' when feedback was being given. Lily reports that these ideas were fun and that it was good to have something (other than herself) to blame.

At the start of our work on behavioural experiments, Lily reported that she found it '100% hard' to argue back with Henry. With this in mind, we embarked on a couple of playful sessions where we used role-play to take it in turns to argue back with Henry. Lily asked if I could take the role of 'Lily' in the first role-play so that I could model the types of things she might like to say back to Henry. Following this, Lily found it much easier to argue back with my comments from Henry. Lily could say 'Go away Henry, you're no use to me', 'Shut-up and leave me alone', 'That's not true', and 'Actually, *you* are wrong!'. In later sessions, Lily would often ask if we could write down what to say to Henry so that she could practise this again at home.

In one session, when Lily expressed worries about Henry's comments being true, we took time to explore this using games and silly questions. We looked at whether thoughts were always true, or just things that pass through our minds. We picked Henry's thoughts and then compared them with other thoughts, such as 'I am a pink giraffe' and 'That car will move if I touch this chair'. Lily was able to see the humour in this and agreed that not all thoughts are true. Lily concluded that it was important to determine if thoughts were based on fact (not feeling) and that this could be resolved by asking oneself logical questions or doing research or surveys to establish other opinions.

Maintaining change

Lily and her parents were encouraged to keep setting experiments and challenging Henry's unhelpful thoughts. At this stage in our work together, Lily's parents became important co-therapists and took the lead in identifying unhelpful cycles and setting new behavioural experiments. Having understood how they might inadvertently maintain OCD cycles through their response to Lily, they were able to step back and make choices about the longer-term management of OCD. This was an important shift and demonstrated that they were now more in control of family life, and OCD was no longer dictating what needed to happen. They no longer needed to offer Lily excessive reassurance or to take part in her distressing rituals. Sessions in the clinic became less frequent and time was used to review progress and to problem-solve any areas of difficulty.

Once Lily had a good understanding of what she needed to do in order to challenge her OCD, it became important to keep track of positive progress and reinforce the changes that she had made. At the start of each session, Lily was asked about how many stickers she had achieved. Stickers were given for goals set within our sessions as well as goals set at home, depending on the daily circumstances. As time went on, full sticker charts were swapped for prizes. In negotiation with her parents, doughnut parties were agreed and Lily found these highly motivating. Lily and Helen now look back on these experiences and report that the charts helped, even if things were not going too well, as they were a reminder that you could do well despite having a temporary blip. Lily became better at praising herself and enjoyed being able to tell Henry that he was a 'lunatic'.

Every few sessions, Lily and I would take the opportunity to look back over our previous work and remind her that she had the knowledge and skills to keep going. These sessions were helpful in increasing Lily's sense of self-efficacy and her sense of hope for the future. With little prompting, Lily wrote lists (action plans) based on things that she felt had worked well. Her most recent list consisted of the externalising techniques (shredding, stamping, or poking Henry in the eye), telling Henry to go away, arguing back with evidence, doing things differently just to confuse Henry, and asking mum to be in a mood with Henry. The last point on the list was important to follow up later in the session when Helen joined us: Lily revealed that she still felt that her family were angry with her, rather than Henry, when she got stuck in an OCD cycle.

Another useful visual method of demonstrating change and inspiring Lily to keep up her hard work was a pie chart of control. Lily drew a pie chart of how much control she perceived herself to have over OCD (see Figure 9.6). In the first pie chart

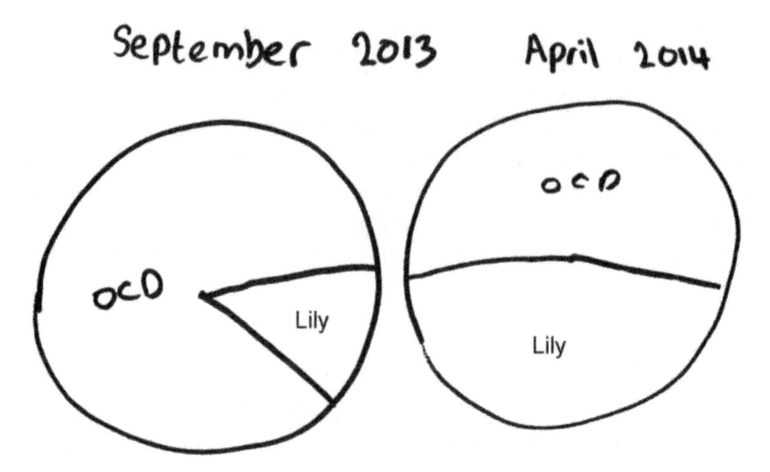

Figure 9.6 Lily's pie chart of control

(September 2013) Lily showed herself as being approximately one-eighth in control. When drawing a pie chart for April 2014, Lily demonstrated that she had taken back nearly half of the control, effectively squashing Henry back out of her mind. Lily still uses these pie charts to remind herself that she should persevere and regain control.

Outcomes

Lily is now 11 years old and has begun her first term at high school. She attends therapy appointments every 2–3 weeks and medication reviews when required. Lily continues to struggle with OCD symptoms and the interplay between OCD and TS. At times Lily finds this incredibly challenging and still questions 'why me?', but she is more able to reflect on her skills and capacities for change.

Overall, Lily has gained good insight into her disorders. She has found the externalised concept of Henry very useful, and everyday conversations still centre on Henry as an unwanted bully – someone to challenge rather than obey. Lily has worked hard to overcome lots of her stuck cycles and rarely engages in verbal rituals that require Helen to repeat 'We're here', 'Hello', or 'Night night'. Lily has also found that her OCD attacks happen less frequently, and that when they do they are more quickly overcome. I have observed Helen gain confidence in being able to say 'No' to Henry's requests and to support Lily's emotional needs without giving in to the demands of OCD. There is also more joined-up family working on tackling OCD thoughts and behaviours.

Lily was pleased to be asked what she thought about our work. Lily stated that she now felt able to tell me anything, and that it felt okay to do so. She was pleased to have someone helping, and now believed in her own skills to fight OCD. Overall, she felt that life was better – it was still hard but she felt much stronger now. She ended this discussion with 'I hope OCD will go away', and while we cannot guarantee that Lily will ever be symptom-free we will continue to offer her time and space to 'drop-kick Henry into the next county'.

Reflections

It has been a pleasure working with Lily and her family, and witnessing their journey from a place where most daily activities were interrupted by OCD to a place where everyone is working hard to regain control and treat 'Henry' as the bully that he really is. It has been a long process, requiring patience and hope from all parties, but the outcomes are now testament to the efficacy of the therapeutic approach and the determination of Lily and her family. Helen reports that 'there is now light at the end of the tunnel'.

When using cognitive behavioural interventions with children, and particularly with Lily's complex presentation, it has been important to be accepting of constantly changing situations and to be comfortable with a slower pace of therapy. Therapy sessions included repetitions of information presented in lots of different ways, and frequent reviews of skills. It was also essential to involve Lily's parents in her therapy, ensuring skills were transferred to situations outside of the clinic, and to reaffirm to Lily that her parents were working with her to break her OCD cycles. I would hypothesise that the outcome would not have been as good had Lily's parents not been able to take on the role of co-therapists.

Finally, it is important to note that this intervention would not have been possible without the support of multi-disciplinary team members. The combination of OCD and TS symptoms caused significant distress for Lily and her family, and it was important for all family members to have a space to reflect on their own feelings and responses. Medical management of OCD and TS was also crucial in alleviating some of Lily's anxiety and tics, thus enabling her to take a more active part in her treatment. This shared care will continue for the foreseeable future.

Conclusion

This chapter has attempted to provide insight into some of the ways in which CBT interventions can be adapted to meet the needs of younger children presenting with OCD. Lily's case is somewhat unusual in that she presents with OCD and TS. Lily has shared her experience of living with these disorders, and illustrations from our work together show how evidence-based therapeutic techniques can be used creatively with good effect. Lily demonstrates how children can learn to make sense of OCD and that they can draw on a range of cognitive behavioural skills, with family support. The case has allowed me to reflect on my skills as a therapist and reminded me that change is possible even in the most complex of cases.

I wish to thank Lily and her family for allowing me to share their story and for their valuable contributions to this case illustration.

Key terms

Behavioural experiments

In OCD, behavioural experiments are set up to test the assumptions one might have about an obsessional thought, that is, testing whether the thought is valid. The aim is for the individual to learn that their feared outcome is not likely to come true and to enable them to achieve a more balanced way of thinking.

Compulsive behaviours

Actions, behaviours or mental rituals performed to relieve the anxiety caused by an obsessional thought: for example, hand-washing due to a persistent fear of catching a disease.

Exposure and response prevention (ERP)

ERP is used in the treatment of anxiety disorders. The individual is confronted with the situation/stimulus that makes them anxious and encouraged to choose not to engage in the compulsive behaviour that would usually have alleviated the anxiety. The aim is for the individual to learn that their anxiety will lessen even if they do not act on their anxious thoughts.

Externalising

A process of referring to the problem in a different way, making it separate from the individual, and allowing new meanings and perspectives to develop.

Obsessional thoughts

Persistent, uncontrollable thoughts, worries or doubts, that are often disturbing to the individual. These might include worries about contamination, illness, humiliation, and they may have unwanted sexual or violent content.

Obsessive compulsive disorder

A disorder characterised by the presence of both obsessions (repetitive thoughts/ images) and compulsions (ritualistic behaviours), often underpinned by significant anxiety and beliefs that something bad might happen.

Psychoeducation

Education offered to individuals to enable them to understand issues related to their mental health problem and empower them to deal with the issues in the best way.

Tics

Tics are sudden twitches, movements, or sounds that people do repeatedly and unintentionally. A person with a motor tic might keep blinking and a person with a vocal tic might make a grunting sound.

Tourette's syndrome

A condition characterised by the presence of vocal and motor tics over a period of 12 months or more, and which often begins in childhood.

Appendix

Obsessive compulsive disorder

The *Diagnostic and Statistical Manual of Mental Disorders*, 5th edition (DSM-5: APA 2013) describes the criteria for a diagnosis of OCD.

- Firstly, both obsessions and compulsions must be present. Obsessions are persistent thoughts, images, or ideas that occur involuntarily and result in an urge to perform some kind of action. Compulsions are the repetitive behaviours performed to alleviate the anxiety or uncomfortable feelings that the obsessions cause. Both the obsessions and compulsions must significantly impact on daily functioning.
- Secondly, obsessions must be repetitive and intrusive, and cause the individual distress. Thoughts are not simply about real-life problems and attempts to suppress the thoughts or images are often unsuccessful.
- Thirdly, compulsions consist of excessive and ritualistic behaviours, e.g. hand-washing, counting, checking. Individuals believe that something bad will happen if the behaviour is not performed. Rituals often take up excessive amounts of time per day. Rituals or mental acts are used as strategies to reduce anxiety caused by the obsessive thoughts.

Tourette's syndrome

DSM-5 describes the criteria for a diagnosis of Tourette's syndrome. For a diagnosis to be made, the following must be present: two or more motor tics (e.g. blinking, twitching) and at least one vocal tic (e.g. humming, throat clearing, shouting out a word). Tics must have been present for 12 months or more, beginning before the age of 18 years, and occur several times a day, every day.

References

American Psychiatric Association (2013) *Diagnostic and Statistical Manual of Mental Disorders* (5th edn). Washington, DC: American Psychiatric Association.

Derisley, J., Heyman, I., Robinson, S. and Turner, C. (2008). *Breaking Free from OCD: A CBT Guide for Young People and Their Families.* London: Jessica Kingsley.

Friedberg, R.D. and McClure, J.M. (2002) *Clinical Practice of Cognitive Therapy with Children and Adolescents: The Nuts and Bolts.* New York: Guilford Press.

Fuggle, P., Dunsmuir, S. and Curry, V. (2013) *CBT with Children, Young People & Families.* London: Sage.

Graham, P. and Reynolds, S. (eds) (2013). *Cognitive Behaviour Therapy for Children and Families* (3rd edn). Cambridge: Cambridge University Press.

OCD-UK (2014). *Tourette's Syndrome (TS)*. Retrieved from http://www.ocduk.org/tourette-syndrome.

O'Kearney, R.T., Anstey, K., von Sanden, C. and Hunt, A. (2010). *The Cochrane Collaboration: Behavioural and Cognitive Behavioural Therapy for Obsessive Compulsive Disorder in Children and Adolescents (Review)*. The Cochrane Collaboration/John Wiley and Sons.

National Institute of Clinical Excellence (2005). *NICE clinical guideline 31. Obsessive-compulsive disorder: Core interventions in the treatment of obsessive compulsive disorder and body dysmorphic disorder.* Retrieved from http://www.nice.org.uk/guidance/cg31/resources/guidance-obsessivecompulsive-disorder-pdf.

Salkovskis, P.M. (1985) Obsessional compulsive problems: A cognitive behavioural analysis. *Behaviour Research and Therapy*, 23: 571–583.

Salkovskis, P.M., Forrester, E. and Richards, C. (1998). Cognitive-behavioural approach to understanding obsessional thinking. *British Journal of Psychiatry*, 173 (suppl. 35): 53–63.

Seiler, L. (2008) *Cool connections with cognitive behavioural therapy: encouraging self-esteem, resilience and well-being in children and young people using CBT approaches.* London: Jessica Kingsley.

Spence S.H. (1998). A measure of anxiety symptoms among children. *Behaviour Research and Therapy*, 36: 545–566.

Stallard, P. (2002) *Think Good, Feel Good: A Cognitive Behaviour Therapy Workbook for Children and Young People.* Chichester: Wiley.

10 Jane – Experience as an inpatient at a specialist unit

Rob Bode and Sarah Russell

Jane is a 13-year-old girl referred for assessment and treatment to a child and adolescent inpatient ward. Jane is the only child of Betty and Armin; they describe themselves as a quiet family who spend most of their time in each other's company. Over the past year Jane has felt unable to attend school, and her family describe her as depressed. Initially this presented as physical complaints of stomach aches and headaches for which extensive investigations revealed no physical causes. Jane describes low mood and lots of worries about attending school. These have led her to feel helpless and hopeless and contributed to thoughts that her life is not worth living. Attempts from the community team to address these issues have proved fruitless, and an intensive inpatient admission was requested.

The inpatient unit to which Jane was referred is a specialist unit, which admits children and young people alongside a parent. The unit's remit is to work with the whole family, recognising that people's difficulties do not exist in a vacuum. This allows us to work closely on familial relationships that, in the language of CBT, might be described as 'maintaining factors'. Jane had been diagnosed with depression and anxiety and prescribed an SSRI antidepressant by a private psychiatrist whom she had been seeing in the community. In addition, she was diagnosed with facial tics and was prescribed a low dose of aripiprazole. Aripiprazole is an atypical antipsychotic, and there is a growing body of evidence that supports its use as a treatment for facial tics (Ghanizadeh 2012). Jane also has a number of other unusual symptoms: she has a very selective diet that revolves chiefly around a specific brand of cheddar cheese, a specific brand of bread, tomato soup and pasta (with cheese), and includes no fruit and vegetables; she has a tendency to walk on the balls of her feet all the time; and she has an interest, which she shares with her father, Armin, in obscure German board games. Owing in part to the above specific tendencies, an additional query of a diagnosis of an autistic spectrum disorder has been raised.

For the purposes of this chapter, I will adhere mainly to the CBT approaches used to address Jane's depressive symptoms. However, as these are so closely bound with her anxiety symptoms, these will be alluded to as well. Jane was unable to say which came first, her depression or anxiety symptoms, and in a sense it does not matter, as, while problems may have originated in the past, they exist in the present. The discussion will also consider factors such as collaboration, empathy and the therapeutic relationship.

Depression in adolescents

Depression alone in children and adolescents is a relatively rare thing. According to Young Minds (2014), 1.4 per cent of 11–16-year-olds are seriously depressed. However, as clinicians we must be open to its existence and accept that it may present in a different way than depression in the adult population. Figure 10.1 presents some of the ways in which symptoms can differ between children and adults.

Diagnosis of depression in children and young people can often be missed, and there is limited evidence that primary screening tools may accurately identify depressed adolescents (Williams *et al.* 2009). Due to this difference in presentation, professionals involved in the care of young people must be alert to alternative presentations. The following points should be considered (see Paient.co.uk 2013):

- Presentation will often occur with somatic symptoms and may also have features of anxiety.
- Depression in young people may sometimes only present as poor functioning at school, socially, or at home.
- Particularly in boys and young men, antisocial behaviour may be a more prominent feature.
- Low mood may be less pervasive than in adults. Rapid mood swings often occur.
- The fact that children are able to enjoy some aspects of their life should not preclude the diagnosis of depression.

While 1.4 per cent (or about 62,000) of 11–16 year-olds are seriously depressed, a larger proportion (4.4 per cent, or about 195,000) of young people have an anxiety

Children and adolescents	**Adults**
Running away from home	Socially withdrawn
Separation anxiety and possibly school refusal	Loss of interest
Complaints of boredom	Low mood
Poor school performance	Poor self-esteem
Antisocial behaviour	Psychomotor retardation
Insomnia (often initial and middle rather than early morning wakening) or hypersomnia	Tearful
	Guilt
	Anxiety
Eating increased or decreased	Anhedonia

Source: Patient.co.uk (2013)

Figure 10.1 A comparison of symptoms of depression in children and adolescents, and in adults

disorder. There is no evidence that one disorder causes the other, but there is clear evidence that many people suffer from both disorders (Regier *et al.* 1998). Moreover, according to the National Institute for Health and Care Excellence (NICE 2009), adolescent females are twice as likely to experience depression as their male counterparts. Children and adolescents with depression also frequently have psychosocial, education and family difficulties (NICE 2005).

CBT for Jane

Establishing collaborative relationships

CBT for Jane took a number of different forms in the inpatient unit. Chiefly, it occurred through a CBT group with other children of a similar age, and more traditional one-to-one sessions with a psychiatrist supervised by a CBT therapist. For the psychiatrist, developing specific evidence-based treatments for children and adolescents represents both an area of personal interest and continuing professional development. CBT is the recommended treatment for mild to moderate depression in children (NICE 2005). Such talking treatments are usually offered before antidepressant medication is considered, but the community team felt that Jane would not be likely to engage with this as she is 'emotionally immature for her age'. Assuming this to be the case, the first task for Jane was to feel comfortable in the environment and to begin to form trusting relationships with the staff team. The presence of her mother on the unit was a great help to her in this regard, although it quickly became apparent that their relationship was somewhat enmeshed and that separation was difficult for them both. As the admission progressed, a more complex picture of low mood and poor self-esteem emerged following separation anxiety, leading to school refusal. This was also set in a context of life long parental anxiety problems.

The CBT group (Mughal 2014), named the 'Let it Go' group by the group members, was designed for a mixture of ages, typically the 5–12 years age range that the ward serves. However, we tend to consider developmental stage a better measure for suitability than the rather arbitrary boundary of age alone. The group introduces the basic model of CBT: how thoughts, feelings and behaviours all inform and impact upon each other. The group uses a number of visual aids as examples to help children to remember these principles and encourages talking as a way of moderating some of the unpleasant feelings. One of the children's favourite groups involves the use of a balloon attached to a hosepipe. The balloon represents the young person who keeps all of their feelings inside and does not talk about them to anyone. The water flowing through the hosepipe represents the build-up of their feelings such as anger, depression or anxiety. The inevitable bursting of the balloon represents the young person's unhelpful behaviour. Despite the seriousness of the topic, the children have great fun when the balloon bursts and covers them (and the staff!) in water. The children who have participated in the exercise tell us that they remember this example better than they would if it had been a solely discussion-based group. Jane was able to talk about this with her family and recognise that her thoughts, feelings and subsequent behaviour affect not only her but also those around her. These groups offer a good basis for

Food	Difficulty
Broccoli	10/10
Carrot	9/10
Blueberries	8/10
Cucumber	7/10
Tomato	6/10
Apple	5/10
Chicken soup	4/10
Strawberries	3/10
Other hard cheese	2/10
New type of cheddar cheese	1/10

Figure 10.2 Example fear ladder for Jane

further one-to-one work and represent both part of the psycho-education and collaborative aspects of CBT, fostering relationships among clients and between staff and clients.

In addition to the CBT group and one-to-one sessions, Jane was given weekly tasks by the nursing team in an attempt to challenge her rigid behaviour patterns and make her more flexible. These have included trying new foods with the aim of improving her diet, and in line with CBT principles an exposure hierarchy was created with foods that she was mildly anxious about trying at the bottom, such as different types of cheese, and working towards greater challenges such as fruit and vegetables. For children, the technical language can be a bit overwhelming, so again visual aids are employed, and an exposure hierarchy becomes a 'fear ladder'. An example of a 'fear ladder' for Jane is illustrated in Figure 10.2.

The CBT model – formulation and goal setting

Initial one-to-one sessions began once Jane had settled into the ward environment and built on the work that had begun in the CBT group. It was clear that Jane was capable of understanding the model, but she could relate best to the model where depressed and anxious feelings arise from thoughts. Jane was also able to understand that some of her behaviours, such as avoidance of situations that triggered negative thoughts and feelings, had contributed to her feelings of depression. Jane felt particularly sad about her shrinking social circle. Behavioural activation became one of the first pieces of 'homework'. The term 'homework', in my experience of working with adults, can have negative connotations, as it is associated with being at school and can therefore feel patronising. For most children, however, it is a normal part of their everyday lives and they are used to the expectations. This was also the case for Jane: she recognised that completing homework agreed in the sessions would be an important aspect of her treatment. In CBT, patients and therapists make mutual decisions about how time will be spent in a session, which problems will be discussed, and which homework assignments patients believe will be helpful (Beck Institute 2014). Jane was asked to write a list of things that she would like to change – these would act as motivators to return to when the work felt difficult. Jane identified the following goals:

1. To be able to go into town at the weekends.
2. To be able to see her friends with whom she had lost touch.
3. To get back into school as she felt that she was missing out.
4. To improve her self-confidence, so that she did not have such negative thoughts about herself.

While Jane was used to spending a lot of time with her family, this was usually in the family home, and thus a beginning point was to spend time with her family while not at home. This formed a part of behavioural activation and began to expose Jane to low amounts of anxiety to which she could habituate. Jane was aware through psycho-education that the unpleasant thoughts and feelings (anxiety) she experienced in social situations would peak before decreasing, but she needed some real-life experiences of this to prove that the theory was correct. Part of her homework following the first session was to go out for a walk with her father. Jane's father, Armin, was much better at providing Jane with reassurance than her mother, Betty. Betty would feel overwhelmed by her daughter's anxiety and was ultimately complicit in helping Jane to avoid situations that worried her or that gave way to depressive thoughts. This in itself is not abnormal for parents – when our children are young a reassuring cuddle will take away all of their worries and upset, but as they grow older, more sophisticated strategies are necessary to promote self-reliance and resilience. This will include the labelling of emotions and how they can be calmly responded to and tolerated. The child learns that if their parent can tolerate these difficult feelings, then they can also learn to tolerate them.

Betty and Armin would use the word 'depression' to describe most of Jane's emotional responses. They believed that asking Jane to do anything that she did not want to do would lead to her feeling depressed, and they had become quite disabled by this belief themselves. Family therapy was offered to the family to begin to understand the wider intergenerational issues. Betty still remained markedly reliant on her own mother for emotional support and felt unable to work in case she was needed by her brother, Jim, who has problems with substance misuse. One of the questions raised in family therapy concerned Jane's inability to go to school – this kept her mother at home (and close to her) and away from Jim. While Betty wanted to help Jim, it caused her great distress, and Jane was aware of how this affected her mother. These sessions also explored what other emotions were occurring in the family and how these in turn affected Jane. Part of this work involved naming emotions that the family felt unbearable, for example, anger.

Identifying automatic thoughts and finding ways to challenge them

The next session began with reviewing the homework. Jane had been into town at the weekend and had also gone for a walk with her father. This had been uneventful; her main worry had been that she would meet people that she knew and they would ask where she had been. When asked in session what she might be able to say, she could not come up with an answer. In exploring these thoughts further, she described her experience in class where some peers had made it clear that they did not like her. Jane believed that this was because she was different and related this to her facial tic. Thus, she believed that if these peers knew she had been in hospital, she would feel even odder. On prompting, Jane was able to identify people in her class whom she liked who treated her kindly. This represented a thinking error or cognitive distortion, namely mental filtering, in which Jane filtered out the possibility that she might bump into people who she liked from her class and who would not think badly of her. Given this worry, time was spent first thinking about how she could answer the question 'where have you been?' and then role-playing meeting a peer. Jane could not think what to say and immediately became tearful – she rated her anxiety as 10/10. At this point Jane was unable to explain how she felt or what she was thinking. The therapist imagined with her that perhaps she was worried about people would think badly of her. Jane nodded in agreement, and the therapist asked:

THERAPIST: What makes you think this?
JANE: If they know I have been off school for depression and anxiety, they will think I am stupid.
THERAPIST: And, if they did think that?
JANE: I would be embarrassed and blush and feel like running away.
THERAPIST: What would it mean if you were embarrassed?
JANE: That I am pathetic.
THERAPIST: What would it mean if you were?
JANE: That no one would want to bother with me, they would give up, you would give up on me.

Jane was able to think about how likely it was that we would give up on her and decided, on balance, that it was unlikely. In time, she was able to generate some explanations to role-play and a second member of staff was invited to be a part of the role-play. All members took it in turns playing different roles. Initially, Jane read the words in a scripted way, but through repetition was able to break away from the script and use eye contact. This was an indication that Jane was beginning to move away from her automatic thoughts and entertain new possibilities.

Homework for the next week was discussed – given the separation difficulties and enmeshed relationship with her mother, spending a night on the ward alone was suggested. Jane became very tearful saying that she felt helpless and not in control. Despite this initial reaction, she was able to calm down quite quickly when reminded of the support that would remain from the staff team and she agreed to undertake the experiment.

Experiments and their results

On reviewing the experiment to stay on the ward without her mother, Jane said that she had 'survived' and had even found it easier than she had expected. When asked to rate herself out of 5 stars as to how well she had managed without her parents, she rated herself with 3 stars. When asked how she would rate a friend who had achieved the same, she said she would give them 5 stars. In contrast, her parents, particularly her mother, had found the separation extremely difficult. Jane began to question the relationship between her own difficulties and those of her family. Jane wanted to discuss this further with her family and felt that family therapy offered the best way to do this.

Further experiments involved sending an email to a friend with the aim of re-establishing lost contacts. Jane had not checked her email since and was already predicting that her friend would not reply because she 'did not want to be friends any more'. This possibility was considered, as part of a Socratic dialogue, but Jane was able to decide that until she checked her email, there would be no point continuing to think about it. Jane was asked about what she felt she had achieved since being admitted to the ward, but said that she found it difficult to recognise her achievements, further adding that she is 'rubbish at everything'. Initially she stated that she believed this 100%, but on reviewing her successes to date she was able to revise this to 90%. Exploring this belief in more detail, Jane felt that she was 5/10 good at maths, 2/10 good at science (although she knows her teachers feel she is good at science) and 3/10 good at English. When asked to consider 'English' more closely, Jane was able to say that she was very good at reading, but was not sure about spelling and sometimes struggled to find the words she wanted. Through breaking down these beliefs into more specific thoughts, Jane revised her score and gave herself 5/10 for English.

The homework options for this session were discussed and Jane agreed to check her email to see if her friend had replied, write a list of her achievements, and to interview staff members about their adolescence – in particular, this was to elicit how many people had felt like an 'outsider' during their teenage years. Jane asked for additional homework activities as she found they helped her to structure some of the evenings when her mother was not present, and she was becoming more confident approaching staff members to ask to interview them.

In reviewing homework at the start of her next session, Jane stated that she had been in touch with her friend, Katy, via email, which she was pleased about. She had forgotten to write down her list of achievements, so this was done in the session. Jane admitted later that she had not forgotten, but that she had found it difficult both to think of things she had achieved and to acknowledge that she can do things well. With guidance and support, Jane was able to come up with a list of achievements and to say that she felt good about some of them. She was asked why she had omitted a football session that she had joined in with from her list of achievements. Jane thought she had done quite badly – however, the group facilitator had felt she was the strongest footballer there. This provided further evidence of Jane's propensity to underrate her abilities. When asked if she believed her teachers and ward staff when they gave her positive feedback, she shrugged; asked if she believed they were all wrong, she smiled, 'probably not'.

Reviewing progress

At this stage, Jane was encouraged to review progress towards her goals. She had been going into town every weekend and was beginning to find this easier. In addition, after re-establishing contact with a friend, Jane had been able to meet up and even to go with her to town. Using the metaphor of a ten-step ladder, Jane was encouraged to consider how many steps towards her goal of going to school she had climbed. She replied '3, I have come to hospital, met other children and started going to the school [pupil referral unit] here'. She agreed that the next step would be to start to reintegrate to her own school. In enquiring about her goal to improve her confidence, Jane thought that she could not have achieved the other goals without being more confident, but felt more confident because she was achieving her goals.

Fun and creativity – Blue and Blob

It made sense to Jane that our thoughts can influence the way we feel about ourselves, so this was examined further. Two creatures were created, which Jane drew on a piece of paper. One creature represented her negative thoughts about herself stating that she is 'totally rubbish at everything' (90% true). This creature was ugly and green with red spots, antennae, a big mouth with teeth and screamed very loudly, and was named 'Blob'. The other creature was small and blue with ears and wings, but had no mouth or eyes and was named 'Blue'. Jane agreed that perhaps Blob was shouting so loudly it was difficult for her to hear if anyone said good things about her. One of Blob's statements was examined again in more detail: being 'rubbish at English' or 3/10. The term 'English' was broken down into its constituent parts – reading, speaking, comprehension, vocabulary, spelling, and expressing oneself (both describing things and expressing thoughts and feelings). Jane was asked to rate herself for each of these parts. The lowest rating was for expressing thoughts and feelings, which she scored herself 6/10 for and her highest for reading, was 9/10. Jane was able to work out the average for these scores as 7.7. She was able to consider how this compared to Blob's score of 3/10 and to state that Blob was probably not right, and to see that she could not take every statement Blob made as a fact. Jane was again asked to rate the statement that she is 'rubbish at everything' – she now rated this as 60% true. When asked how she would rate a friend who had achieved the same, she said she would give them 5 stars.

To end the session a range of skills was listed that included being good at English, science and maths, but also included being good at art, working things out, being creative, compassionate, understanding, honest, being able to look after yourself and so on. Jane could see that no one could be good at everything.

Homework was discussed and agreed – to continue the list of achievements, to give 'Blue' a voice and to practise listening to him, to carry on interviewing staff about their teenage years and to examine the statement 'I am rubbish at swimming', looking for evidence to support or contradict this statement.

Managing anxious predictions: More work with Blue and Blob

For homework, Jane had interviewed a staff member, and had continued to list her achievements, but had not collected evidence for or against 'I am rubbish at swimming'. Jane stated that she had been too busy to do this and wanted to 'look' for the evidence while at the pool. The interviews of staff members had revealed that self-doubting thoughts and the feeling of 'not fitting in' were more common than she had thought. The list of achievements was added to in session and included being kind, sociable, motivated, paying attention, and completing work. Jane was reminded that a couple of sessions ago, she had believed that she was '100% rubbish at everything' and asked if that belief had changed – she now felt this to be 75% true. Some time was spent thinking about thoughts and how sometimes they can be true and sometimes untrue. She was reminded of Blob and Blue and stated that she found it hard not to believe Blob as he 'shouts' so loudly.

As a visit to her home school was imminent, Jane's predictions of how this would go were considered. Blob's views were that she would 'run out crying', 'people will talk about me', 'others will say nasty things about me', 'teachers will tell me that my work is not as expected for my age' and 'Katy will not want to be friends with me'. Jane considered which of Blob's predictions might be accurate – she thought probably none of them, except that maybe people would be talking about her. She was able to consider that probably people were talking about her and maybe it was ordinary that people were curious about her. Furthermore, Jane was able to see that going to school would give her the opportunity to confirm or refute some of these thoughts (uncertainty), but that not attending would not give any opportunity (but would be a certain result). The difficultly of tolerating uncertainty was acknowledged, but so was Jane's ability to improve at things that she initially found difficult. Homework was to arrange to meet Katy to watch *Doctor Who* or play Xbox together as these were shared interests.

Adolescence and uncertainty: unpacking anxious thoughts

When increasing the number of nights she was to spend without her mum was discussed, Jane used a similar technique to help her to manage her anxiety; she was offered the choice of some time on her own, but opted to stay in the session. The therapist wondered if a lot of 'Blob talk' (her negative thoughts about herself) was going on. Jane agreed, but said it was different. Eventually she wrote 'being on my own makes me worse, I feel depressed all the time'. She also revealed that she felt a lot of life was not worth living, but she would not act on this thought because of her parents. These thoughts had existed for many years but had become stronger since she had been admitted. Together the question why being away from her mum made her feel so low was considered: was she worried about her mum, or did she feel that she was letting her down in some way? Jane was unsure. She was able to acknowledge that she had been on a residential trip in primary school, but had not felt as bad as this, so what had changed?

Jane was growing up; she had become more aware of the instabilities in her family, specifically issues with her uncle who has addiction problems, but also not feeling as if she was a child or an adult, and of not belonging anywhere. The therapist reflected on the trust that had developed between them and that feeling safe enough to disclose these feelings is an important step and allows therapy to be a 'safe space' where such scary thoughts and feelings can be examined. Jane was asked to consider why we might encourage staying on the ward on her own. After some thought, she said 'it's supposed to increase my confidence and independence'. When asked what would help to increase her self-confidence she hesitantly acknowledged 'doing things for myself, being self-sufficient'. It is an interesting parallel that Jane's uncle, even as an adult, is heavily reliant on his sister, Jane's mother, and thus is not completely self-sufficient.

Towards the end of the session, discussion turned to planning school reintegration. Jane became visibly more relaxed at this point, and had some ideas of her own to contribute. This change in Jane's response from distress to desire further demonstrates the development of the therapeutic relationship as well as Jane's progress. She seemed engaged and motivated and clearly able to voice her views on the process. These ideas were taken back to the team and initial school visits were planned around Jane's strengths, starting with art and ICT.

Evidence of change: getting back to school

Jane felt that the school visit had been 'okay'. She still experienced 'Blob thoughts' very strongly prior to going, but these settled down quite quickly. Jane was able to acknowledge that the lessons were actually 'quite fun' and offered some further suggestions about how her attendance could increase. She was also able to talk about what would be most difficult – this included being taken to her school by her mum rather than staff members and attending classes in subjects that she felt were more challenging for her. The increased nights alone on the ward were reviewed, and Jane felt they had gone well. She had enjoyed the feeling of independence when planning her evenings for herself. In addition, she denied feeling sad at these times. In discussing a recent family therapy session, the therapist acknowledged that Jane had made her laugh with her particularly dry sense of humour. Jane was able, for the first time in therapy to acknowledge that she knew this was a positive aspect of herself – a clear and independent step away from 'I am rubbish at everything'. This turned the conversation to the difficulties that Jane can have accepting praise. Jane gave an example of an English teacher telling her that she had done 'very well in an essay'. Jane was not able to consider why this was so difficult, but could accept it better when rephrased as recognition of the effort and progress that she had made. After rephrasing, she was able to consider that achievement of perfection was therefore not necessary in order to receive praise.

In discussing further plans for school reintegration, Jane was asked if she thought that she or her mum was most anxious about her going to school. Jane felt it was her mum, and that this lead to her worrying about her mum, which made separating difficult. When asked what she thought her mum was worried about she said 'she is worried that I am worried'. It was agreed that the family therapy sessions would be the best forum to discuss this cyclical phenomenon. The session ended by adding to Jane's list of achievements and qualities.

Review and reflection: the final session

In reviewing homework, further interviewing of staff about their teenage years had been completed and she had extracted particular themes from these discussions. These were that the teenage years were not easy for anyone. Some people preferred to belong to groups and others did not, and most people felt that they had not fitted in. This had been in contrast to her predictions that no one else could understand how she felt. Jane was able to see that getting to know people better gave her a much better sense of what they thought than just 'looking from the outside'. She felt the interviews had helped her to form a different view of 'how things should be'. The perceived discrepancy between the view of 'how things should be' and 'how things are' has been a common theme in much of Jane's distress. Therefore, she determined, 'I do not necessarily need to fit in'. She could consider that everyone is different and everyone has qualities and is special in some way, but no one possesses all qualities at once, therefore, no one is perfect.

Jane spoke about her evenings without her mother. She felt that these were much better, though not great. She felt that they had increased her self-reliance, which she feels is an important part of feeling confident. In reviewing her stay on the inpatient ward, Jane produced two images to describe her time. The first was of three roaring lions decreasing in size from left to right (Figure 10.3). The lions represented how scary her stay with us was, with the final lion being more like a pussycat. The second image (not shown) was of a flower with each of the leaves and petals containing things that she has learnt from her stay, entitled 'Things that have helped me gain confidence'. These included:

Talking to more people – kids my own age and staff members
Being at the ward school
Doing more things with Mum and Dad, like going into town more often and going bowling

Figure 10.3 Jane's roaring lions

Trying new activities like football, baking and dancing
Trying new foods
Staying on my own
Being able to accept praise and accept that I'm not bad at everything
Analysing bad thoughts and defining that most of them are wrong
Learning to understand anxiety – it goes up at the start and down at the end
Learning not to compare myself to amazing people, like Leonardo Di Vinci

Conclusion

Unfortunately, in psychiatry's current paradigm, it is almost exclusively necessary to be of serious risk to oneself or others to gain admission to an inpatient bed. However, this case reminds us of the need to retain some capacity to admit people who do not pose such risks. Much of this depends on the definition of the term 'risk'. Jane risked missing out on her education, which in turn would impact on her ability to gain employment that feels meaningful to her. This would no doubt have compounded her difficulties, which, as has been alluded to, are already similar to those of her mother. Thus, the risk of this continuing through generations exists. For Jane, the ward provided a safe and containing environment that was non-threatening and non-judgemental. Here, to continue her analogy, she was able to form some roots that ultimately allowed her to grow emotionally and to blossom. One of the challenges of changes achieved in any setting is how to maintain these after therapy has ended. As discussed earlier, the remit of the ward is to work with the whole family and in doing so to address potential maintaining factors. As Jane's and her family's distress has decreased, there is a risk that their motivation to change or to maintain their gains could wane. Equally, the freedom from distress could also provide the continued motivation to sustain the changes that they have all worked so hard to create.

References

Beck Institute (2014) *Goals of Cognitive Therapy*. Available at http://www.beckinstitute.org/cognitive-behavioral-therapy-goals/ (accessed 23 November 2014).

Ghanizadeh, A. (2012) A systemic review of aripiprazole for the treatment of children and adolescents with tic disorders. *Neurosciences*, 17(3): 200–204.

Mughal, F. (2014) The "Let it Go" Group. Unpublished.

National Institute for Health and Care Excellence (2005) *Depression in Children and Young People: Identification and Management in Primary, Community and Secondary Care*. NICE Clinal Guideline 28. Available at http://www.nice.org.uk/guidance/cg28/chapter/patient-centred-care# (accessed 5 November 2014).

National Institute for Health and Care Excellence (2009) *Depression in Children*, Clinical Knowledge Summaries. Available at http://cks.nice.org.uk/depression-in-children (accessed 5 November 2014).

Paient.co.uk (2013) *Depression in Children and Adolescents*. Available at http://www.patient.co.uk/doctor/depression-in-children-and-adolescents (accessed 11 November 2014).

Regier, D.A., Rae, D.S., Narrow, W.E., Kaelber, C.T. and Schatzberg, A.F. (1998) Prevalence of anxiety disorders and their comorbidity with mood and addictive disorders. *British Journal of Psychiatry*, 34 (suppl.): 24–28.

Williams, S.B., O'Connor, E.A., Eder, M. *et al.* (2009) Screening for child and adolescent depression in primary care settings: a systematic evidence review for the US Preventive Services Task Force. *Pediatrics*, 123(4): e716–e735.

Young Minds (2014) *Mental Health Statistics*. Available at http://www.youngminds.org.uk/training_services/policy/mental_health_statistics (accessed 5 November 2014).

11 Robert – Cerebral palsy

Alison Coad

Robert is a 22-year-old man who was diagnosed with cerebral palsy at the age of 2. A definition of cerebral palsy is provided at the end of this chapter. Robert lives with his mum and dad and their two dogs; he also has an older sister who lives with her partner in the same city. The family is close, and Robert sees his sister regularly. All of the family help to support Robert in his day-to-day activities, for example by giving him lifts to appointments and social events. Robert's physical symptoms are relatively mild and he is able to walk unaided, although he does experience problems with eyesight, balance and co-ordination. Robert also experiences a high level of anxiety, and some situations, such as travelling on the bus or being in a crowded public place, can induce panic attacks.

Robert's mum reported that she had a normal pregnancy and delivery, but that she noticed that he was 'not very lively as a baby'. When he attended playschool, his teacher noticed that he tended to be withdrawn and that he found it difficult to interact with other children. His developmental milestones were delayed – he did not walk until he was 21 months old, and he was referred to a speech therapist at the age of 2 owing to difficulties in acquiring language. The speech therapist referred him for further assessments at the local community paediatrics service. He was assessed by an occupational therapist and by a paediatrician. He was diagnosed with dyspraxia and continued to receive support from the service until he reached the age of 12. At the age of 7, Robert was also referred to the local child and adolescent mental health service (CAMHS) service as he had developed a phobic fear of loud noises. He received treatment from a psychologist, which helped him to manage his symptoms in the short term. Thereafter, although he had a statement of special educational needs, he did not receive any professional input. Robert attended mainstream school and achieved 10 GCSEs, although he struggled academically and socially. Robert's mum stated that 'he was constantly bullied at high school' and that she felt that he lived with 'a constant feeling of threat'. He left school at the age of 16 and enrolled at a local college to study animal care, where he achieved a merit at BTEC diploma level 2 and a distinction in an introductory biology course. Robert describes this experience as being very positive – he developed confidence and independence, and felt very comfortable in the environment.

Since leaving college Robert has struggled to find structure and purposeful activity in his life. He does not feel confident enough to apply for paid employment, as his anxiety and his physical symptoms make it difficult for him to consider a role in a busy workplace. He is a volunteer at a local charity shop, which he greatly enjoys, and is also very interested in music. He plays guitar and has been a member of a number of bands, occasionally gigging at local events. Robert enjoys writing songs and performing them. He also has a keen interest in cookery and does a lot of cooking at home. He regularly undertakes cooking projects to raise money for a local charity for the homeless. He has a strong social conscience, and is acutely aware of the fact that there are others who are less fortunate than himself.

Psychological problems, including anxiety and difficulties in peer relationships, are relatively common for those diagnosed with cerebral palsy (Parkes *et al.* 2008). A fear of loud noises and an exaggerated startle reflex can also be a source of embarrassment and anxiety. A number of blogs make reference to this – the following extract describes symptoms very similar to those experienced by Robert:

> I feel like sometimes I'm forced to face my fears. I don't even know what my fears are anymore exactly, which sounds really stupid, but I think I'm forced to face them so often that they no longer [seem clear]. They're stupid little things too, like ... startling when I know there is a loud noise coming and being laughed at for it.
>
> (Erin, 23 May 2010. Chalk and Cheese: Life as a Teenager With Cerebral Palsy, http://bit.ly/1Ib8QRX)

This symptom is thought to be linked to sensory processing or motor problems and is not, therefore, directly linked to anxiety. It was this issue that led Robert to seek further therapy, as it was affecting his quality of life and his ability to engage in day-to-day activities. He had become very self-conscious about his reaction to loud noises, which compounded his anxiety.

Robert and I met when a family friend suggested that I might be able to help him to work on these fears. At the age of 22, Robert no longer qualified for help from CAMHS, and although the local mental health service provides a youth service which caters for the needs of those up to the age of 25, Robert's symptoms were not severe enough to meet the criteria of that service. I therefore met Robert on a privately funded basis, although this left me feeling conflicted as he is in receipt of benefits and has a very small income. We negotiated a small fee per session which Robert felt was fair, and which, as Robert's mum pointed out, helped him to feel independent in his ability to fund his own treatment.

Early meetings: partnership working, collaboration and pitching things at the right level

Robert attended his first appointment at my clinic. He was accompanied by his parents. He explained that he had decided to seek help with his phobia as he was becoming increasingly aware of the ways in which it was limiting his enjoyment of life. Naturally, his parents were also concerned, reporting that Robert's mood had become low and that he seemed to find it difficult to motivate himself to do things that he had achieved relatively easily in the past – travelling on a bus, for example. Robert was aware of the ways in which his anxieties were affecting him, and had sought help through the local Wellbeing Service. Unfortunately he did not feel comfortable with his therapist and did not return after his initial appointment. Following an hour's discussion, during which I was able to gather basic assessment information and Robert had the chance to get to know me a little, we agreed that we would work together on a weekly basis in the first instance. I explained that I would work with Robert to establish some clear goals for therapy, and that we would use graded exposure techniques to help him to tackle his fears. Robert's previous therapist in CAMHS had worked with him in this way, so he was familiar with the idea, and knew that it was manageable for him. He had some very positive memories of sessions at the local CAMHS clinic which involved the use of party poppers to provide the loud noise. Robert's sister had joined in with the sessions and had encouraged him to move towards the source of the noise until he had been able to sit next to her when she set off the party popper. Robert remained tolerant of party poppers, but found it difficult to generalise his learning to other situations. He also continued to experience anxiety about unexpected loud noises, which affected his confidence in a wide range of social situations, from walking down to the local shop to attending performances at the theatre or cinema. By the end of our first meeting, we had established a clear idea of how we could work together and what we could expect of each other.

One of our first joint decisions was that we would carry out our sessions in public places, rather than at Robert's home or at my clinic. We agreed that Robert needed opportunities to be out in public with someone other than a family member as this would enable him to identify specific fears. (When with his family, Robert felt safe and protected – and he was aware that he would be more likely to avoid challenging situations.) Being out in public helped Robert to gather evidence about the likelihood of the occurrence of sudden loud noises – and of how he would be able to manage the anxiety that these events could trigger. It also enabled him to identify other anxiety-provoking situations that he might want to work on. Looking back over around 15 sessions which we have undertaken 'out and about', Robert acknowledges that there have been very few situations where he has felt unable to manage his anxiety; and there have been no problems with unexpected loud noises so far. We have a long-term plan to attend a fireworks display together, although we need to do some more work on day-to-day goals before we get to this!

Our initial outings involved tasks such as visiting shops, going to cafés and ordering coffee, and walking in crowded environments together. Robert created a hierarchy of tasks that he wanted to be able to achieve, starting with shopping in small quiet shops and building up to visiting the city's main shopping mall and a busy café. This hierarchy is illustrated in Figure 11.1.

We agreed on an anxiety rating system (0–10) which we could use as shorthand between us while we were in the midst of experiments. 'What number?' is an easier and more discreet question than 'How are you feeling now?' or 'How's the anxiety?' Robert wanted to be able to do the things that he saw others of his age doing: he did not want to be identified as 'someone who needs extra help'. It was therefore important that the activities that we worked on together were as spontaneous as possible, and that we had ways to adapt what we were doing without Robert feeling that he had in some way failed or made a mistake. The collaborative nature of our work is captured in the following text message, which illustrates Robert's increasing ability to add to the agenda for our sessions:

> Maybe we could make the next appointment a chat in the city … Next following appointment maybe work on buses when I'm feeling more confident about it
>
> (16 March 2014)

Numbers refer to marks out of 10, with 10 representing the worst fear and zero representing no fear.

Activity	Score
Going on the bus	9
Watch a play at the theatre	7
Open mic night	6
Shopping mall on my own	6
Go for a coffee with Alison	6
Visit the market with Alison	5
Watch a film at the cinema	5
Shopping mall with someone else	5
Go into the baker's with Alison to buy a pasty	4

Figure 11.1 Robert's first hierarchy

Fun, creativity and discovery: the balloon experiment, and a visit to the theatre

Robert and I had agreed very clearly that the pace of our work would be determined by him. Over the weeks it became apparent to both of us that Robert had a tendency to avoid situations that triggered his fear of public embarrassment. The quotation above, which suggests putting off the bus journey to a later date, is an example of this. His social anxiety was maintained by self-focused attention (Clark and Wells 1995); he was convinced that other people would notice his symptoms of anxiety, and judge him as being odd or weak. Our first goal was therefore to enable Robert to feel more comfortable when he was out in public. He acknowledged that there had been times in the recent past when he had felt a great deal more confident. His experiences as a student at a local higher education college, in particular, had been helpful to him in developing social confidence and in feeling that he was able to live his life in a way that connected him to other young people of his age. For the first time in his memory of formal education, he felt part of a peer group who did not judge him. Since leaving college, however, Robert's confidence had declined and he and his family noticed that his fear of loud noises had become more of a problem for him. Robert's mum described family days out which had resulted in panic for Robert, and distress for his parents who felt helpless and frustrated by the situation. A day trip to a local history day unexpectedly included a replication of cannon fire, and Robert could not cope with the level of noise and had to leave; and a Halloween prank, when friends of Robert's sister burst into the house shouting and laughing, was vividly recalled as being traumatic. Robert explained how these events left him feeling inadequate and weak, and 'a nuisance'. His family struggled to understand how to support him and to understand why his responses were so acute. We therefore agreed that some work on this fear – which we both felt was at the level of a phobia – would support our aim of improving Robert's social confidence. Using the work undertaken in CAMHS as a starting point, we devised an experiment which would enable Robert to increase his tolerance of loud noises. In preparing for the experiment, I undertook some research and discovered that hypersensitivity to sensory stimuli can be a part of the symptom profile for cerebral palsy. I shared this information with Robert and he was surprised and reassured to learn that he was not alone with this worry. This gave him added confidence to tackle our balloon experiment.

The balloon experiment

We agreed that this experiment should be conducted at Robert's home, as it was one of the most anxiety-provoking challenges that we had undertaken, scoring 8/10 on the anxiety scale. The experiment involved exposure response prevention (ERP), that is, working our way up a hierarchy of tasks which became increasingly challenging, while helping Robert to change his response to the fear stimulus. In short, this means sticking with the situation rather than trying to escape it, so that the anxiety response progressively lessens. The stages of the experiment, and the results of each stage, are described in Figure 11.2.

By the second session of ERP, Robert was able to hold an inflated balloon and pop it with a pin. At the outset of the experiment, Robert was very critical of himself and became frustrated when his anxiety prevented him from completing every stage within one session: 'It's stupid, I feel so stupid … it's just a balloon, I know it can't hurt me, but

Stage 1-making a loud noise with a pan and a wooden spoon

Step	Initial response	Response after 5 min
Robert hitting pan (with spoon)	2	2
Alison hitting pan in hallway–loudly	7	2
Alison hitting pan in room–quietly	1	0
Alison hitting pan in room–loudly	7	4
Alison hitting pan next to R–quietly	2	1
Alison hitting pan next to R–loudly	8	4

Stage 2-the balloon experiment

Step	Week 1	Week 2
Alison blowing up balloon	4	0
Alison popping balloon in next room, telling R when to expect	3	0
Alison popping balloon in next room, not telling R when	8	2
Alison popping balloon in same room, telling R when to expect	7	2
Alison popping balloon in same room, not telling R when	5	1
R blowing up balloon	6	2
R popping balloon	not applicable	2

Figure 11.2 Robert's hierarchy: the balloon experiment

I just can't do it.' We talked about the experience of phobic anxiety, and I reiterated the points that we had covered prior to the experiment: phobias induce intense fear, and fear is a very basic response which engages the 'instinctive' brain. Robert was able to acknowledge this, and agreed that we would repeat the experiment at our next meeting a week later. The second session produced some dramatic results – a significant drop in anxiety levels which Robert had not been expecting, and which reduced him to tears. He simply could not believe that he had achieved so much in such a short space of time.

In order to remind Robert of the steps that we took in the balloon experiment, I recorded the steps in a series of video clips, and provided him with copies of the clips which he could look over between sessions. Later that day, I received the following text message from Robert:

> Thanks so much for today Alison it means so much for me to get over this phobia.
>
> (21 February 2014)

A visit to the theatre

Another of Robert's goals was to be able to attend a theatre performance. Although he was happy to visit a theatre for live music events, Robert was extremely anxious about the idea of watching a play. When we discussed these worries in a little more depth, it became apparent that Robert's anxiety stemmed from a mixture of fears – unexpected loud noises, crowds of people, a formal seating arrangement which might make a quick exit difficult, and the fear of 'panicking and showing myself up'. Once again we thought about breaking the task down into manageable steps and we came up with the idea of asking for a backstage tour of a local small theatre, to give Robert the chance to imagine himself as part of the audience and to demystify the process. I agreed to make contact with the venue manager and a date was agreed.

Robert was a little nervous as we made our way to the theatre, as he was unsure what to expect. I anticipated a brief chat about the history of the theatre and a tour of the empty auditorium. In fact, we were given a detailed tour including backstage, green room, props room and costume wardrobe, plus a chance to walk out on stage and to look at the sound and light equipment. I was fascinated by the whole experience and was caught up in the enthusiasm of the theatre manager and his staff. Robert, as I learned later, was also fascinated but, unbeknown to me at the time, a number of aspects of the experience were very challenging for him. The costume wardrobe was located at the very top of the building and to reach it we had to climb a series of tiny staircases. Robert managed to do this without any obvious difficulty, although I was aware that enclosed spaces combined with meeting a number of new people might trigger higher levels of anxiety. The staircases were also quite tricky to negotiate as they were so narrow and steep, and I was mindful of Robert's sight and balance problems.

After the visit we had a 'debrief' when Robert was able to tell me that he had struggled with feelings of panic when we climbed up to the costume wardrobe. He had carried on with the tour rather than disclose his anxiety to me because he did not want to feel embarrassed or appear ungrateful to the theatre staff. We had an interesting discussion about the line between pushing through anxiety and avoiding situations that would induce anxiety. Robert felt that he had managed to achieve things that he would not have volunteered to do, and was able to recognise that sometimes it was possible to push through anxiety even though his instinctive response was to escape. I was also able to confirm that his feelings of panic had not been evident, even though I had been alert to the possibility and had been observing him for signs of stress. This gave Robert some food for thought in respect of his fears about the way that others perceived him when he felt anxious. He was also able to be honest about his response to the trip: 'I don't know if I'd be able to do that again and I'm not sure about going to the theatre … but I'm really pleased I managed to get through today.' We agreed that this experiment had probably been a little more challenging than we had imagined it would be, but that we had both learned from the experience – and in the process, had some fun and learned a lot about theatre.

Change methods – understanding more about thoughts, feelings and behaviours

Much of the work described above is based on behavioural change – the focus was very much on improving Robert's functioning as an independent young adult. Part of the rationale for the use of challenges and experiments was also to help Robert to gain a clear understanding of the ways in which his view of himself, of the world and of other people (Beck's cognitive triad) could influence what he felt able to do. One of the difficulties that Robert struggled with in his daily life was motivation. He described how he experienced phases of low mood which made the simplest of daily activities – getting up at a regular time, eating well and general self-care - difficult to achieve. On these days, Robert reported that he would find it difficult to get out of bed, and when he did get up he tended not to pay attention to self-care tasks such as eating and drinking. The physical sensations which resulted from low blood glucose and inadequate hydration made Robert even more lethargic and low in mood. We talked about the ways in which Robert could improve his care for himself, and spent time thinking about the influence of physical symptoms such as hunger, thirst and tiredness. The following text message demonstrates how Robert has taken this on board and, most importantly, has recognised that bad days don't have to mean disaster:

> today has not been too good I woke up late this morning and have not had a drink all day. Yesterday woke up early and had lots of drink and felt loads better. I am not going to be harsh on myself over today though as things can still improve. I am going to have a shower drink lots of fluids and have something to eat in a bit which should make me feel much better
>
> (1 August 2014)

A text the following day, in response to a message from me asking how Robert was feeling, confirmed that the strategy was successful:

> Today is much better thanks
>
> (2 August 2014)

Setting daily tasks such as completing household chores, planning and cooking a meal or taking the dogs for a walk also became part of Robert's regular routine. At times it is still difficult for Robert to stick to these objectives, but the difficult days have become less frequent, and Robert feels that he has strategies to tackle his low mood before it becomes too established. These strategies include practical steps such as the daily objectives described above (this is sometimes referred to as activity scheduling), and also an increased awareness of difficult thoughts and how to respond to them. Robert has noticed that he sometimes experiences negative thoughts about himself such as 'You're weak', 'You're never going to be really independent' and 'You're not as good as other people'. Through our work together, Robert has been able to challenge these thoughts by gathering evidence that does not support them. We have achieved this through talking about Robert's achievements, both in and out of sessions, and by testing out the anxious thoughts through the experiments described above. An example of the ways in which Robert has successfully challenged anxious thoughts is demonstrated by the following text messages which Robert sent me as we made arrangements to try a journey on the bus together:

> I have been so happy these past weeks that I think I could also fit in a bus journey if that's ok with you?
>
> I was thinking we could take the bus from the bottom of our road to [the local shopping area] to start with? I'm feeling so good now I'm a new person
>
> (15 August 2014)

We also have a shared interest in music and literature, which has helped Robert to recognise that he has a connection to the experiences of others. Discussing the impact of a novel such as Harper Lee's *To Kill A Mockingbird* (a favourite of both of us) has provided a shared language, both between Robert and myself and between us both and a wider population of readers. Music serves a similar function. Robert writes and performs his own songs, and having had the opportunity to see him on stage, I have witnessed the way in which the desire to perform can override everyday anxiety. Music and literature enable Robert to recognise himself as a member of society – a person who has both an inner and an outer world. This is an important aspect of the cognitive change which is helping Robert to see the world in a new way. The acknowledgement of shared interests and experiences reduces the sense of 'being different' which has been so unsettling for Robert. As his ability to focus attention on the world around him grows, the anxiety which stems from unhelpful thoughts and feelings (Robert's internal world) reduces.

Pulling things together: formulation

While writing this case study, I realised that I have not shared the concept of formulation with Robert. I have thought about Robert's situation from a range of perspectives – as a cognitive behaviour therapist, where diagnoses such as specific phobia and social anxiety provided a starting point; as a clinician with a special interest in anxiety and depression in young people; as a parent, with all of the protective tendencies which are part of that role; and as an individual who has also found the world overwhelming at times. Shared interests in music and literature add another dimension to the therapeutic relationship. For me, formulation provides a 'road map' to guide my thinking, and to work out connections between the various aspects of the narrative of an individual. A disorder-specific model is too rigid for the work that Robert and I have undertaken, although models such as Clark and Wells (1995) have helped me to understand important aspects of Robert's experience. The most useful formulation for Robert is one which takes account of a range of factors, and which recognises the impact of physical, emotional and social factors. Moorey's (2010) six aspects formulation is a useful model for this and is used as the basis for the formulation illustrated in Figure 11.3.

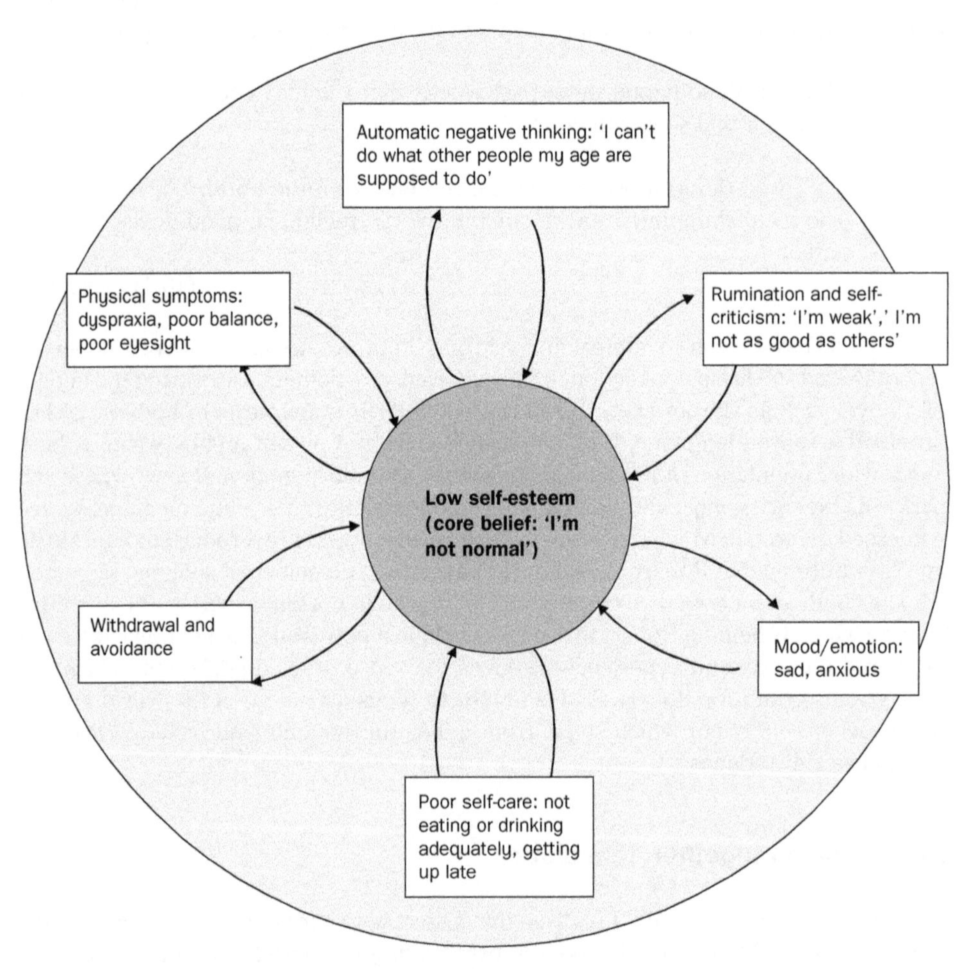

Figure 11.3 Robert's experience of cerebral palsy

Plans for the future

Robert and I recognise that our work is ongoing, and that it is likely that we will continue to meet for some time yet. Our appointments have decreased in frequency, and we have reached a stage where Robert sets his own goals and asks for my support when he feels he needs reminders and recaps of strategies that have proved useful for him. 'Booster' therapy sessions are often helpful, especially for young people, who are developing emotionally and intellectually. Therapeutic techniques may need to be adapted as the individual's skills grow and their needs change. Robert's latest targets, for example, include using a taxi and shopping in larger, busier stores independently. Our appointments are arranged according to Robert's needs, giving him control over what he chooses to work on and when.

Robert hopes to make a career using his cookery skills and at the time of writing is investigating the possibility of finding an apprenticeship in the catering trade. A final quotation from Robert captures his sense of achievement and provides a summary that is moving in its simplicity and clarity:

> I have been much happier since we last met and have done many things I thought not possible.
>
> (28 July 2014)

Postscript

During the process of working together on this case study, Robert has become more aware of the role which cerebral palsy has played in the development of his anxiety. As a part of this process he decided to read an autobiography written by Francesca Martinez, a stand-up comedian and actress who, to use her personal term for cerebral palsy, is 'wobbly' (Martinez 2014). Robert invited me to read Francesca's account as he felt that the book could help me to understand his experiences:

> [the book] is really funny at times but also included a lot of things which affect me. I was wondering whether you might be interested in taking a look yourself in order to better understand the condition.

I have read Francesca's book and not only have I learned a great deal, but I thoroughly enjoyed it too. Robert and I are reformulating our approach to give more emphasis to the effects of cerebral palsy on his life. For the first time, Robert has made clear connections between his physical health, his resulting social isolation, and the effects of this on his mental health. Francesca's open and honest account of her experiences, good and bad, has inspired Robert and has enabled him to see what is happening for him in a different light. We have also been able to identify a core belief which is the source of much anxiety for Robert ('I'm not normal'). We are agreed that our next sessions will focus on gradually modifying this belief.

This seems to me to be a perfect example of the value of narrative accounts, and of thinking creatively. It also demonstrates the ways in which collaboration, curiosity and shared learning can lead to therapeutic change.

Glossary

Cerebral palsy. A condition that affects muscle control and movement. It is usually caused by an injury to the brain before, during or after birth. Children with cerebral palsy have difficulties in controlling muscles and movements as they grow and develop. In the UK, cerebral palsy affects about one in every 400 children. It can affect people from all social backgrounds and ethnic groups. There is no cure for cerebral palsy, but physiotherapy and other therapies can often help people with cerebral palsy become more independent (see http://www.scope.co.uk).

References

Clark, D.M. and Wells, A. (1995) A cognitive model of social phobia. In R.G. Heimberg (ed.) *Social phobia: Diagnosis, assessment, and treatment.* New York: Guilford Press.

Martinez, F. (2014) *What the **** is Normal?!* London: Virgin Books.

Moorey, S. (2010) The six cycles model: Growing a 'vicious flower' for depression. *Behavioural and Cognitive Psychotherapy*, 38: 173–184.

Parkes, J., White-Koning, M., Dickinson, H.O., Thyen, U., Arnaud, C., Beckung, E., Fauconnier, J., Marcelli, M., McManus, V., Michelsen, S. I., Parkinson, K. and Colver, A. (2008) Psychological problems in children with cerebral palsy: a cross-sectional European study. *Journal of Child Psychology and Psychiatry*, 49: 405–413.

12 Hannah – Epilepsy

Alison Coad

Background

Hannah is a 20-year-old woman who was diagnosed with childhood absence epilepsy (CAE) at the age of 6. At the age of 18, Hannah's symptoms changed and she began to experience tonic-clonic seizures. Around 10 per cent of young people diagnosed with CAE will go on experience seizures in adulthood.

Epilepsy is defined as 'a common neurological disorder characterised by recurring seizures' (National Institute for Health and Care Excellence (NICE) 2012: 7). A seizure 'happens when there is a sudden burst of intense electrical activity in the brain. This is often referred to as epileptic activity. The epileptic activity causes a temporary disruption to the way the brain normally works, so the brain's messages become mixed up.' It is estimated that over 600,000 people in the UK live with a diagnosis of epilepsy (Epilepsy Action 2013).

Initially, Hannah's symptoms were well controlled by medication and the most troublesome issues were absence seizures, which are characterised by a brief loss of awareness which can often go unnoticed, even by the person experiencing them. At the time of Hannah's diagnosis, her paediatrician was confident that her symptoms would resolve as she matured, and that by adolescence she would be seizure-free. She was able to attend mainstream school without any problems and was successful in gaining GCSEs and A levels. However, when Hannah left home to go to university at the age of 18, she began to experience more severe symptoms and had a series of serious seizures which required hospital attendance. It became clear that her epilepsy was unlikely to resolve as had been hoped and that Hannah needed to undergo further tests and treatment. Understandably, both Hannah and her parents found this to be very distressing. After completing one term at university, Hannah decided to give up her course and return home until her symptoms could be stabilised.

Hannah lives with her parents and her younger brother, Sam, in a village just outside a major city. Hannah's parents are both medical professionals. The family are close and have a lot of contact with extended family, in particular with Hannah's maternal grandmother and aunt. Hannah's maternal grandfather also experienced symptoms of epilepsy, although this was the result of a head injury. In his later life, Hannah's grandfather was also diagnosed with dementia and needed specialist residential care. Hannah stated that at times she was fearful of visiting her grandfather, as she found it difficult to witness his epilepsy; in spite of this Hannah remained deeply loyal to her grandfather and expressed great affection for him. She remembered the way in which her grandfather's seizures could be very difficult to manage and wondered if this memory made it particularly difficult for Hannah's mum to witness her daughter's seizures:

> if [grandad] had a fit, he didn't know his strength … I think that scared [mum] so maybe that puts her off [when I have a fit]. I know she's thinking about it but she won't tell me.

Following her withdrawal from her university art course, Hannah took the decision to study locally with the aim of training to become a nurse. She enrolled at the local college on a part-time foundation science course and also continued to work part-time as an administrator at a local medical practice.

Hannah was referred to me following her return from university as her mother was concerned about the effect of the impact of frequent seizures on Hannah's mood. Hannah's neurologist adjusted her medication, which reduced the frequency of seizures but did not eliminate them completely. As a consequence Hannah became very anxious about undertaking activities that she had previously managed without concern. Everyday activities such as travelling on public transport, buying a cup of coffee and being able to hold her newborn cousin became fraught with anxiety. Hannah was fearful of embarrassment, but also of injuring herself or others as a result of a seizure. She lost confidence and began to exhibit symptoms of clinical depression, for which her GP prescribed antidepressant medication.

There is evidence to suggest links between epilepsy and common psychiatric diagnoses such as anxiety and depression, and more recently research has been undertaken into possible links between panic attacks and seizures (Munger Clary 2014). A diagnosis of chronic illness has implications for many aspects of the affected individual's life – not just in terms of health, but also with regard to education, employment opportunities and social interactions. It is not surprising to learn that a strong correlation exists between chronic illness and psychological difficulties (see, for example, Eiser 2000). I had a lot of experience in the treatment of depression, but no knowledge of epilepsy. I had a lot to learn, but the positive aspect of my lack of knowledge was that Hannah and I were in some ways on an equal footing, each with our respective areas of expertise.

Building a relationship: joining our expertise

Hannah presented as a mature and reflective young woman with very strong personal values. She acknowledged that attending therapy felt a little strange, as she was such an independent person who had always been able to resolve difficulties with the support of her family and friends. These factors are recognised as important in the management of epilepsy symptoms (NICE 2012), and it was apparent from the outset that Hannah was secure in the knowledge that her loved ones would support her. However, she was also able to recognise that she needed some help in clarifying her thoughts and feelings following the dramatic changes in her symptoms, and the effects of those changes on her daily life. Hannah described a close relationship with her parents and talked about how guilty she felt for the worry that her epilepsy had caused them, particularly in the last weeks before she returned home from university. She was also very disappointed at having to give up her studies, and fearful about what this decision would mean for her future. I had no experience of working with young people with epilepsy, and so had my own concerns about whether I would be able to offer Hannah the right support. Our first few sessions were therefore a learning experience for both of us. Hannah described the way in which the reactions of those around her sometimes added to her distress when she experienced a seizure. On one occasion, for example, a fellow student had told Hannah that witnessing Hannah's seizure had 'left her traumatised'. This compounded Hannah's sense of anxiety, and also the feelings of guilt which she experienced as a result of her epilepsy. At the opposite end of the scale, it was also difficult for Hannah when those around her were over-protective. Hannah described a recent situation in the workplace when she had admitted to feeling unwell – this had resulted in repeated enquiries about her well-being, to the point where

> I thought they were going to put everyone's coats on the floor around me in case I had a fit. It was so embarrassing.

The effect of both experiences was to increase Hannah's tendency to hide her symptoms whenever possible, and to hide herself from public view if she suspected that a fit was about to occur. As Hannah acknowledged, this response could lead to increased risk of harm – fits can lead to loss of consciousness, with obvious implications for the safety of the individual concerned. On one occasion, Hannah experienced warning signs of a seizure while she was revising in a quiet room at college. Warning signs can include experiencing unusual smells or tastes, a general feeling of unease, and tingling sensations. Hannah's response to this was to head to the toilets and lock herself into a cubicle where she experienced a complex partial seizure. Fortunately, Hannah recovered consciousness without having sustained any serious injury, and she was able to contact her mother, who arranged to collect her from college. On returning home, Hannah described what had happened to her father, who was very concerned to hear of Hannah's decision to lock herself into a toilet cubicle. He explained that a patient of his had done the same and had fallen to the floor during a seizure; this resulted in a blocked airway. In the time it took to unlock the cubicle, the patient had died of asphyxia. Hannah described her father's account as 'a wake-up call'. She agreed with her father that her actions could have put her at risk; should the situation arise again, she might still go to the toilets, but she would not lock herself into a cubicle. As Hannah realised, her fear of embarrassment had affected her ability to prioritise her safety. Although at this stage she did not feel able to take the risk of having a seizure in public, or to seek help when she experienced early symptoms, she recognised that her father's concerns were valid and adjusted her behaviour accordingly. This is a good example of the way in which Hannah's growing maturity led to a shift in perspective and behaviour. Hannah simultaneously acknowledged her parents' concerns and her need to take increasing responsibility for her own safety. The ability to hold both issues in her mind was indicative of a level of acceptance of the complexity of the situation which, to me, boded well for her ability to manage a rapidly shifting profile of symptoms. This point is explored further below, as a part of the discussion relating to cognitive and behavioural change.

Hannah was acutely aware of the dual impact on her parents of not only adjusting to her leaving home, but also the coincidence of this key life event with the dramatic change in her symptoms. From early on in our relationship, I was therefore aware of the importance of understanding my own concerns about Hannah's health and equipping myself with the knowledge that I needed to be able to relate to her with confidence. I undertook some research about how to respond if Hannah experienced a seizure during one of our sessions, and talked this through with Hannah to check that I was on the right lines. Hannah was patient with me during this process and, although I suspect it was tedious for her to field my very basic questions, did not betray any signs of dismay. I was grateful to Hannah for her tolerance and for the reassurance that she offered; for me, there was a sense of a reversal of roles, which fitted well with my desire to establish a truly collaborative relationship. Along the same lines, I also recognised the importance of treating Hannah as an independent young adult. I remained alert to the possibility that I might adopt a parental role in response to my concerns to keep Hannah safe.

Change methods: behavioural and cognitive strategies

Given the fact that there appeared to be a link between increased stress and more frequent seizures, I needed to review my standard approaches to the management of anxiety symptoms. Treatment strategies for anxiety generally involve gradual exposure to stressful situations, with the aim of increasing tolerance of both physical and emotional symptoms of stress. The client is then enabled to remain within situations which have previously been avoided. This is a process known as exposure response prevention. For Hannah, these experiments carried a risk of inducing a seizure. The standard question 'what's the worst that can happen?', which encourages the client to acknowledge and hopefully challenge catastrophic thinking, therefore held a very different meaning for Hannah, and for me as a professional responsible for her care. Depending on the circumstances, 'the worst that could happen' involved a risk of serious injury. We therefore needed to be creative, but also relatively cautious, when working on strategies for behavioural change. Hannah acknowledged that she was restricting her activities as a result of her fear of having a seizure. The ways in which this affected her day-to-day life varied from tasks as simple as holding a cup of hot coffee to taking decisions based on subtle distinctions in physical symptoms (for example, if Hannah experienced a feeling of lightheadedness, she needed to establish whether this was this panic, or a precursor to a seizure). I needed to learn from Hannah's expert knowledge of her own symptoms, and to make sure that I understood the ways in which Hannah and her family had learned to manage the balance between safety and being able to enjoy family activities such as travelling and sailing. A key part of this process was eliciting the meaning of Hannah's fearful thoughts, in order that we could work out how best to manage them. A degree of acceptance was certainly necessary – there were undoubtedly valid grounds for some of Hannah's fears. However, we also needed to be alert to unhelpful patterns of thoughts, and perhaps look at ways in which Hannah might learn to respond differently to intrusive thoughts. Mindfulness techniques, which enable the individual to 'take a step back' from difficult thoughts,

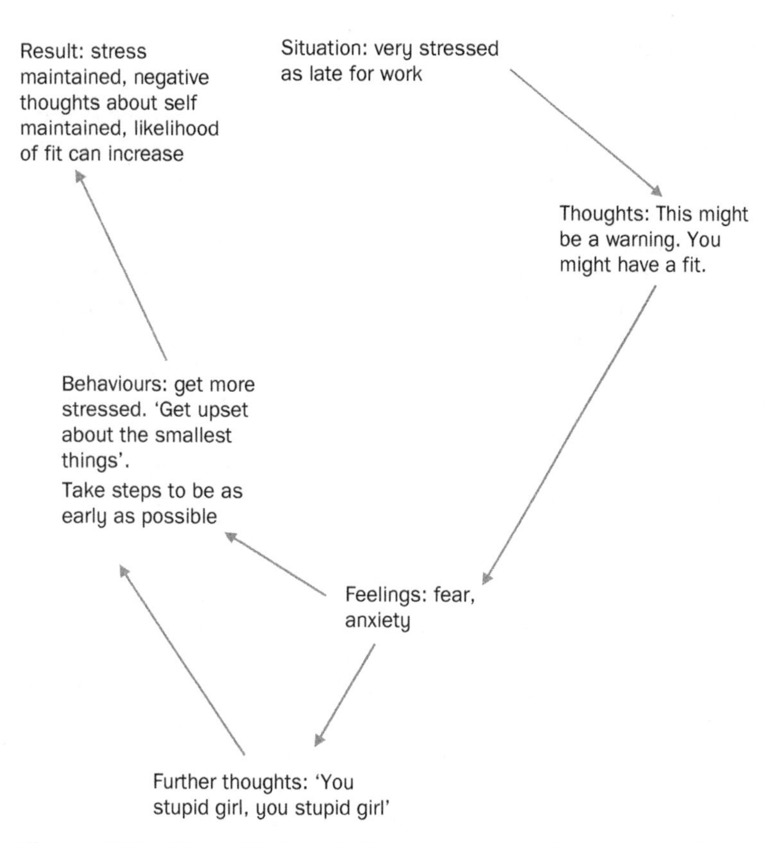

Figure 12.1 Hannah's formulation: a typical maintenance cycle

was one approach which I felt might be helpful; Hannah was able to use some techniques from mindfulness to help her to cope with insomnia.

We devised a basic formulation derived from our discussions about the activities that Hannah realised that she was avoiding as a result of her anxiety. A diagram of this formulation is shown in Figure 12.1.

Hannah worked on her avoidance at her own pace. Owing to the unpredictable nature of her seizures, she continued to experience high levels of anxiety, but she was largely successful at maintaining her achievements. Although anxiety can lead to severe and debilitating symptoms, including physical symptoms, repeated exposure to anxiety-provoking situations usually leads to habituation and an associated reduction in anxiety levels. For Hannah, anxiety regularly served a genuinely protective function. If a seizure could result in serious injury or death, then it is appropriate that the brain should register a threat and respond accordingly. For Hannah, it was not a simple process to distinguish between genuine danger and false alarms, and it took a lot of courage to repeat activities such as holding hot coffee in a public place. Hannah's family were very encouraging, and helped her to achieve goals which were essential for her to participate in family activities – for example, climbing into the rubber dinghy which was the means of reaching the family's sailing boat. When she had achieved this, Hannah reported that she cried with joy.

Creative elements

In contrast to my work with many of my young patients, all of the therapy sessions arranged with Hannah took place within the clinic room. Although I felt that we developed a good rapport over the course of our sessions, which were punctuated by easy 'non-task' discussions and lots of evidence of humour, I did not suggest strategies such as behavioural experiments in public places. In retrospect, I recognise that I was less directive and much more speculative in my approach than usual. Perhaps this was related to the fact that Hannah was a mature and confident young woman with a very supportive network of family and close friends. It soon became clear that the aim of our sessions was to enable Hannah to arrive at her own solutions, with a light touch from me here and there. Theoretically, this is the way I would like every therapeutic relationship to be. Realistically, every client comes to therapy with a unique set of skills, circumstances and levels of support, and it is essential for the therapist to tailor their input to fit these needs. I realise on reflection that my work with Hannah emphasised gaining an intellectual understanding of her situation. There was a lot of checking understanding, and rehearsing key points such as 'avoidance perpetuates anxiety'. It was a surprise to me that I had accepted this without question; as other case studies in this volume demonstrate, my approach often involves work outside the clinic to enhance 'real-life' learning. Our work centred on developing a shared understanding of Hannah's experience of epilepsy, and on constructing a model for the future which worked with the uncertainty of changing symptoms. The elements of creativity within our sessions related to the development of new perspectives, rather than novel ways to explore those perspectives (or novel ways to deliver therapy). In order to understand what led to me adopting what could be seen as a more conventional approach to therapy, I spent some time constructing a formulation and reformulation. These are illustrated in Figures 12.2 and 2.3.

Comparing this to some of the early formulations I worked on with Hannah (see Figure 12.1), it seems that a parallel process was occurring here. This is a term which usually refers to the way in which the relationship between client and therapist is

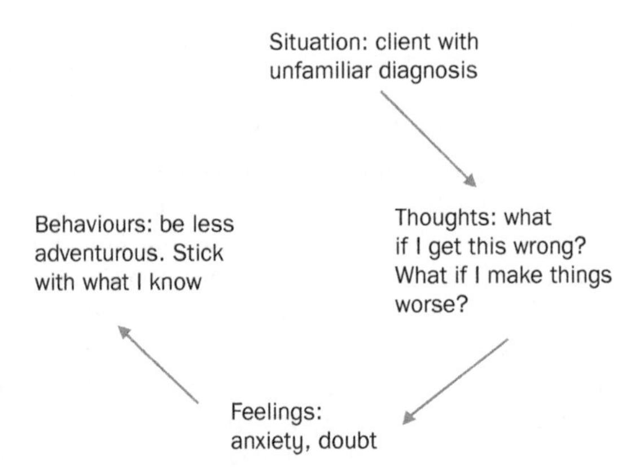

Figure 12.2 The therapist's formulation, stage 1

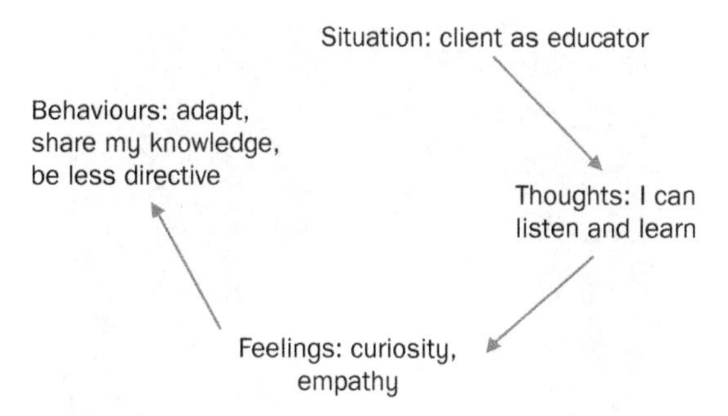

Figure 12.3 The therapist's formulation, stage 2

mirrored in the relationship between therapist and supervisor. In this instance, the issues that I took to supervision did not acknowledge the way in which my approach had been shaped by my fear of 'getting something wrong.' In writing this case study, I have become much more aware of Hannah's skill in concealing uncertainty and how my reactions both accommodated this and tapped into my own anxieties. I was reminded of my surprise when I invited Hannah to complete a routine questionnaire, which screens for anxiety, depression, risk and overall well-being and functioning (CORE-10). Her responses to the questionnaire suggested that she was experiencing clinically significant levels of anxiety and depression. The fact that this was a surprise to me is a further indication of the position I had taken within the therapeutic relationship, and how much I wanted to see the capable and resilient aspects of Hannah's character. Over the course of therapy, I was able to acknowledge these issues more effectively, as Figure 12.3 shows.

Helen's story: enhancing understanding through narrative

On 9 March 2014, a feature about epilepsy appeared as a cover story in the *Observer* New Review. The feature included a first-person account of living with epilepsy, written by a young woman named Helen Stephens, accompanied by a series of photographs taken by Helen's boyfriend, Matt Thompson. Some of these photographs captured Helen's expression moments after a seizure, and the narrative which accompanied them was powerful. As I read the article, my understanding of my conversations with Hannah shifted. I had heard Hannah describe her feelings following a seizure, and had tried my best to empathise. Helen's account, alongside such striking photographs, presented with devastating clarity the impact of a tonic-clonic seizure:

> Today I had a tonic-clonic seizure, the textbook hey-look-at-me-I'm-epileptic kind of seizure, convulsions, teeth-gnashing, groaning – all the big boys!
>
> It started, as it always does, with the rising feeling – a sickness and despair coming from my toes, like the feeling of nightmares – crawling all up my body and paralysing me so that I couldn't call for help. Then the dread closed in all around me and everything went fuzzy and unreal.

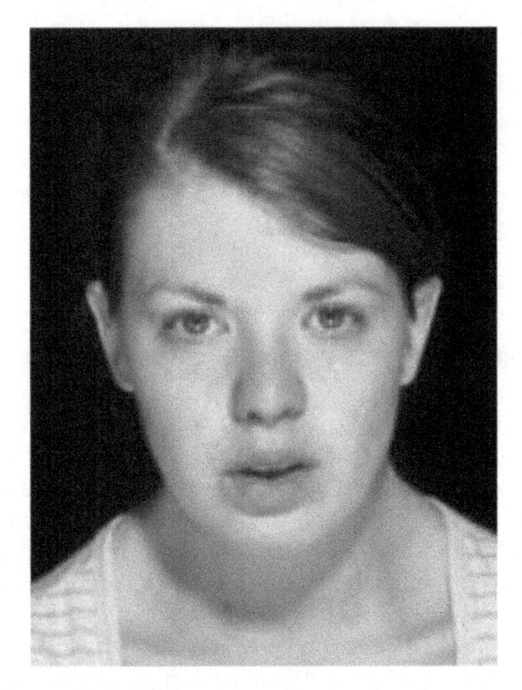

Figure 12.4 Helen immediately after the seizure

> The seizure's never the worst bit, though. The worst bit's when I come to and I see the faces of the people I love. It must be pretty horrific for them to see me all twisted and spitting like that. After every seizure my body mends me, but the guilt is always the last thing to heal.
>
> (Stephens 2014)

The photograph of Helen taken immediately after this seizure is shown in Figure 12.4.

Helen's story gained a lot of attention on social media and was highly praised by organisations such as Epilepsy Action (www.epilepsy.org.uk) for tackling the stigma and misunderstanding surrounding the condition. At our next session, Hannah described the article as 'a fantastic piece of literature that needs to be shared'. She went on to explain:

> I recognise that look, I've seen that post-fit look so many times when I look in the mirror … that grey look, and just that … look of emptiness. You can feel empty, but it's not often that you can look it as well … maybe, just maybe, this will help people to understand.

Reading Helen's story gave me a vivid new perspective on the lived experience of epilepsy, offering me a glimpse of the physical and emotional impact of seizures. It illuminated the accounts which Hannah had provided, and greatly enhanced my understanding. One of the aspects I appreciated most was that Hannah and I had found the story independently, outside our therapeutic relationship, and had been able to draw different things from it. This piece of writing helped me to acknowledge the severity of Hannah's difficulties, while simultaneously offering ways to accept this and to recognise the optimism that can grow from acceptance. Helen Stephens found that better adherence to her drug regime, awareness of the impact of her menstrual cycle and changes to her diet made major difference to her ability to manage her symptoms. As we worked together, Hannah's acceptance of her situation grew, leading her to explore new options for treatment.

Negotiating further change: looking forward

During our last sessions, Hannah was in the process of investigating new treatments which could help to reduce the severity of her epilepsy. This had not been entirely comfortable for Hannah; she had been shocked when, during a routine appointment, her specialist epilepsy nurse had raised the possibility of surgical intervention:

> I thought I was on the road to recovery ... I had [my future] planned out... and then I find out I may need big surgery. ... it was a big shock, and something that I wasn't prepared to hear.

Hannah recognised that she had been holding on to the reassurances that she had been given when she was first diagnosed, when it was hoped that she would 'grow out' of her symptoms, as many children do:

> I was promised that it [the absence epilepsy] would go and it didn't. It got worse. I think part of what I'm experiencing is disbelief – I held on to that 'truth' for so long.

There was also the possibility of more invasive treatments which carried a degree of risk and which therefore led to further uncertainty. These included vagus nerve stimulation, as well as the possibility of brain surgery raised by her specialist nurse. Hannah needed to be able to negotiate these uncertainties, but also to respond to her parents' concerns about the potential risks to the procedures.

Alongside issues specific to epilepsy, Hannah was experiencing life transitions which mark the move into adulthood: defining a separate, independent life outside the safety of her family, and forming significant attachments outside the family as a part of that process. During the time that we worked together Hannah entered into a serious romantic relationship, which influenced her life choices and which enabled her to shape her ideas about her future. The relationship was a long-distance one, which brought various challenges including regular long journeys on public transport (something which caused Hannah a degree of anxiety) and the impact of frequent separations from a loved one. Hannah recognised that her needs fluctuated and that at times, she felt a strong need to be cared for by her family:

> I just want them to be there for me, to give me hugs ... to look after me if I'm at my worst ... I want them to tuck me up in bed if they see that I'm not right.

At other times, the need for independence was equally evident. Hannah described her wish to attend medical appointments without her parents, a choice she had been offered in the past but which she had not felt able to take. She also talked about her plans to move away from home to live with her boyfriend:

> Mum and dad will be happy for me to move away once my health is stable … [which means] when I'm not having regular fits. … I think they're a bit scared … [at] the prospect of me moving away. But I think they've realised that it's going to happen someday and I can't keep holding off for ever.

At the time of writing, Hannah had recently been admitted to a specialist neurology hospital to undergo video telemetry. This is a very detailed test which involves close scrutiny of the patient via a continuous EEG and video recording of any seizure activity. Information is gathered over a period of days, with the objective of gaining sufficient detail to plan future treatment, including brain surgery if this is deemed appropriate.

Conclusion

Hannah continues to seek answers to her questions about her epilepsy, while simultaneously working towards her chosen future as a nursing professional. She has acknowledged confusions and contradictions in her experiences, and has put a great deal of effort into defining realistic life goals. This is a narrative without a neat conclusion, but it is one which demonstrates how resilience grows through acceptance and understanding. It is fitting to conclude this case study with some reflections from Hannah on her experiences:

> This epilepsy experience has redefined me. I wish it could have happened in another way, but now … I just want to find out what's going on. … It doesn't faze me. I don't care how long it takes. I just want to find out.

The author wishes to thank Matt Thompson for generously permitting the use of his photograph of Helen Stephens.

Glossary

Behavioural experiments. Behavioural experiments are experiential activities undertaken in or between sessions. They are designed based on a cognitive formulation of a problem. The primary purpose is to gather information which tests the validity of the client's beliefs, develop or test new beliefs or develop the formulation (Bennett-Levy *et al.* 2004).

Childhood absence epilepsy. 'This is a common epilepsy syndrome starting in early childhood. These seizures can happen in many different epilepsy syndromes occurring in childhood and adolescence. The seizures of childhood absence epilepsy usually start between the ages of four [and] nine years of age, and happen slightly more often in girls than boys. They can also happen many times a day, from 20 up to several hundred. A typical absence seizure consists of a sudden loss of awareness' (Epilepsy Action 2012).

Complex partial seizure. Complex partial seizures lead to the patient losing their sense of awareness. They cannot remember what happened after the seizure has passed. These seizures may also involve physical movements such as rubbing hands together, waving arms or chewing/swallowing movements.

EEG. An electroencephalogram or EEG is one of the tests used to help diagnose epilepsy. It 'records the electrical activity of the brain by picking up electrical signals from the brain cells. These signals are picked up by electrodes attached to the head and recorded on paper or on a computer. The recording shows how the brain is working' (Epilepsy Society 2015).

Exposure response prevention. A type of behavioural experiment that involves being exposed to a feared situation, and then sticking with the situation, rather than avoiding it or trying to escape it. As a result, anxiety reduces over time.

Habituation. The end result of successful exposure response prevention experiment, when the feared situation no longer induces anxiety.

Mindfulness. An approach to life which encourages focus on the here and now, while learning to accept and observe thoughts (as opposed to engaging with thoughts). Mindfulness is one of the approaches known as 'third wave' CBT.

Specialist epilepsy nurse. A nurse member of the epilepsy clinic team who has specialist training in, and knowledge of, epilepsy. The specialist nurse offers appointments between consultant reviews (which normally take place annually or six-monthly).

Tonic-clonic seizure. A seizure which has two distinct phases: tonic, where the individual loses consciousness and their muscles become stiff; and clonic, where the individual's limbs jerk, and they may experience symptoms such as biting the tongue or losing control of bladder or bowels.

Vagus nerve stimulation. Vagus nerve stimulation therapy 'uses a pulse generator to send mild electrical stimulations to the vagus nerve with the aim of reducing the number, length and severity of seizures' (Epilepsy Society 2012).

Video telemetry. 'Videotelemetry is a special type of EEG (brainwave) investigation. The brainwaves are recorded usually for several days along using with a video camera. This is a much longer recording than a standard EEG. Videotelemetry can only be performed as an in-patient as it requires specialised equipment and specially trained staff usually in a purpose-built unit. The advantage of videotelemetry is that if you have an attack then the brainwaves and video are recorded together. This can often be very helpful with coming to a diagnosis or further treatment' (British Society for Clinical Neurophysiology, no date).

References

Bennett-Levy, J., Butler, G., Fennell, M., Hackmann, A., Mueller, M. and Westbrook, D. (eds) (2004) Oxford Guide to Behavioural Experiments in Cognitive Therapy. Oxford: Oxford University Press.

British Society for Clinical Neurophysiology (no date) My Videotelemetry EEG Investigation. Available at: http://www.bscn.org.uk/content.aspx?Group=patients&Page=patient_video (accessed 6 February 2015).

Eiser, C. (2000) The psychological impact of chronic illness on children's development. In A. Closs (ed.), *The Education of Children with Medical Conditions*. London: David Fulton.

Epilepsy Action (2012) *Childhood Absence Epilepsy*. Available at: https://www.epilepsy.org.uk/info/childhood-absence-epilepsy (accessed 6 February 2015).

Epilepsy Action (2013) *What Is Epilepsy?* Available at: https://www.epilepsy.org.uk/info/what-is-epilepsy (accessed 6 February 2015).

Epilepsy Society (2012) *Vagus Nerve Stimulation.* Available at: http://www.epilepsysociety.org.uk/vagus-nerve-stimulation#.VVWAok3bLcs (accessed 6 February 2015).

Epilepsy Society (2015) *EEG (Electroencephalogram).* Available at: http://www.epilepsysociety.org.uk/eeg-electroencephalogram#.VVWDJk3bLcs (accessed 15 May 2015).

Munger Clary, H. (2014) Anxiety and epilepsy: What neurologists and epileptologists should know. *Current Neurology and Neuroscience Reports.* Available at: http://link.springer.com/article/10.1007/s11910-014-0445 (accessed 13 May 2015).

National Institute for Health and Care Excellence (2012) *The Epilepsies: The Diagnosis and Management of the Epilepsies in Adults and Children in Primary and Secondary Care.* NICE Guideline CG137. Available at http://www.nice.org.uk/guidance/cg137 (accessed 6 February 2015).

Stephens, H. (2014) How I faced up to epilepsy: Helen Stephens' photo diary. *Observer,* 9 March. Available at: http://www.theguardian.com/society/2014/mar/09/how-i-faced-up-to-epilepsy-helen-stephens-photo-diary (accessed 6 February 2015).

13 Sophia – post-traumatic stress disorder

Sarah Rogers

This chapter explores the use of cognitive behavioural therapy (CBT) in work undertaken with Sophia, a young person presenting with post-traumatic stress disorder (PTSD). Sophia's case is introduced in some detail to illustrate the complexities of working with trauma and to provide some insight into Sophia's lived experience of this distressing disorder. The skills used during each stage of therapy are discussed and, in each section, adaptations to the process of therapy when working with young people are highlighted. Sophia is a highly articulate individual and has contributed to this chapter, providing first-hand accounts of her experience of living with PTSD and her subsequent journey through therapy. She was keen to show others that you can get through PTSD and that 'there is light at the end of the tunnel'. As the chapter draws to a close, I will reflect on my experiences of working with Sophia and give an update on her progress.

Sophia

Sophia is 15 years old and the eldest child in her family. Her parents separated when she was 2 years old and, due to a difficult relationship with her mother, she went to live with her father, stepmother, and half-brother several years later. The family house is on the outskirts of the city with good access to public transport, shops, schools, and other amenities. Sophia has a strong relationship with her father, describing him as someone whom she can always rely upon. Contact with her biological mother is fractious and intermittent, and visits are mostly initiated by Sophia in an effort to maintain relationships with other family members. Sophia attends the local high school and is completing her GCSEs.

Sophia took the brave step of seeking a consultation with her general practitioner who subsequently referred her to the local child and adolescent mental health service (CAMHS). Sophia disclosed experiences of physical abuse that took place when she was 5 or 6 years old and the resulting difficulties that were affecting her life, including symptoms of anxiety and panic, and harming herself by cutting her forearms as a way of coping with these feelings.

At Sophia's first CAMHS appointment a range of difficulties were identified, including low mood, tearfulness, problems with sleep, and self-harm. Sophia disclosed that she was frequently the recipient of verbal bullying from peers at school, who would make comments about the scars on her arms and insinuate that she had a mental illness. Further exploration revealed that Sophia frequently experienced nightmares, flashbacks, and a sensation of pain in her legs. She spoke of increasing feelings of irritability and of an overwhelming sense that she would be better off if she were to end her life. Many of these difficulties had been present for approximately a year but had worsened significantly on a chance sighting of the perpetrator of the historical physical abuse. A diagnosis of PTSD with depression was given: evidence suggests that PTSD and depression frequently co-occur and individuals with one disorder have increased susceptibility to the other (O'Donnell *et al.* 2004; Spinhoven *et al.* 2014).

Despite her difficulties, Sophia demonstrated many strengths and there were several factors that enabled her to maintain her resilience. Sophia spoke of her love of singing, something she enjoyed in and out of school. She was attaining good grades at school and had a best friend whose support she could rely on. She also had a strong relationship with her father and his wife, and they were keen to support her in any way they could.

Considering the evidence base (Ehlers *et al.*, 2005) and current clinical guidelines (National Institute for Health and Care Excellence, 2005), Sophia was referred for trauma-focused cognitive behavioural therapy (TF-CBT). Sophia was clear that her symptoms of PTSD pre-dated her symptoms of depression and she was keen to tackle the root cause of her difficulties. It was hypothesised that TF-CBT would have greater efficacy than CBT for depression in treating Sophia's symptoms. This was the beginning of my 14-month journey with Sophia.

Engagement and assessment

My contact with Sophia began before our first planned appointment, following a concerned telephone call from a teacher at her school. Sophia had broken down in class and had admitted that she had 'had enough' and had briefly considered taking several paracetamol tablets. I telephoned Sophia later that day and we spoke about her struggles with nightmares and muddled thoughts. I was struck by Sophia's ability to think rationally and articulate her concerns, considering the distress she was experiencing. We spoke at length about risks (overdoses) and protective factors (relationships with dad, stepmum and best friend) and identified a plan for staying safe until our first meeting. Sophia was given contact telephone numbers should there be a further crisis.

Sophia's appointments took place in an outpatient clinic. As is usual, when working with young people, the choice of being seen alone or with a family member was offered and Sophia chose to be seen alone. As Sophia was nearly 16, consideration was given to both her capacity to make choices for herself and the legal age for consent to treatment. Sophia's wishes and feelings about including parents or sharing information with them were taken into consideration throughout therapy and when self-harming behaviours became a concern.

To begin our work together, it seemed important to consider Sophia's strengths as well as her difficulties and, as the initial assessment had already been undertaken, I took the opportunity to get to know her as an individual, not just as a young person in crisis. It also felt important to make Sophia feel comfortable at her first appointment within a mental health service, knowing that peers had taunted her about her having a 'mental illness'. We talked about her interests and I learned more about her wish to further her singing skills in the future, perhaps in opera or the West End.

Once Sophia felt comfortable talking, attention was turned to the problems with which she was referred. Sophia described her difficulties with sleep and nightmares, and the worsening of her PTSD symptoms 8 months previously when she saw the male perpetrator of her abuse. She explained: 'The memories were locked away before this.' Sophia spoke about flashbacks that were triggered by people smoking cigarettes and seeing or touching her own legs. In order to cope, Sophia had developed several strategies including avoiding smokers, always wearing trousers, and not looking at her body while washing.

At the first appointment and throughout our work together, I was struck by Sophia's courage and ability to discuss difficult issues and her resolve to face problems head-on. Sophia went on to talk about the context of the physical abuse and explained that her mother's former partner used to stub his cigarettes out on her legs, on a regular basis. Sophia's mother denied reports of this abuse and tried to find alternative explanations for the scars on Sophia's legs. To this day, Sophia does not perceive her mother to have ever believed her story. This lack of understanding and connection with her mother played an important role in the maintenance of and subsequent recovery from her PTSD.

CBT models assume that problems are maintained by maladaptive thinking styles and unhelpful coping behaviours, and that by identifying links between thoughts, feelings, and behaviours one can work on making changes that will lead to better coping in the future. Changing how you think will change what you feel, which in turn will influence what you do. As we had easily established the behavioural changes that had occurred since the emergence of PTSD, it was important next to consider the emotional and cognitive changes. Sophia described the abuse as having left her feeling worthless, of having a sense of not belonging, and of feeling damaged. Sophia explained that she prided herself on being a strong and independent person and admitted that she had spent 9 years 'trying to keep a brave face on' and resolving never to cry. It was no longer easy to maintain these resolutions.

Sophia agreed to come back for a further appointment in order to reflect on these discussions and consider how she would like to proceed with therapy that fitted around her own individual needs. The next session began with the completion of a Trauma-Symptom Checklist for Children (TSCC; Briere, 1996), as a baseline measure of her difficulties. It is good practice to use standardised measures in sessions, both to add weight to clinical impressions regarding diagnosis and to provide measurable data that can be used to assess problem severity before and after therapy. The TSCC confirmed clinically significant symptoms of post-traumatic stress and depression. In order to ensure a mutual understanding of the problems, we focused on psycho-education about PTSD and depression (causes and maintenance), and Sophia was given leaflets to take home so that she could refer back to the information in her own time. For PTSD, we used the analogy of memories being scattered quickly into the wrong place, just like shopping having been thrown into a cupboard for convenience – at a later date, however, items tumble back out of the cupboard and need to be re-shelved.

Lastly, we explored the nature of TF-CBT, during which Sophia expressed concerns that she would get worse before she got better. She used a metaphor to explain her position, saying that her problems had been crammed into a box for 9 years and letting it all out now would undo the effort she had put in to keep it all in the box. It was useful, at this point, to use an analogy once told to me by a colleague: trauma leaves an infected wound which hurts if you touch it, so you therefore try to ignore or avoid it. To get better you need to begin the process of acknowledging and then gradually draining the wound. (Depending on the young person, the wording used in this analogy can be made more or less disgusting: it is a useful way of engaging young people in the early stage of a process of change.) We discussed the importance of building up coping strategies (diaphragmatic breathing, alternatives to self-harm), of including her family in any support plan, and ensuring sessions were planned well with clear boundaries.

Formulation

In order to begin our work in a collaborative manner, Sophia and I considered her PTSD symptoms in the context of the general cognitive model of PTSD by Westbrook *et al.* (2007), and spent time putting this into a diagrammatic format (Figure 13.1). For Sophia, this model was easier to relate to than the more commonly used model of Ehlers and Clark (2000), which is discussed in more detail in a later section. Sophia was keen to understand her perceived feelings of 'stuckness,' and the diagram allowed us to see how a vicious cycle is maintained.

We established that there were a number of triggers that evoked Sophia's trauma memories, including interactions with her mother, seeing the perpetrator or his daughter (who attended her school), seeing the scars on her legs, and seeing anyone smoking cigarettes. Elicited memories were vivid, and Sophia described seeing the events in real time as pictures, like a videotape being played over and over again. She also described detailed realistic dreams, which caused her to feel threatened. These experiences resulted in an overestimation of danger and heightened feelings of anxiety, including physiological symptoms (racing heart, nausea, and tingling legs) and worries about whether other people would see and judge her scars. In order to avoid the anxiety caused by the memories, Sophia engaged in a number of safety behaviours, including checking over her shoulder, avoiding the shopping mall, and wearing tights or trousers every day. She also admitted that cutting herself was a way of avoiding the emotional pain. Engaging in these safety behaviours meant that Sophia did not learn that she could do these things without increased threat, repeated abuse, or unmanageable emotions occurring. The result was failure to process the traumatic memories which meant the cycle continued. Sophia's goals were therefore to reduce the frequency of flashbacks and dreams, and to decrease all safety behaviours.

Therapy session planning and considerations

In order to begin trauma-focused work, consideration was given to a number of factors. Most important, perhaps, was ensuring that Sophia was currently in a safe place and that she had good support systems around her. This meant that there were no current experiences of trauma and that there was a stable family home with supportive

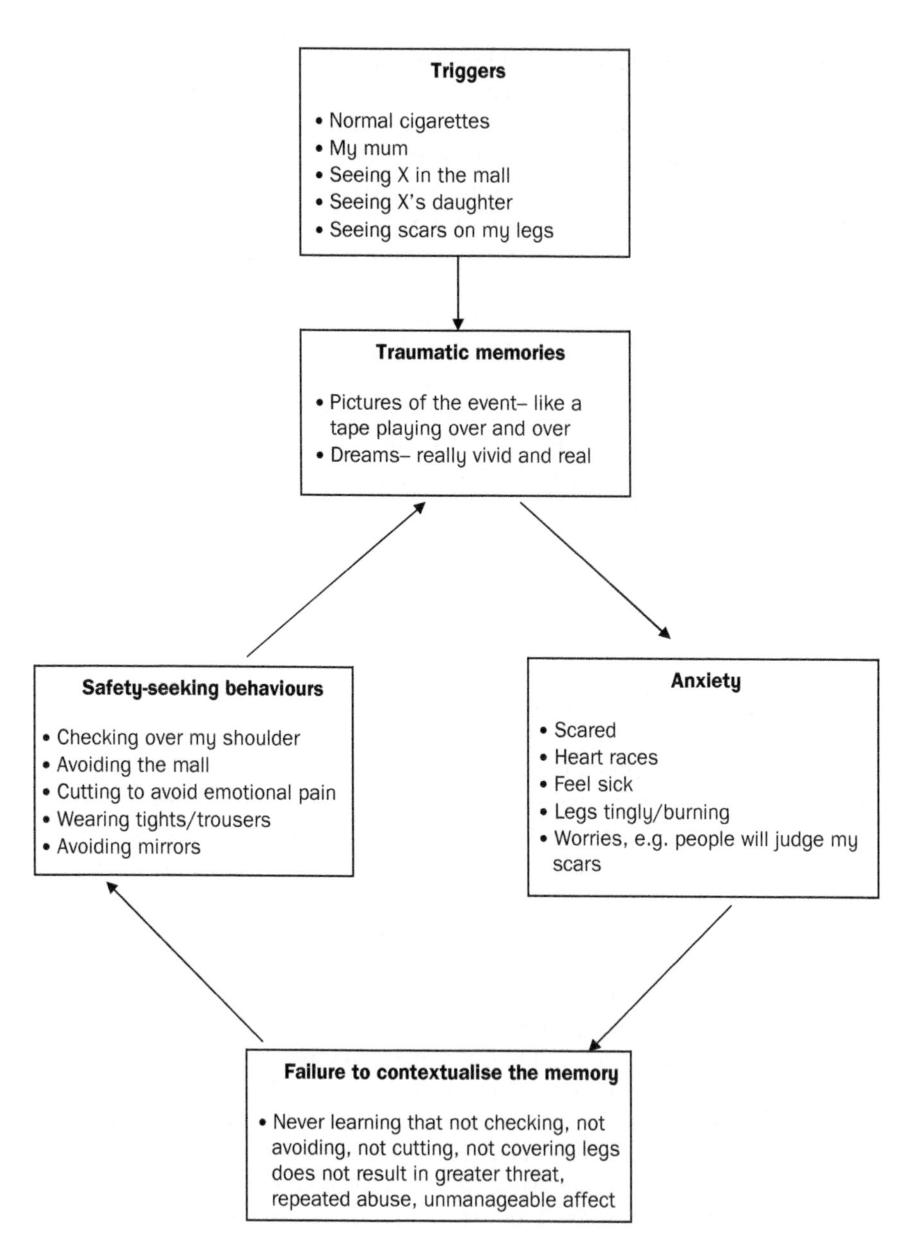

Figure 13.1 Sophia's PTSD in the context of the Westbrook *et al.* (2007) general cognitive model of PTSD

parents. There were no concerns about any aspects of Sophia's safety. Also important to Sophia was her ability to cope with peers at school, and to ensure she had good friends whom she could confide in if she wished.

As Sophia was in her final year at school, issues relating to the frequency and timing of sessions were important to address. In the early stages of therapy, appointments were frequent to enable Sophia to build up coping skills to ensure there were no long periods of time during which she would be left feeling isolated and distressed. As the trauma work progressed and Sophia was engaged in GCSE examinations, trauma-therapy breaks were introduced and replaced with supportive counselling sessions. This enabled Sophia to raise issues relating to emotional distress but ensured she was not left in a position where trauma memories would interfere with her academic work at this critical time. Trauma-focused sessions were reinstigated once the exams were finished.

Before TF-CBT took place, time was taken to ensure that Sophia had the resources to cope with sessions that would evoke difficult thoughts and feelings. This included skills-building in managing panic and providing Sophia with a range of alternatives to self-harm. Time was taken to plan the session structure, with agendas typically consisting of a brief review at the start of the session. This was followed by trauma-focused work, then at least 10 minutes of debriefing, relaxation and a change of topic at the end to ensure Sophia did not leave the session in distress. During critical periods in Sophia's therapy, sessions were extended to 90 minutes, to ensure ample time was given to address key points, modify maladaptive appraisals, and ensure emotions were managed in a contained way.

Cognitive and behavioural techniques

Ehlers and Clark (2000) provide a helpful cognitive model of PTSD. They propose that PTSD occurs if an individual processes the traumatic event or its outcomes in a way that leads to a sense of current perceived threat. For example, if a person in a car crash recalls only seeing a white van moments before the crash they might go on to appraise all white vans as dangerous and as posing more threat when they next go out for a drive. When an individual continues to experience this sense of ongoing threat this leads to intrusive memories of the original trauma, heightened bodily arousal, and strong emotions. In an effort to manage these troublesome experiences, unhelpful cognitive and behavioural strategies are often employed, such excessively checking mirrors or avoiding certain roads, but these are only effective in the short term. Ultimately, these strategies prevent changes occurring in the thoughts and beliefs about the trauma, and prevent change in the trauma memory itself. Ehlers and Clark identify that intervention needs to focus on change in three areas: the trauma memory needs to be elaborated (explored in detail) and put into the context of past and subsequent experiences; problematic appraisals of the trauma, outcomes, and current threat need to be modified; and unhelpful cognitive and behavioural strategies (safety behaviours) need to be dropped. Sofia's therapy encompassed ideas from each of these three areas.

Elaborating and integrating memories

Sophia's trauma-focused sessions began with work that centred on elaborating memories and putting them back into a context which consisted of information relating to time, place, and subsequent outcomes. This meant thinking about the trauma in as much detail as possible and ensuring the memory had an ending that was consistent with the actual event, as well as a conclusion that considered Sophia's current circumstances and safety. Sophia was given options about how we could start this work together and she chose to narrate her story, from a first-person perspective, giving as many details as she felt able. Sophia's parents were made aware of the likely distress this work would cause and they were available to take Sophia home whenever she was ready.

On the first occasion, Sophia gave a full account of her early childhood experiences, including events leading up to the physical abuse and feelings thereafter. Feeling proud of having achieved this, Sophia undertook a second session, this time undertaking imaginal reliving of her experience. This meant narrating the details of her experience whilst imagining herself back in the original situation, with the original thoughts, emotions, and sensations. Sophia tolerated this process well and was able to recount specific conversations, feelings of anxiety and dread, and visual details of her surroundings, for example the perpetrator's clothes and decoration in the room.

Reflecting on this process, discrepancies between the perpetrator's words and actions were highlighted, as was the implied threat which Sophia understood to mean that she should not tell anybody about the abuse. Sophia discovered that her 'videotape' did not have an ending; instead she found a 30-minute period of blankness before she recalled her mother returning to the scene. With this in mind, we engaged in a further period of reliving, and on reaching the end of her narrative Sophia was encouraged to visualise a safe ending. There is a growing literature on the use of imagery techniques (Hackmann *et al.* 2011), including its use in PTSD. The safe ending that Sophia described was arriving back at her current home, sitting on the sofa with her father, and enjoying a hot chocolate in front of the television.

Imaginal reliving continued in further sessions, interspersed with skills building and emotion management (see below). Sophia began to identify that there were two hotspots in her experience of the events: one relating to the perceived cause of the abuse (breaking an ornament) which led to the perpetrator walking into the room, and one relating to experience of the first cigarette burn. Attention was paid to these areas of the trauma narrative and Sophia was encouraged to imagine and discuss these areas in as much detail as she could.

As is typical of cognitive therapy protocols, homework formed a significant part of Sophia's learning experience. In relation to our early sessions, Sophia chose to begin a written narrative of her experience, at home on her computer. Initially Sophia found this much more difficult than she had anticipated: she was honest in admitting that she had avoided doing it as she feared the difficult thoughts and feelings that it was likely to evoke. We spent time exploring these issues in session, and Sophia identified that she would feel more able to begin this task with support. Thus, the written narrative commenced in session with Sophia writing at her own pace, the words she had previously used when giving her story verbally. Prompts and open questions were used when she felt stuck. We checked in on this homework at the start of each session and noticed that Sophia was able to recount the details of her trauma very fluently but was achieving this by avoiding the perpetrator's name. While she was able to say this out loud during our sessions, it was unbearable to see it written down while at home on her own. We used this opportunity to become more creative in our work together and began introducing the perpetrator's name in a less threatening way. Sophia wrote the name repeatedly on the whiteboard until the task became boring, and on another occasion made a clay face to represent him and used this to demonstrate exactly what she thought of him (you can use your imagination here). These tasks freed Sophia to process meanings associated with the name and to incorporate this into her written trauma narrative.

Modifying maladaptive appraisals

Woven throughout the trauma narrative work were tasks aimed at identifying maladaptive (unhelpful) appraisals. Although these appraisals were understandable at the time of the abuse (when Sophia was 6 years of age), they were no longer valid. Sophia showed skill in identifying negative automatic thoughts related to the trauma hotspots, which had now generalised to different areas of her everyday life, for example: 'I've done something wrong', 'It's my fault', 'I can never do anything right', and 'I don't deserve to be alive'. Core beliefs were also revealed with little prompting: 'I deserve it' and 'I am a horrible person'. We reflected on how Sophia had continued to experience feelings of shame because of her belief about the abuse being her fault, whilst the reactions of the perpetrator had led her to fear punishment for anything she might do wrong. As time had gone on, not being believed by her mother also led her to doubt her own credibility and her place in the family. Sophia summarised the result of all these experiences using a metaphor that described herself as being 'a million smashed pieces' which were 'not fixable'.

Work addressing maladaptive appraisals began with a focus on Sophia's perception of herself as a person. It was noticed that Sophia often spoke of herself in negative terms and she found it difficult to identify more positive aspects of her character. To consider these issues in more detail, Sophia engaged in a task where she was asked to draw a poster to depict herself. Sophia's response was to write words of varying sizes and colours on a large sheet of paper – the words depicted her perceived characteristics. On analysis, we noticed that negative characteristics were often in large print or capital letters, whereas positive characteristics were smaller. Sophia was encouraged to think about what the poster would look like if it had been drawn by her friends.

These insights led us into a couple of sessions where we explored Sophia's ability to be kind and compassionate towards herself. We agreed to use some techniques derived from compassion-focused therapy (Gilbert 2010; Lee 2012) to work on this issue. This began with the creation of a compassionate image, something that would evoke a sense of ideal compassion and non-judgement towards self. Using guided imagery, Sophia chose the image of 'Dog' – a creature who would always be there to listen and provide comfort. 'Dog' was subsequently used as a 'safe image' when trauma was addressed.

Further cognitive work on maladaptive appraisals took the form of challenging unhelpful thoughts, seeking evidence for the validity of thoughts, and exploring alternative meanings for thoughts or events. Using Socratic questioning, Sophia was encouraged to think about her previous position as a 6-year-old child suffering abuse and her position now as a 15-year-old who was achieving significant life goals. Based on her trauma narrative, Sophia was able to describe her thoughts and beliefs (e.g. 'It's my fault') and to rate how much she believed them (95%). Sophia reflected on differences between the two situations, noting that she was now older, more assertive, and that in now knowing all the details of the abuse her father would keep her safe. Sophia was also asked to think about the power differences between the adult abuser and the 6-year-old child, and to consider different positions for blame and motive. Sophia subsequently opted to take the position of the 'White Queen' (from Alice in Wonderland; see the poem at the end of this chapter) to argue why the perpetrator of the abuse was in the wrong and concluded that he was a psychopath who showed no remorse. Sophia re-rated her beliefs towards the end of therapy and it was wonderful to see that her belief relating to the abuse being her own fault had diminished (0%).

Addressing safety behaviours

As identified in the formulation, there were a number of avoidance behaviours that Sophia needed to address in order to break the PTSD cycle. Sophia was introduced to the idea of creating a hierarchy of goals, a process by which she could systematically challenge her unhelpful behaviours. Sophia identified that there were two separate issues that needed addressing: her avoidance of cigarettes and her avoidance of the burns on her legs. She felt these were very personal issues and opted to work on these independently through homework tasks.

To address her avoidance of cigarettes, Sophia worked on gradually spending more time with her father when he was smoking outside. Addressing issues related to her scarring was more complicated, as this required both an acceptance of past events and a shift in self-image. Sophia set goals at her own pace and began with seeking everyday opportunities for looking at, and not judging, her own legs. Following this, Sophia challenged herself to touch her legs – initially while not looking, but then whilst she was bathing or putting on lotion. Finally, there were goals related to other people being able to see her legs, with challenges including wearing short pyjamas at home and, eventually, having bare legs in public. It is important to note here that Sophia's skills in leading her own therapy are exceptional: in my experience of working with other young people, more support and guidance is often necessary.

Emotion management

During our work together, Sophia and I had to put the trauma-focused work 'on hold' a number of times in order to focus on risk management and emotion regulation. There were times when Sophia was using self-harm (cutting her arms) as a means of coping with distress. Also, throughout most of our time together, Sophia experienced significant feelings of depression and had fleeting thoughts of suicide (but no plans to end her life). Sophia had been writing in her diary and wrote poems throughout her therapy, which provided some insight into her experiences. An extract from the start of one poem reflects her early relationship with self-harm:

My scars they tell a story,
most of you don't know.
The pain I have to be in,
for me to stoop so low.
To take the razor blade,
cut deep into my skin,
watch the blood pour out,
my world just caving in.

Self-harm it proves to be, a never-ending war,
a few seconds of quick release,
a mark to prove forever more.

Some of you will think, oh look attention-seeking,
but some of you will know, exactly how I'm feeling.

Risk issues were managed in a number of ways, including discussion about short- and long-term consequences of self-harm, exploring vicious cycles interlinking mood and trauma, making risk management plans (which included family members), and managing physiological symptoms of anxiety and depression. Due to ongoing depressive symptoms Sophia was also prescribed antidepressant medication a year into our work together. Over time, Sophia's mood stabilised and this enabled us to return to the more challenging aspects of our trauma-focused work.

It is important to note here that, even with planned therapy breaks and work on emotion management, progress in reducing PTSD and depression symptoms was not straightforward. Events outside our control often got in the way but at least provided opportunities for reviewing triggers and the efficacy of coping strategies. Examples included unhelpful contacts between Sophia and her mother, and another unexpected sighting of the perpetrator of the abuse in the shopping mall. However, as a second extract from Sophia's poem reveals, there was certainly reason to be hopeful about change:

My scars are slowly fading,
they remind me of where I've been.
Never to go back there,
the horrid place I've seen.

They remind me I am strong,
stronger now you see.
I don't want to go back,
to the place where I had been.

Outcome and reflections on change

Sophia is now 17 years of age. It has been several months since we completed our trauma-focused work and a lot of changes have taken place, both in respect of PTSD and for Sophia on a more personal level.

Reflecting back on Sophia's PTSD formulation, it is rewarding to see that the original 'stuck' cycle has been broken at every step. Through contextualising the trauma memories and reducing safety-seeking behaviours, Sophia has found that the old 'videotape' no longer plays and she does not experience vivid dreams related to the trauma. Her anxiety related to the trauma has reduced and Sophia feels confident that she would be able to act in a different way should she ever encounter the perpetrator again. Sophia no longer checks over her shoulder, she is able to go shopping in the city, and her proudest moment of all was wearing a skirt (with no tights) during a music performance. In addition to these observations and reflections, such changes are also supported by the more formal TSCC measure, with both PTSD and depression scores falling in the average range.

While Sophia's difficulties with PTSD have resolved, she has continued to experience difficulties relating to mood management, including a reoccurrence of self-harm. Sophia is engaging in opportunities to enable her to manage this new period in her life, including retaking Year 12, attending an emotion-regulation group, and taking different medication under the supervision of a psychiatrist.

From my point of view, it has been a humbling experience to hear Sophia's personal accounts of trauma and to be part of her journey towards recovery. Sophia's case has highlighted the complexities of working with co-morbid difficulties (depression, self-harm) and the importance of working with the systems around the client that keep them safe (for Sophia this was her family and good friends). Within a CAMHS, the support of other staff is also invaluable both in respect of ensuring that Sophia received the best care and that, through supervision, I was providing effective, individualised, evidence-based therapy.

Sophia has taken the opportunity to reflect on her experiences since writing this chapter:

> When I first started therapy I was very sceptical – I wasn't sure it could help me at all. I was in a very dark place, I felt like everything was falling apart and I didn't believe I would get better. But CBT helped me immensely. It helped me to pinpoint the parts of the trauma I was still suffering from, which meant I could then go on to work towards overcoming them.

Summary

This chapter has provided an account of the cognitive behavioural treatment of PTSD, through the case illustration of Sophia (a 15-year-old attending a CAMHS). Details of Sophia's presenting difficulties, her case formulation, and the trauma-focused work undertaken are discussed at length. Therapy skills and processes are described throughout the text, and I hope that Sophia's case has given some insight into the way in which work can be adapted when working with young people. I wish to thank

Sophia for her valuable contributions and will conclude with a poem she wrote that eloquently summarises her journey.

Just Like Wonderland

Just like wonderland, wonderland I say.
It's where I dream of everyday.
No one gets judged, gets judged you see,
I wish I could be Alice, she's prettier than me.

I met the Mad Hatter in my dream,
And well, I guess he's a lot like me.
Hurt and in pain, but covers it well,
He covers it with laughter and a spell.

I don't have magic on my side,
But my smile works just as fine.
Give me a top hat and wacky hair,
I'd be the mad hatter, what's left to compare?

He's friends with a hare, a hare you see,
This hare was just as crazy as me.
Made me realise, I'm not insane,
I should not let my craziness cause me shame.

The Hatter and Hare, taught me well,
Being different can just be swell.

I met the Wise Old Caterpillar,
This caterpillar said to me,
'Stop being silly and smile for me.
It may be hard, but things get better.'
Then he handed me a letter.

The letter read, in big black writing,
You have people who love you darling.
Don't end it now, carry on smiling.
I know how you're feeling, please stop hiding.

The words he spoke, may be true,
But I didn't listen, I continue . . .

Continued down the deep dark hole,
Pitch black and an awful smell.

Tweedle Dee and Tweedle Dum,
Held me up and that was fun.
Took me to an enchanted place,
But somehow I still hate this space.

I met the Cheshire Cat on my travels,
His floating head caused me no troubles.
His constant smile was so pretty you see,
I wondered if it would look good on me.

Things started cheering up you see,
And that was when I met the White Queen.
She looked in to my eyes, and smiled at me,
Darling you're not ugly, not ugly you see.

She handed me a mirror and inside I saw,
A scared, trapped girl, nothing more.
Look closely she smiled, a lovely grin,
I stare at the mirror, it sucked me in.

I met the Red Queen in this mirror,
Empty and lifeless she made me enter,
Into a place I don't want to be,
For goodness sake, I just want to be happy.

I found a little bottle, this bottle was tempting,
DRINK ME it screamed. I was shaking.
I knew if I took it, I wouldn't awake,
So I walked out of the door and ate a cake.

I saw the Mad Hatter a second time,
He said he was proud and then went shy.
You ate the cake instead of the drink,
It took great strength, now stop being bleak.

I reached the end, where the Red Queen stood,
'Off with her head', she screamed, 'I shh'd'.

I turned around and then I saw, the White Queen at this war.
Then I realised, I realised you see,
No one will ever defeat me.

I thought this to myself, I won't let you down,
This is where I'll earn my crown,
For the people I love who mean the world to me,
I'll end this battle sufficiently.

I took out my sword, I cut off her head.
Gone forever, forever dead.

I woke up the next morning, all became clear.
Now you're dead, you're dead my dear.
I can't even love you, not at all,
Just biological, it means nothing at all.

I'll never forget the dream I had, for I'll return you can be sure of that.
I'll close my eyes and rest my head.
I'll go to a land where the Red Queen's dead.

(Sophia, 2013; reproduced with permission of the author)

Glossary

Compassionate image. An image that generates a feeling of being cared for, without any judgement. The aim of the image is to evoke kinder and more supportive thoughts towards oneself. Images are unique to the individual and might include angels, animals, or objects with more personal meanings.

Emotion regulation. In this case, this refers to the conscious control of emotion, such that a thought leads to the employment of a particular behaviour in order to manage an emotional state. An example would be instructing oneself to engage in a deep breathing technique in order to manage feelings of anxiety or panic. Used as a coping mechanism, conscious emotion regulation techniques will prevent engagement in unhelpful or harmful strategies.

Flashbacks. Sudden, vivid, recollections of past events. In PTSD these occur frequently and involve the individual re-experiencing details of the traumatic event as if it were happening in the here and now.

Hotspots. These refer to detailed moments within a trauma memory that are most closely linked with significant emotions or distress. Hotspots are areas of the trauma that require targeted work in understanding their meaning and ensuring memory details are accurately updated.

Imaginal reliving. A technique in which the individual visualises the traumatic event while describing what is happening, along with details of their thoughts and feelings in that moment. Reliving is repeated over a number of exposure sessions.

Protective factors. Factors that serve to minimise the occurrence of a problem or risk, for example development of a mental health disorder or acting on suicidal thoughts. These might include personal characteristics or beliefs, attachment to a supportive family, and good peer relationships.

Psycho-education. Education offered to individuals to enable them to understand issues related to their mental health problem and empower them to deal with the issues in the best way.

PTSD. A trauma and stress-related disorder causing significant distress or impairment following exposure to a traumatic event (such as possible death, threat or actual injury). Individuals with PTSD typically experience flashbacks, nightmares, and changes in arousal and emotional responses.

Risks. Factors that are likely to increase the chances of harm towards oneself or others. Risks might include injury through self-harm behaviours or suicide. Such risks are moderated by occurrence of issues such as low mood, low self-esteem, poor family relationships, bullying, and poor socio-economic status.

Safety behaviours. Behaviours or mental activities that are employed in an attempt to minimise or prevent something bad from happening. For example, carrying a sick bag around in a pocket to prevent sickness, as this strategy appears to have prevented sickness on all previous occasions. Safety behaviours prevent learning as each 'safe' outcome is attributed directly to the safety behaviour.

Socratic questioning. The use of therapeutic questions to guide the individual towards a conclusion, without any direct instruction. This enables the individual to use their own abilities and skills to solve problems, without reliance on the therapist providing the answers.

Trauma-focused cognitive behavioural therapy (TF-CBT). TF-CBT is an evidence-based therapy for the treatment of PTSD. It involves modification of emotional and behavioural responses to the traumatic event in addition to addressing distorted beliefs and attributions. TF-CBT often involves the individual giving a narrative of their trauma while engaging in imaginal reliving (imagined exposure) sessions.

Trauma Symptom Checklist for Children. A self-report questionnaire assessing post-trauma symptoms in children aged 8–16 years. Six clinical scales measure anxiety, depression, post-traumatic stress, sexual concerns, dissociation, and anger.

Appendix: Post-traumatic stress disorder

PTSD is now referred to as a trauma and stress-related disorder. The *Diagnostic and Statistical Manual of Mental Disorders* (DSM-5; American Psychiatric Association 2013) describes the criteria for a diagnosis of PTSD (in adults and children over the age of 5 years) as including history of exposure to a traumatic event (such as possible death, threatened or actual injury or violence) either directly or as a witness, and symptoms from four other categories.

1. The event is persistently re-experienced through intrusive memories, nightmares, or dissociative reactions. This includes physiological reactions and distress.
2. The person avoids trauma-related stimuli, including thoughts or external reminders (people, places, objects, etc.).
3. There are alterations in cognition and mood, some of which include: inability to recall details of the event, negative/distorted beliefs about the world, negative emotions (fear, anger, shame), or reduced interest in activities.
4. Alterations in arousal and reactivity, including irritability/aggression, hypervigilance, exaggerated startle response, poor concentration, or poor sleep.

Symptoms must have been present for more than 1 month and there must be significant distress or functional impairment.

References

American Psychiatric Association (2013) *Diagnostic and Statistical Manual of Mental Disorders* (5th edn). Washington, DC: American Psychiatric Association.

Briere, J. (1996) *Trauma Symptom Checklist for Children (TSCC), Professional Manual.* Odessa, FL: Psychological Assessment Resources.

Ehlers, A. and Clark, D.M. (2000) A cognitive model of posttraumatic stress disorder. *Behaviour Research and Therapy*, 38: 319–45.

Ehlers, A., Clark, D.M., Hackmann, A., McManus, F. and Fennell, M. (2005) Cognitive therapy for post-traumatic stress disorder: development and evaluation. *Behaviour Research and Therapy*, 43: 413–31.

Gilbert, P. (2010) *The Compassionate Mind.* London: Constable.

Hackmann, A., Bennett-Levy, J. and Holmes, E.A. (2011) *Oxford Guide to Imagery in Cognitive Therapy.* Oxford: Oxford University Press.

National Institute for Health and Care Excellence (2005) *Post-traumatic Stress Disorder (PTSD). The Management of PTSD in Adults and Children in Primary and Secondary Care.* NICE Clinical Guideline 26. Available at http://www.nice.org.uk/guidance/cg26/resources/guidance-posttraumatic-stress-disorder-ptsd-pdf.

O'Donnell, M.L., Creamer, M., and Pattison, P. (2004) Post traumatic stress disorder and depression following trauma: understanding co-morbidity. *American Journal of Psychiatry*, 161: 1390–6.

Spinhoven, P., Penninx, P.W., van Hemert, A.M., de Rooij, M. and Elzinga, B.M. (2014) Co-morbidity of PTSD in anxiety and depressive disorders: prevalence and shared risk factors. *Child Abuse and Neglect*, 38(8): 1320–30.

Westbrook, D., Kennerley, H. and Kirk, J. (2007) *An Introduction to Cognitive Behaviour Therapy: Skills and Applications.* London: Sage.

14 Stephanie – Social anxiety and physical health

Jenny Smerdon

Background

This chapter describes my work with Stephanie, a young person aged 15 whom I have been working with using cognitive behavioural therapy (CBT) to address social anxiety. As the main emphasis of the chapter will be looking at Stephanie's account of these experiences, I have tried to incorporate her voice into the work.

Stephanie has fibrodysplasia ossificans progressiva (FOP) a condition which involves, in Stephanie's words, the 'calcification of muscles. If trauma happens to my muscles, they will calcify and basically turn into bone. In rare cases, people might be able to move a part of their body that they haven't been able to move for years – it's unpredictable – quite different for different people.'

In this chapter I will explore Stephanie's experience of social anxiety: how Stephanie's condition impacted upon the development of her social anxiety and the treatment of it using CBT.

Stephanie lives with her parents Wayne and Emily and her younger siblings, Jasmine, Tom and Raphael. She is currently studying GCSEs and is predicted to obtain As and A*s. There have been discussions with her about her studying at a top university, which Stephanie says 'I would really like to do as I like to achieve the best that I can'. She is very artistic, despite her limited movement and enjoys 'anything creative'. She is interested in Japanese culture, particularly music and art, and is teaching herself to speak Japanese. Her thoughts of careers involve writing, fashion design or counselling (her friends often confide their difficulties in her). We have reflected on the diversity of these ideas and how they demonstrate the breadth of her interests and her ambition for the future. She describes herself as being very caring and states that she would 'never put myself before others'. She sees herself as sociable: 'I really enjoy being with people. It's ironic as I love having company, despite the fact that I have social anxiety.'

Stephanie was first diagnosed with FOP when she was 18 months old. She is now in a mechanised wheelchair, with limited movement in her arms, legs and face. Despite this, she manages to maintain her school work, including written and art work. Reflecting on how her condition impacts upon her, Stephanie observes that

> it does make it harder to do the normal things – getting around, even simple things like changing clothes can be a really big matter. I can't do anything or go anywhere without a parent because they know what I'm like condition-wise and what I need.

At school, Stephanie has a teaching assistant who stays with her. While Stephanie's lessons are part of the mainstream school, in break time she prefers to stay in the unit for young people with special needs. She does this partly because of concerns that she might be injured in the hectic corridors and partly for social reasons:

> I like all the buzz of people, but if surrounded by people I don't know, then I can feel pretty uncomfortable.

While friends will visit her in the unit, her separation from her academic peers during breaks further emphasises the sense of separateness for her:

> In a way, I would like to go out there in breaks, but they don't really understand my different needs, for example my different eating habits, and so I would rather come here where people accept my differences and I feel more comfortable.

I first met Stephanie approximately 1½ years ago. I work in a community paediatric nursing and psychology service which supports children and young people with non-malignant life-limiting and life-threatening conditions. The clinical psychology team have a broad remit, working with anyone in the family system who is experiencing psychological difficulties as a consequence of the child or young person's condition. Examples of the sorts of work we do include: acceptance of diagnoses; procedural anxiety; medication non-adherence; post-traumatic stress disorder; anxiety conditions; depression; and systemic issues.

Stephanie's community nurse referred Stephanie to clinical psychology because she was experiencing a 'flare-up' in her condition. The primary symptom of this flare-up was that she was not able to eat solid food, causing her and her family some distress. We spent the first six sessions addressing this with the family. The main difficulty was that Stephanie did not want to stop eating solid food, but her family and medical team were concerned that she might choke. Finding a middle ground was identified as a helpful solution – providing Stephanie with a sense of choice and control over what she ate, yet her agreeing to not eat anything identified as particularly risky. During these sessions, Stephanie discussed her difficulties of talking in class and her desire to address this therapeutically.

Stephanie and I have met on 16 subsequent occasions over a 12-month period to address social anxiety. The course of therapy has taken longer than other social anxiety cases, which typically last up to 14 sessions over a 4-month period (National Institute for Health and Care Excellence (NICE) 2013). We have struggled to meet as frequently and regularly as the guidelines (NICE 2013) recommend, largely owing to practical constraints. We agreed to hold sessions in school because Stephanie's busy household meant that meeting in private at home was difficult. We needed to accommodate Stephanie's fortnightly school timetable and my own complex working arrangements. Holidays and cancellations meant that we frequently had a 4-week break, which certainly affected continuity. We have met with Stephanie's family for review sessions on a regular basis. This has been helpful in monitoring progress (the family have noticed a definite increase in Stephanie's confidence), but because the majority of work has been in school, we have not been able to enlist their support in quite the way we might have done.

Early meetings, engagement, empathy and collaboration

Reflecting on our early meetings, Stephanie struggled to remember that my original remit was to address eating issues. Although the nurse who referred Stephanie had hoped that Stephanie would use our sessions to reflect on the impact of her condition, Stephanie was clear that she did not want to do this. While acknowledging that her condition did limit aspects of her life – for instance, she did not feel able to go into town with friends in case she experienced physical difficulties – Stephanie said she was accepting of her condition.

Stephanie said that she first noticed symptoms of social anxiety approximately 3 years ago when she overheard some girls, whom she had thought of as friends, making unkind comments about her. She talked about the pain of hearing such comments; the erosion of trust in others and her sadness about the impact of such an experience, because she likes being sociable. Since then, she said that she has become more aware of how her disability has made her stand out. At school, she thought new teachers made assumptions about her intelligence because she was in a wheelchair, speaking to her in overly simple terms. These experiences have compounded her sense that people will make judgements about her because of her condition and she developed the rule that 'I should only speak when I know that I won't stumble, otherwise I believe that people will think of me as stupid'. Such beliefs that others will make negative evaluations about individuals based on performance are common in individuals with social anxiety (Blöte *et al.* 2014).

Throughout our sessions Stephanie has enjoyed artistic activities, including drawing manga, origami and loom bands (see Figure 14.1). Having this external focus has been helpful to Stephanie in lessening her discomfort in talking about herself while not affecting her ability to engage in our conversations. Use of whiteboards and large pieces of paper to draw formulations and maintenance cycles has had similar effect (see Figure 14.2).

As part of the engagement process, it was important to develop a narrative of Stephanie beyond 'the problem' so that we could use the 'non-problem talk' to strengthen our relationship. As a result, she felt that 'I could speak more freely, not feel that the relationship is forced – it is a lot easier to speak when feeling comfortable'. In order to establish a constructive and collaborative relationship with young people, I find there is often a need to spend time helping them understand the difference between a therapeutic relationship and their other existing relationships with adults where there is typically a power bias towards adults such as parents and teachers (Fuggle *et al.* 2013). Therefore Stephanie and I spent some time just getting to know each other and understanding the CBT principle of collaboration (Beck 2011).

While Stephanie has always appeared happy to spend time with me, it took her some time to be open about her thoughts and feelings. When I first met with Stephanie's family, her mother talked about how Stephanie does not confide in her when experiencing difficulties or pain. Stephanie agreed that she does not like to cause anxiety or

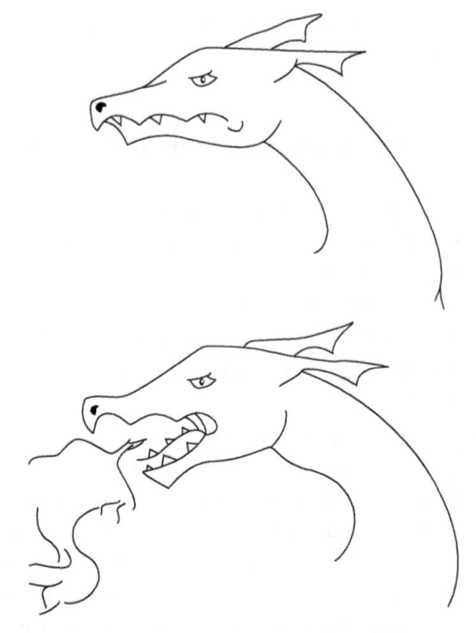

Figure 14.1 Stephanie's drawings of dragons

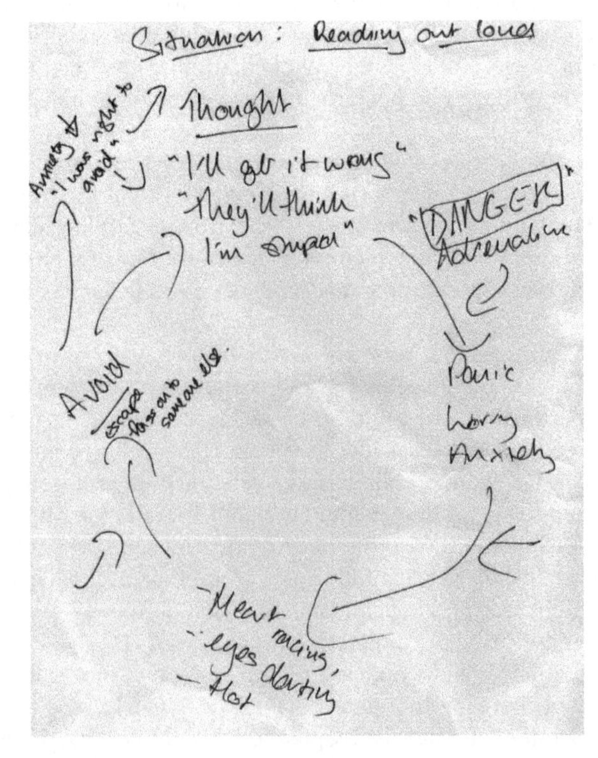

Figure 14.2 Example of a maintenance cycle drawn in session

draw attention to herself. As a consequence, I wondered whether there were times earlier in our relationship when Stephanie had 'gone along' with our discussions because she did not feel able to tell me that she was uncomfortable. Her rule not to put herself before others perhaps made it more difficult for her to openly say 'no' to me. Given how anxiety-provoking intervention for social anxiety can be, I was concerned that unless Stephanie was able to be open about how she was finding our sessions, I might end up coercing her into work that she did not feel able to refuse for fear of upsetting me. To address this, much to her discomfort, we enacted role-plays involving her giving me negative feedback. The aim of this exercise was to help her to formulate what words she might use, and for me to demonstrate that I will not respond negatively. On further discussion, Stephanie said that she

> feels uncomfortable when giving negative feedback as I think that it might be seen as being mean and it is important to me to be a nice person. I would feel that I had let myself down if I hurt someone else.

We have explored this belief and the times when it might be necessary to give negative feedback and have also spent some time challenging the belief that 'giving negative feedback is mean'. Stephanie recognised that

> there are times when I need to let people know if I don't want something to happen to make sure that I am not made to do something I don't want to do – I will then speak out.

As is often the case with treating social anxiety, when Stephanie understood that the intervention would involve conducting behavioural experiments to test her beliefs about herself in social situations, there was clearly a reluctance to start the work. She talked about the risks associated with the more challenging tasks, while also acknowledging the potential benefits. To address this ambivalence, we conducted a motivational interviewing exercise, in which we looked at the pros and cons of using CBT to address the social anxiety. The main risks which Stephanie identified in carrying out the work were:

- The more you talk the more likely you will be asked questions.
- There is more potential to be judged as stupid.
- People will think that I am too keen.

The advantages she identified for doing the work were:

- I will be able to get my opinions across.
- I can let others know that I am actively engaged in learning.
- People will get to know me better.
- I will need to be able to do public speaking for future studies.

Following this exercise Stephanie decided that the benefits to doing the work outweighed the risks and that she wanted to start the therapy.

We agreed to work using the Clark and Wells's (1995) model for social anxiety. There is emerging research to suggest that more generic anxiety programmes perform less well with social anxiety than with other anxiety conditions in young people, and that disorder-specific treatment programmes are more effective with social anxiety (Cresswell *et al.* 2014; Hodson *et al.* 2008; NICE 2013). Stephanie immediately grasped the model, stating that it was a

> relief to know what was happening. The model is a good representation of my feelings – fitting in really well – exactly mapping what is happening to me in terms of my thoughts and actions.

She found it helpful to learn that it is the third most common anxiety disorder (Kessler *et al.* 2005):

> It being common also makes me feel glad I'm not the only person with the disorder – that I can share experiences with other people suffering the same thing.

As part of the assessment Stephanie identified that the main goals she wanted to achieve were to 'be able to talk out loud in class on a regular basis' and 'to perform my oral exam in English GCSE'.

Summary of the Clark and Wells (1995) model of social anxiety

Clark's (2005) treatment protocol for working with social anxiety using the Clark and Wells (1995) model involves first helping the individual understand the model (see Figure 14.3) and individualising it with the client. Stephanie's individualised version of the model is presented in Figure 14.4.

In brief, the model proposes that when individuals with social anxiety enter a feared situation, certain assumptions are activated. These typically relate to: requiring excessively high standards for social performance; perception of threat experienced as a consequence of certain performances; and negative beliefs about oneself (Clark, 2005). In Stephanie's case, she held the assumptions that

> if I speak in class and stumble people will think I am stupid; if I go red people will think I am stupid; they will laugh at me; I will get it wrong; people will think I am too keen.

On activation of these assumptions the individual tends to experience physical symptoms of anxiety. Cognitively, the individual shifts the focus of attention to detailed internal self-monitoring and uses the information derived to judge how he or she is perceived by others – again in Stephanie's case, 'I am going red' and 'I am stumbling'. Clark (2005: 195) terms this self-focus 'processing of self as a social object'.

To help cope with the perceived threat experienced in social situations, often individuals will develop safety behaviours to mitigate the potential for harm. Stephanie

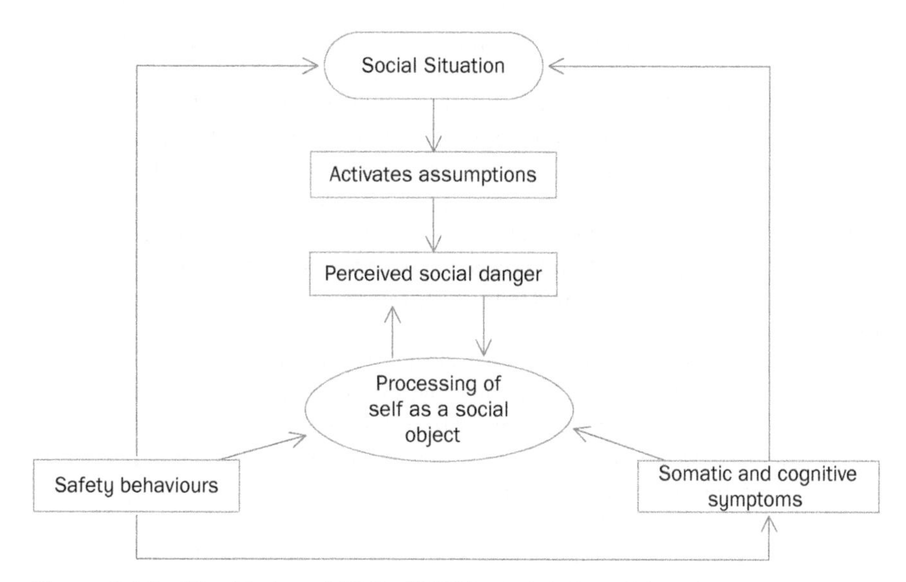

Figure 14.3 The Clark and Wells (1995) model of social anxiety

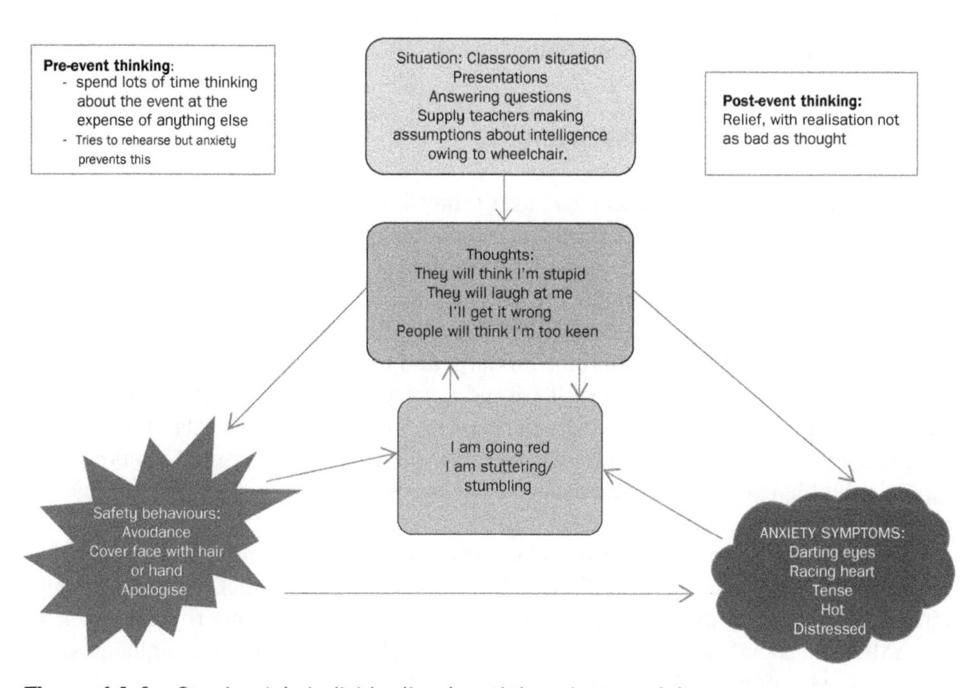

Figure 14.4 Stephanie's individualised social anxiety model

avoided talking in class by telling the teacher to ask someone else. When she was unable to avoid it, she would cover her face with her hair and hand; try to rehearse what to say; and apologise repeatedly. Stephanie believed these behaviours prevented people from seeing her redness and anxiety and made them less likely to judge her as being stupid. A key part of change for her was recognising that her safety behaviours actually drew attention to rather than away from her and that rehearsing in her mind interfered with the fluency of her performance, exacerbating the stumbling.

The physical symptoms of anxiety that Stephanie experienced gave further feedback that the situation she was in was threatening and needed to be avoided to lessen the danger.

Another key aspect of the Clark and Wells (1995) model is pre- and post-event processing, when individuals spend time anticipating events and ruminating about them afterwards, often with a negative appraisal of either their anticipated or actual performance. Stephanie' spent considerable time in advance of social events thinking about the situation and the potential outcome. As a consequence, she would try to rehearse what she wanted to say, 'but I find I can't rehearse because I just keep thinking what's going to go wrong'. If she stumbled she would afterwards ruminate about the event, believing that 'I have failed and people think I am stupid'.

Our intervention involved training Stephanie to shift her focus of attention from internal to external events; to drop safety behaviours and test her beliefs using guided discovery and behavioural experiments. We used role-play, social skills training, video feedback and real-life experimentation (Clark 2005).

Creativity, self-efficacy, discovery, fun

As the intervention for social anxiety using the Clark and Wells (1995) model can be highly anxiety-provoking, making the sessions fun can be difficult. Stephanie found behavioural experiments challenging and 'enough of a task for me not to want to do them'. She understood the rationale for the work in testing her beliefs, but would often try to avoid experiments by using distraction. We used the model to help Stephanie understand how avoidance maintains anxiety, and to emphasise the fact that change would be more difficult to achieve if we did not try to test the beliefs. From further discussion, Stephanie agreed that she perhaps needed more time to relax into the session and agreed to allocate 10 minutes each session for chat. These 10 minutes were typically highly entertaining, and served to enhance engagement and develop a sense of fun in the room.

Likewise, Stephanie's use of drawing during the session also helped to make the sessions less intense for her (see Figure 14.1). We recently externalised social anxiety – Figure 14.5 shows Stephanie's depiction. This has helped Stephanie to see herself as separate from social anxiety and not defined by it. She has started to imagine pushing Social Anxiety off a cliff before trying experiments.

We have also used social media for Stephanie to conduct a survey looking at people's perceptions of others when they stumble. As described later in the chapter, a previous attempt at a survey in person had been unsuccessful because Stephanie found it too anxiety-provoking. While using social media has an element of avoidance

Figure 14.5 Social anxiety as personified by Stephanie

(it enables Stephanie to avoid doing a survey with her peers, which is more anxiety-provoking), because the aim of the survey was simply to collect others' views about what happens when people stumble over their words we agreed that there was still value in doing the survey online.

Setting up experiments in general is more challenging for Stephanie. Her physical condition meant that it was harder to be spontaneous in how we conducted the experiments. Any experiments outside the school or home required careful planning to ensure there was adequate transport and care. To date, the focus of our work has been to address the goal relating to talking in public at school and we have therefore remained in school. However, Stephanie has recently expressed interest in broadening the work to other social situations. If we develop this idea, it could provide opportunities to be more creative with experiments – for example, practising public speaking in forums other than school.

We have developed a graded hierarchy to support Stephanie in her work towards her ultimate goal (see Figure 14.6) but because some steps were too anxiety-provoking for her, we revised the hierarchy to make it more manageable. We enlisted her teaching assistant, Ruby, to support her in some tasks. For instance, one of the steps identified by Stephanie has been to speak to her teachers about the social anxiety (until recently she had not wanted me to involve her teachers) to explain why she did not speak in class. Ruby facilitated this by asking the teachers if Stephanie could speak to them. Stephanie was amazed that none of her teachers were aware that she experiences social anxiety and all expressed a high regard for her class contributions. This experience led to a demonstrable shift in Stephanie's cognition that 'everyone will see me going red and think that I am stupid' because clearly teachers had not noticed, indicating to Stephanie that 'while I think everyone can see how anxious I am, actually they don't seem to know'.

After carrying out this task Stephanie's belief that 'everyone will see me going red and think that I am stupid' shifted from 90 per cent strength of belief to 40 per cent. Stephanie said that it was unlikely that she would have been able to conduct this task without Ruby's support, as asking to speak to the teachers in the first place was too big a step to take. Making it smaller through Ruby asking if the teacher could speak to me first, made this much easier.

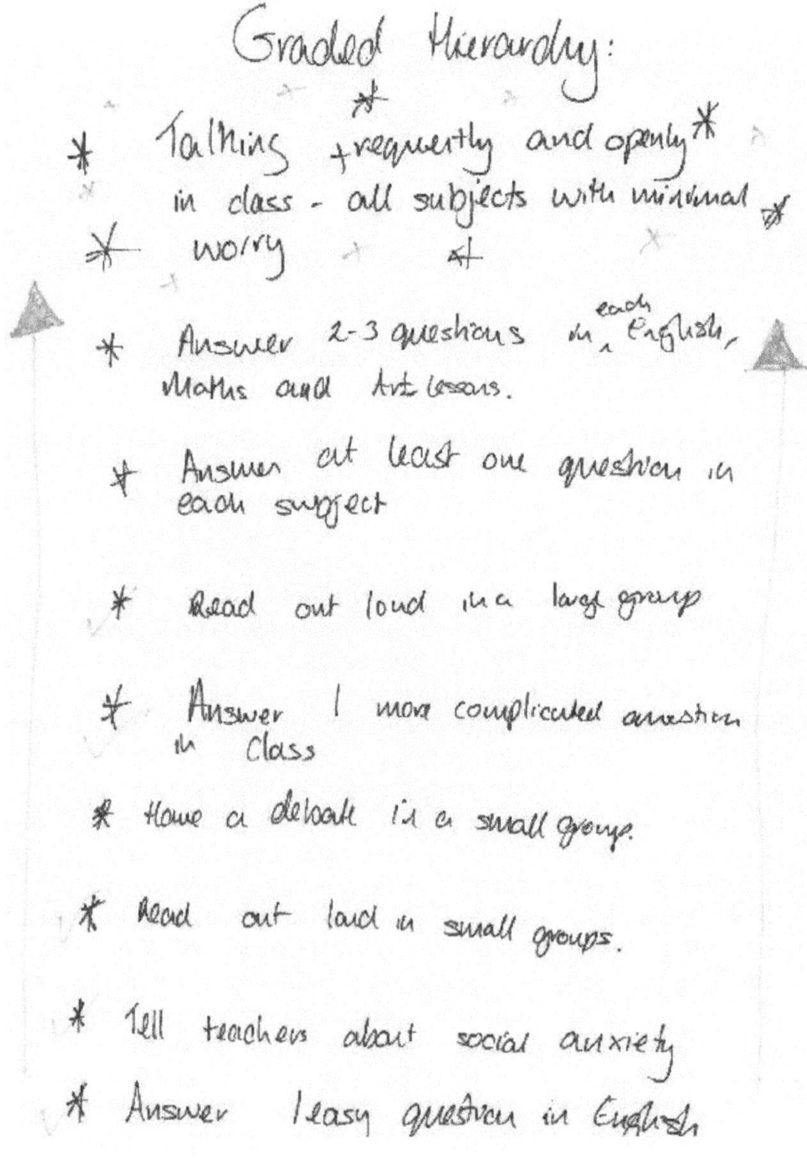

Figure 14.6 Stephanie's graded hierarchy drawn in an early session

Skills: methods for cognitive and behavioural change

Stephanie engaged well with CBT, stating that the formulation-driven, goal-focused, problem- solving approach was perfect for her. She understands the relationship between her thoughts, feelings and behaviours and appreciates the function of experiments to test and modify unhelpful beliefs. She sees the purpose of the between-session tasks 'as they further challenge my beliefs [and] I have to do them if I want to challenge the different issues', recognising the need to practise skills between sessions – but admits that 'I don't like doing them'.

She liked the structure of the sessions (the 10-minute chat; feedback from previous week and home tasks; main session content, typically an exercise to actively bring change; home tasks and feedback) and the methodical way in which topics are addressed. She understands the collaborative nature of the work, particularly her part in setting the agenda, which, helps to give her a sense of ownership of the sessions.

In terms of the Clark and Wells (1995) model of social anxiety, Stephanie demonstrated a sound understanding of the key elements of the model. She understood the role of avoidance and safety behaviours and described her experiences as 'perfectly mapping on to the model'. She also saw the benefits of shifting her attention from an internal to an external focus (Mörtberg *et al.* 2015).

Examples of our intervention

To help Stephanie understand the maintaining role of self-focus in perpetuating her social anxiety, we arranged a series of experiments gradually shifting her focus from herself to what was happening externally. We did this by Stephanie reading out loud – first, while focusing on what was happening internally; secondly, by focusing externally on the words, initially just with me as an audience, then with the video camera to provide direct feedback about how she was looking and how she was feeling, and finally in front of Ruby and another teacher. Concurrently, we worked on dropping the safety behaviours of putting her hand and hair in front of her face and apologising. Stephanie's predictions before the experiments were:

(i) I will go very red (she identified how red by finding a red colour in the room);
(ii) I will stumble more when focusing on myself than when I just focus on the words;
(iii) people watching will be able to see how anxious I am feeling and will think I am stupid.
(iv) people will notice me more if I don't hide my face with my hand.

Through watching the video, Stephanie was able to see that she was not as red as she had predicted. She was also able to see that her safety behaviours of hiding her face drew attention to her rather than away from her. Furthermore, when she focused on what was happening to her internally, she stumbled on her words more than when she just focused on the words. Finally, the two teachers who watched her said she looked calm and read beautifully. When relating this back to the model, Stephanie could find no evidence, at least in this experiment, for the belief 'they will think I am stupid'. She was also able to see how her performance was actually enhanced by not rehearsing as she was speaking.

Further work helping Stephanie to practice shifting her focus externally has been to practise with her family, having conversations focusing on what is happening internally and then doing the same while concentrating her attention externally. Again she reported to being more fluent when simply concentrating on the conversation and finding the experience more enjoyable. She has dropped the safety behaviour of covering her face when talking in class but is yet to take the next step of answering questions without rehearsal.

To help Stephanie re-evaluate her sense of social danger – which told her that people would think she was stupid if she went red or stumbled over her words – we set up a survey looking at people's judgements about others going red. Stephanie found this too anxiety-provoking to do – instead she observed others' reactions when someone else goes red; similarly noticing the effect when people (for example, teachers or live TV presenters) stumble over their words. Stephanie observed that 'no-one noticed, or if they did – it didn't matter, people didn't see them as any less intelligent as a result'. I have used self-disclosure of times when I have muddled my words when giving presentations or done something embarrassing (a frequent occurrence!) and there being no adverse consequences. We have tried the experiment of Stephanie deliberately stumbling over her words when talking to others, and while she is able to do that with me, this has been too big a step to do elsewhere so far.

Although we have struggled to devise between-session tasks that Stephanie has felt able to do, now that teachers are aware of her social anxiety they can support any future plan in place.

Evaluation of intervention

There has been a demonstrable shift in Stephanie's beliefs since the start of intervention: her belief 'They will see me go red/hear me stumble and think that I am stupid' has fallen from 90% true at the beginning of treatment to 40% currently; 'They will laugh at me' from 80% to 20%; 'I will get it wrong' from 80% to 60%; and 'People will think I am too keen' from 80% to 40%. Her goal-based outcome ratings have shifted from 4/10 to 7.5/10 (where 10 represents achievement of goal) and her score no longer indicates social anxiety for the Revised Child Anxiety and Depression Scale (Chorpita *et al.* 2000). She has achieved several major milestones – she has answered questions in class; she has read Shakespeare in front of the class; she has recorded an oral test and she has been able to list from memory World Cup football teams in class.

While this progress has been considerable and Stephanie acknowledges this, she still experiences considerable anxiety when speaking in public and does not wholly acknowledge the progress she has made. I discuss this further in the next section.

Formulation and reformulation

In a recent re-evaluation of the formulation, Stephanie identified the role of perfectionism in maintaining her anxiety. While she is unable to find evidence of value judgements being made of others when they stumble their words, and understands that everyone makes mistakes, she believes she needs to set higher standards for herself because others already make judgements about her intelligence owing to her being in a wheelchair. To help to address this, Stephanie has agreed for me to speak to her class tutor to ensure that all supply teachers are informed about her ability. We have also agreed to meet for a further four sessions to work on the maintaining role of perfectionism, attempting to modify the rule 'I must not make any mistakes or people will think me stupid' to 'I will always do my best but it is OK to make mistakes at times' (see Egan *et al.* 2011).

The role of avoidance has always had prominence in our discussions, but we may not have given sufficient notice to the fact that others perhaps also allow Stephanie to avoid certain public speaking tasks because of her physical health; Stephanie has alluded to this possibly being the case. The degree to which this is a factor is unclear, but enlisting teachers' support in any future experiments may help to address this if it is identified as a problem.

We have discussed how the spacing between sessions has perhaps hindered progress – particularly in the practising of between-session exercises. While Stephanie is often motivated to try strategies immediately after the sessions, this motivation understandably drops and anxiety increases as time elapses before the next session. We have agreed to try to make the sessions weekly to maintain any developments made.

Finally, we have discussed the possibility of conducting an imagery rescripting exercise to address the original event that Stephanie identified as triggering her social anxiety. There is increasing evidence to show that this can be a helpful intervention to carry out with individuals with social anxiety (e.g. Wild and Clark 2011), and Stephanie has said that the image of that original event is still prominent in her mind.

Conclusion

I have very much enjoyed working with Stephanie. Clearly her physical condition has contributed to the development and maintenance of her social anxiety. I know that some aspects of our intervention have been more challenging for Stephanie because it has required her to ask others for help, which is something she struggles to do. She has demonstrated huge progress and is now doing things that she said she would not have done a year earlier – for example,

> before I never spoke out in class – I can now say short sentences out loud without being completely overwhelmed with thoughts that stopped me speaking out in the first place.

Perhaps now the greatest challenge is helping her to accept this progress. She is an extremely intelligent and bright individual with a strong academic future, and there is every chance that she will both meet and surpass expectations in terms of her achievements. As is usually the case with my work, I have learnt just as much as I have imparted in our sessions.

References

Beck, J.S. (2011) *Cognitive Behaviour Therapy: Basics and Beyond.* New York: Guilford Press.

Blöte, A.W., Miers, A.C., Heyne, D.A., Clark, D.M. and Westenberg, P.M. (2014) The relation between social anxiety and audience perception: examining Clark and Wells' (1995) model among adolescents. *Behavioural and Cognitive Psychotherapy,* 42: 555–67.

Chorpita, B F., Yim, L., Moffitt, C., Umemoto, L.A. and Francis, S.E. (2000) Assessment of symptoms of DSM-IV anxiety and depression in children: a revised child anxiety and depression scale. *Behaviour Research and Therapy,* 38: 835–55.

Clark, D.M. and Wells, A. (1995) A cognitive model of social phobia. In R.G. Heimberg, M.R. Liebowitz, D.A. Hope and F.R. Schneier (eds) *Social Phobia: Diagnosis, Assessment and Treatment* (pp.69–93). New York: Guilford Press.

Clark, D.M. (2005) A cognitive perspective on social phobia. In W.R. Crozier and L.F. Alden (eds) *The Essential Handbook of Social Anxiety for Clinicians* (pp. 193–218). Chichester: John Wiley & Sons.

Creswell, C., Waite, P. and Cooper, P.J. (2014) Assessment and management of anxiety disorders in children and adolescents. *Archives of Disease in Childhood,* 99: 674–8.

Egan, S.J., Wade, T.D. and Shafran, R.(2011) Perfectionism as a transdiagnostic process: a clinical review. *Clinical Psychology Review,* 31: 203–12.

Fuggle, P., Dunsmuir, S. and Curry, V. (2013) *CBT with Children, Young People & Families.* London: Sage.

Hodson, K.J., McManus, F.V., Clark, D.M. and Doll, H. (2008) Can Clark and Wells' (1995) model of social phobia be applied to young people? *Behavioural and Cognitive Psychotherapy,* 36: 449–61.

Kessler, R.C., Berglund, P., Demler, O., Jin, R., Merikangas, K.R. and Walters, E.E. (2005) Lifetime prevalence and age-of-onset distributions of DSM-IV disorders in the National Comorbidity Survey Replication. *Archives of General Psychiatry,* 62: 593–602.

Mörtberg, E., Hoffart, A., Boecking, B. and Clark, D.M. (2015) Shifting the focus of one's attention mediates improvement in cognitive therapy for social anxiety disorder. *Behavioural and Cognitive Psychotherapy,* 43: 63–73.

National Institute for Health and Care Excellence (2013) *Social Anxiety Disorder: Recognitçion, Assessment and Treatment.* NICE Clinical Guideline CG159. Available at www.nice.org.uk/CG159 (accessed 5 May 2015).

Wild, J. and Clark, D.M. (2011) Imagery rescripting of early traumatic memories in social phobia. *Cognitive and Behavioral Practice,* 18: 433–43.

Index

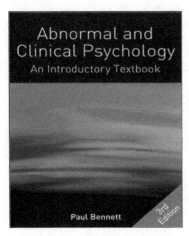